Advanced Automated Software Testing:

Frameworks for Refined Practice

Izzat Alsmadi
Yarmouk University, Jordan

Managing Director:	Lindsay Johnston
Senior Editorial Director:	Heather Probst
Book Production Manager:	Sean Woznicki
Development Manager:	Joel Gamon
Acquisitions Editor:	Erika Gallagher
Typesetters:	Adrienne Freeland
Print Coordinator:	Jamie Snavely
Cover Design:	Nick Newcomer, Greg Snader

Published in the United States of America by
Information Science Reference (an imprint of IGI Global)
701 E. Chocolate Avenue
Hershey PA 17033
Tel: 717-533-8845
Fax: 717-533-8661
E-mail: cust@igi-global.com
Web site: http://www.igi-global.com

Library of Congress Cataloging-in-Publication Data

Advanced automated software testing: frameworks for refined practice / Izzat Alsmadi, editor.
    p. cm.
  Includes bibliographical references and index.
  Summary: "This book discusses the current state of test automation practices, as it includes
chapters related to software test automation and its validity and applicability in different domains"--
Provided by publisher.
  ISBN 978-1-4666-0089-8 (hardcover) -- ISBN 978-1-4666-0090-4 (ebook) -- ISBN 978-1-4666-
0091-1 (print & perpetual access) 1. Computer software--Testing--Automation. I. Alsmadi, Izzat,
1972-
  QA76.76.T48A38 2012
  005.3028'7--dc23
                                    2011042036
British Cataloguing in Publication Data
A Cataloguing in Publication record for this book is available from the British Library.

All work contributed to this book is new, previously-unpublished material. The views expressed in
this book are those of the authors, but not necessarily of the publisher.

List of Reviewers

Eslam Maghayreh, *Yarmouk University, Jordan*
Daniel Bolanos, *University of Colorado, USA*
Seifedine Kadry, *American University of the Middle East, Kuwait*
Natarajan Meghanathan, *Jackson State University, USA*
Saqib Saeed, *University of Siegen, Germany*
Kamaljeet Sandhu, *University of New England, Australia*
Thomas Bauer, *Fraunhofer IESE, Germany*
Robert Eschbach, *Fraunhofer IESE, Germany*
Praveen Ranjan Srivastava, *Birla Institute of Technology and Science Pilani, India*

Table of Contents

Detailed Table of Contents

Chapter 1
How Much Automation can be Done in Testing? 1
Izzat Alsmadi, Yarmouk University, Jordan

It is widely acknowledged that software testing stage is a stage in the software project that is time and resources' consuming. In addition, this stage comes late in the project, usually at the time where pressure of delivery is high. Those are some reasons why major research projects in testing focus on methods to automate one or more of activities in this stage. In this chapter, description of all sub stages in software testing is explained along with possible methods to automate activities in this sub stage. The focus in this chapter is on the user interface of the software as it is one of the major components that receives a large percentage of testing. A question always raised in testing is whether full test automation is possible and if that can be feasible, possible and applicable. While 100% test automation is theoretic and impractical, given all types of activities that may occur in testing, it is hoped that a maximum coverage in test automation will be visible soon.

Chapter 2
On the Application of Automated Software Testing Techniques to the Development and Maintenance of Speech Recognition Systems........................ 30
Daniel Bolanos, University of Colorado at Boulder, USA

This chapter provides practitioners in the field with a set of guidelines to help them through the process of elaborating an adequate automated testing framework to competently test automatic speech recognition systems. Thorough this chapter the testing process of such a system is analyzed from different angles, and different methods and techniques are proposed that are well suited for this task.

Ensuring the correctness of a distributed program is not an easy task. Testing and formal methods can play a significant role in this regard. However, testing does not allow for formal specification of the properties to be checked. On the other hand, formal methods verify that a model of a distributed system satisfies certain properties that are formally specified. However, formal methods do not guarantee that a particular implementation of the system under consideration will also satisfy all of the necessary properties. Runtime verification tries to combine some of the advantages of testing and some of the advantages of formal methods. Runtime verification works on a particular implementation of the system and at the same time it allows us to specify the properties of interest formally. In this chapter we have talked about runtime verification of distributed programs. The main components of a runtime verification framework have been presented and discussed in some details. The reasons that make runtime verification of distributed programs a difficult task have been discussed. A summarization of some of the techniques presented in the literature to simplify runtime verification of distributed programs has also been presented.

System maintenance is a general term required to keep a system running properly. The system could be a computer system, mechanical system, or other system. The maintenance in this sense is related to the deterioration of the system due to its usage and age. This context of maintenance does not apply to software, where the deterioration due to the usage and age don't make sense. Conventionally, the maintenance of software is concerned with modifications related to software system. These modifications come from the user needs, error correction, improvement of performance, adapt to a changed environment, and optimization.

Chapter 5

The high-level contribution of this book chapter is to illustrate how to conduct static code analysis of a software program and mitigate the vulnerabilities associated with the program. The automated tools used to test for software security are the Source Code Analyzer and Audit Workbench, developed by Fortify, Inc. The first two sections of the chapter are comprised of (i) An introduction to Static Code Analysis and its usefulness in testing for Software Security and (ii) An introduction to the Source Code Analyzer and the Audit Workbench tools and how to use them to conduct static code analysis. The authors then present a detailed case study of static code analysis conducted on a File Reader program (developed in Java) using these automated tools. The specific software vulnerabilities that are discovered, analyzed, and mitigated include: (i) Denial of Service, (ii) System Information Leak, (iii) Unreleased Resource (in the context of Streams), and (iv) Path Manipulation. The authors discuss the potential risk in having each of these vulnerabilities in a software program and provide the solutions (and the Java code) to mitigate these vulnerabilities. The proposed solutions for each of these four vulnerabilities are more generic and could be used to correct such vulnerabilities in software developed in any other programming language.

Test Case prioritization consists of proper organization and scheduling of the test cases in a specific sequence. Regression testing is an important issue and concept during software maintenance process, but due to scarcity of resources re-execution of all test cases, is not possible during regression testing. Hence in version or revision specific regression testing, it is more important to execute those test cases that are beneficial. In this chapter, a new prioritization technique is proposed for version specific regression testing using Cuckoo Search Algorithm. This technique prioritizes the test cases based on lines of code where the code is modified.

Chapter 7

Pervasive systems and increased reliance on embedded systems requires that the underlying software is properly tested and has in-built high quality. The approaches often adopted to realize software systems have inherent weaknesses that have resulted in less robust software applications. The requirement of reliable software suggests that quality needs to be instilled at all stages of a software development paradigms, especially at the testing stages of the development cycle ensuring that quality attributes and parameters are taken into account when designing and developing software. In this respect, numerous tools, techniques, and methodologies have also been proposed. In this chapter, the authors present and review different methodologies employed to improve the software quality during the software development lifecycle.

Chapter 8

The standard-compliant development of component-based embedded systems calls for systematic coverage of product requirements and for testing component interactions at the system integration stage. System functionality is represented by a set of complex distributed functions, i.e., functions that are spread across several system components. This chapter presents a novel automated model-based testing approach for distributed functions that uses informal system requirements and component behavior models. The test modeling notation makes it possible to model component interactions and composite functions with defined pre- and post-conditions. Test cases are automatically generated as scenarios of distributed functions represented by sequences of component interactions.

Testing e-learning websites may provide an insight to characteristics that are useful and others that are not so useful to the users. From a technical or systems development perspective, such understanding may not be known till it is finally tested and used by the users. Therefore this research aims to explore the effectiveness of e-learning websites in relation to user's perceptions (either positive or negative) that are developed when interacting with e-learning system and the features that they have to use.

This research is about testing the effectiveness of Web-based e-services system. The problem facing the department is the staff resistance to accept and use e-services in their work. There are technical issues that impact negatively on staff users of the e-services system. Case analysis reveals that there are wider issues stemming from the interaction with the system which has a low impact on e-services acceptance. E-services drivers such as user training and experience, motivation, perceived usefulness and ease of use, acceptance, and usage were not clearly understood by the technical development team, hence not integrated when implementing the e-services system.

Preface

Software testing is required to assess the quality of the developed software. However, it consumes a critical amount of time and resources, often delaying the software release date and increasing the overall cost. The answer to this problem is effective test automation, which is expected to meet the need for effective software testing, while reducing amount of required time and resources. There exists a need for an edited publication illuminating the current state of test automation practices.

In this book, several authors produced chapters related to software test automation and its validity and applicability in different domains. Authors showed how test automation could be used in those different domains and in the different tasks and stages of software testing.

In the first chapter, Izzat Alsmadi introduced a general test automation framework that includes the automation of activities in all software testing stages (e.g. test case design, test case generation, execution, verification, prioritization, etc.). He focused on testing applications' user interfaces. In the chapter, he used model based testing to convert the application user interface into an XML file or model where test automation activities can be easily implemented. Test cases were then generated automatically from the XML file. They were then executed on the actual application. Results were verified based on defining original accepted results with expected ones. While 100% test automation may not be always feasible, nonetheless, the more tasks that can be automated, the more saving is achieved on software project time and resources.

In Chapter 2, Daniel Bolanos focused on software test automation techniques in the field of speech recognition. The chapter demonstrated the process followed during the development of a new generation speech recognition system that is expected to be released as an open source project. The author discussed testing approaches and methodologies followed to test the program through all its components and stages. The aim of the chapter is to provide practitioners in the field with a set of guidelines to help them through the process of elaborating an adequate automated testing framework to competently test Automatic Speech Recognition (ASR) systems. The chapter first described using the unit testing library CxxTest in speech recognition testing. Mock objects are used to simulate or substitute using components that are not ready yet. One of the major units to test in speech recognition system is the decoding network which is a graph that contains all the lexical units that are in the recognition vocabulary. Most of the decoding time is spent traversing the decoding network, so testing it thoroughly is crucial. The chapter then described testing the token expansion process. On the system testing level, the author described black box testing approach for a speech recognition system. The system is tested first through its ability to accept valid inputs and reject invalid inputs. Black box testing also includes testing the configuration file setting and command line parameters related to initialization, environment, et cetera. System testing also includes testing the correctness and validity of outputs or results. Application Programming Interfaces (APIs) are also important to test in systems or programs that have relations with hardware, operation system, database, or external systems such as the speech recognition system.

In Chapter 3, Eslam Al Maghayreh described automatic runtime testing or verification techniques on distributed systems. Runtime verification is a technique that combines formal verification and traditional testing. Testing and verification of a program statically does not guarantee that no new errors will appear at run time. The static time is the time before the compilation of the program, and the runtime is the time where the program is dynamically used after it has been successfully compiled. Runtime verification is more practical than other verification methods such as model checking and testing. Runtime verification combines the advantages of formal methods and traditional testing as it verifies the implementation of the system directly rather than verifying a model of the system as done in model checking. After the description of run time verification and its characteristics in comparison with static checking or testing, the author presents a model for a distributed program. Formal methods approaches and techniques relevant to the chapter are described. The author explores some of the logics used to formally specify the properties that a programmer may need to check and presents the main approaches used to verify distributed programs. Later on, author briefly describes the difficulties of checking global properties of distributed programs. Possible solutions for the state explosion problem are then described in later sections. Examples of strategies described to solve such problem include: exploiting the structure of the property, atomicity and program slicing. A brief description for a tool that can be used for runtime verification of distributed programs concludes the chapter.

In Chapter 4, Seifedine Kadry focused his chapter on regression testing and maintenance aspects of software testing. Conventionally, the maintenance of software is concerned with modifications related to software system. These modifications come from the user needs, error correction, improvement of performance, adapt to a changed environment, and optimization. In the chapter, author discussed maintenance aspects, needs, and costs. In the scope of software maintenance, author described levels of testing unit and system, along with integration testing approaches. As an important testing to maintenance activity, author described debugging which is an activity that comes after detecting errors in order to find their causes and fix them. The author then talks about test automation and started by discussing some of the important questions to answer regarding to test automation. For example, test cases number of repetition, reuse, relevancy, and effort are important questions to answer before deciding whether a test activity should be automated or not. Using a case study, he accordingly proposed drawing a decision tree for making decision on automation based on the answers of those questions. All the proposed questions have a discrete number of answers: 'High', 'Medium' or 'Low', which are represented in the tree by the letters "H," "M," and "L." The author then discussed regression testing as a major activity in maintenance testing. He discussed several possible regression testing strategies: retest-all, regression test selection, prioritization, hybrid, and risk analysis. He then proposed a technique to combine regression testing based on risk analysis and automation techniques to obtain more improvement on the test cost-effectiveness by optimizing the number of cases that should be automated and the number of cases that should we calculate their risk exposures.

In Chapter 5, Natarajan Meghanathan and Alexander Geoghegan focused their chapter on testing software security with a case study on a file reader program written in Java. They followed the static code analysis in order to test possible vulnerabilities associated with the program. They used a source code analyzer and audit workbench, developed by Fortify, Inc. They first introduced static code analysis and its usefulness in testing security aspects of the Software. They then introduced the tool used in the study and how it can be used for source code analysis. Later on in the chapter, they presented a detailed case study of static code analysis conducted on a file reader program (developed in Java) using the described automated tools. They focused on certain security aspects to evaluate. Those include: Denial of Service, System Information Leak, Unreleased Resource, and Path Manipulation. They discussed the potential risk in having each one of these vulnerabilities in a software program and tried to provide the solutions (and the Java code) to mitigate these vulnerabilities. The proposed solutions for each of these four vulnerabilities are more generic and could be used to correct such vulnerabilities in software developed in any other programming language.

In Chapter 6, Praveen Srivastava, D.V. Reddy, Srikanth Reddy, Ch. Ramaraju, and I. Nath discussed test case prioritization using Cuckoo search algorithm. Test case prioritization includes using techniques to select a subset of the test cases (that are usually large) wherein this subset can be an effective representative of the overall test cases in terms of coverage. This is done due to the scarcity of resources available for testing and the small amount of time usually available for such activity. In this chapter a new test case prioritization technique is proposed for version specific regression testing using Cuckoo search algorithm. This technique prioritizes the test cases based on lines of code where the code is modified. The authors introduced first test case prioritization and related work in the area. They then introduced Cuckoo search algorithm for automating the selection and prioritization of test cases. To determine the effectiveness of this approach, the implementation of the algorithm is done on the sample program in Java.

The proposed algorithm was tested on real time software (some of in house development and few of open sources). They showed effective test case selection using the proposed algorithm. They compared (on the basis of redundant test case, complexity of a programme, dependent test cases, etc.) the proposed algorithm with traditional approaches on test case prioritization. Since Cuckoo search is an optimized algorithm, test case prioritization algorithm based on cuckoo search have better results over procedural methods.

In Chapter 7, Saqib Saeed, Farrukh Khawaja, and Zaigham Mahmoud wrote a chapter on software quality methodologies. They present and review different methodologies employed to improve the software quality during the software development lifecycle. In the start, they discussed with a background the meaning and attributes of software quality. In the next section, they discussed software quality elements through the development lifecycle and all stages: project initiation, project planning, requirement, design, coding, testing, configuration management, evolution, or maintenance. They discussed those different stages with focus on quality elements based on the activities that occur in each stage along with goals and objectives. In a separate section, they then discussed several quality methodologies. In the first part on quality, they discussed software quality standards. Those are important to set goals and objectives in which progress and evaluation can be measured based on international standards such as ISO9000, a set of standards for both software products and processes. Examples of those standards mentioned besides ISO include: IEEE software engineering standards, CMM, TL 9000, etc. On a related subject, authors discussed software metrics as tool to measure and quantize software attributes. Without software metrics, it is not possible to measure the level of quality of software. Review and inspection activities are also described as human methods to evaluate the progress and the observation and following of standards. In the next section different methods of software testing are described. Software audits are also described in this chapter as an important tool to identify the discrepancy much earlier in a software development lifecycle approach.

In the eighth chapter, Thomas Bauer and Robert Eschbach talk about model based testing of distributed systems. They present a novel automated model-based testing approach for distributed functions that uses informal system requirements and component behavior models. The test modeling notation makes it possible to model component interactions and composite functions with defined pre- and post-conditions. Test cases are automatically generated as scenarios of distributed functions represented by sequences of component interactions. A generic approach for efficient quality assurance is model-based testing, which deals with the automated generation or selection of test cases from models. A large variety of models have been used and adapted for automated test case generation. Integration testing is frequently supported by different kinds of models. . Distributed systems are systems that consist of multiple autonomous computers or processes that communicate through a computer network or a communication middleware. Components are system parts with defined interfaces and functionalities. Authors discussed Component Based Testing (CBT) as one software development methodology used to build a software from ready components. In their case study, authors discussed an automotive example and other CBT systems related to automotive control systems. They showed the different distributed functions of the case study and their relationships in an acyclic hierarchical function graph. In later steps, the graph is the basis for the derivation of the functional model. The function graph is retrieved from the system requirements specification by mapping chapters, sections, paragraphs, and cross-references to graph nodes and transitions between them. The graph is acyclic to avoid design flaws. Functions may be referenced by multiple functions. Authors also have an extensive related work for model based testing specifically in the automotive systems. They described a model based on pre and post conditions. The second modeling notation used for describing the composition of functions is an operational notation. In the approach, the modeling notation CSP is used. This is a formal notation for describing, analyzing, and verifying systems consisting of concurrent, communicating processes. The combination of CSP and B uses the B machines to specify abstract system states and operations and CSP models to coordinate the execution of operations. The third modeling notation used for describing the composition of functions is a transition-based notation. Transition-based notations describe the control logic of components with their major states and actions which lead to state transitions. Functional and component models are analyzed statically to retrieve model faults and inconsistencies. The model shall not contain any deadlocks and all relevant system states shall be reachable. Furthermore, it has to be assured that each function referred to in the high-level functional models is represented in the low-level component models, i.e., with start states, end states, and defined paths. Based on the functional model, the integration strategy is defined. The integration strategy determines the system assembly order. Test cases are automatically generated from the reduced models for each integration step (4). Different coverage criteria are proposed for the test case generation. The generation starts with the reduced functional models. Integration approaches are also discussed as important elements of model based testing. The integration order determines the order of system assembly for integration testing.

For the testing approach, a function-driven bottom-up integration strategy is used. The objective is to integrate and test the functions according to their order in the function graph. For the test case generation, an approach based on stepwise coverage and considering all three model types is proposed. Test cases are generated for each configuration step from its reduced test models. Test cases are automatically generated from the test models. A set of coverage criteria has been proposed for the different modeling notations. Future work will comprise the improvement of the tool chain and further application of the method in industrial case studies.

In the ninth chapter, Kamaljeet Sandhu discussed testing e-learning websites. The chapter aims to explore the effectiveness of e-learning websites in relation to user's perceptions that are developed when interacting with e-learning system and the features that they have to use. The chapter first described a literature review and popular tools in e-learning. The aim of the study is to investigate the adoption of Web-based learning on websites amongst users. This led to the development of converging lines of inquiry, a process of triangulation. The case study examines the testing of Web-based framework of the University of Australia (not the real name). International students have the option to lodge an admission application through either of: Web-based e-service on the Internet, phone, fax, or in person. The main aim of this approach is to test users' information experience on websites. The user perception of Web electronic service is a burden and acted as a barrier to their work. The users learnt that it increased the workload, slowed the work process, and brought in complexity to the task. The department did not implement electronic services or introduce technology into jobs at the same time. The chapter includes also details on users' in the case study and their perception and evaluation of the e-learning tool WebCT.

In Chapter 10, Kamaljeet Sandhu talked about testing the effectiveness of Web based e-services. There are technical issues that impact negatively on users of the e-services. Case analysis reveals that there are wider issues stemming from the interaction with the system which has a low impact on e-services acceptance. E-Services drivers such as user training and experience, motivation, perceived usefulness and ease of use, acceptance, and usage were not clearly understood by the technical development team, hence not integrated when implementing the e-services system. The chapter focused on evaluating an educational website from the perspective on providing and evaluating services. The case study examines the Web Electronic Service framework of the University of Australia (not the real name). The department is in the process of developing and implementing Web-based e-service system. The focus was on evaluating the website user interface and users' perception and acceptance of the user interface and their ability to understand and use those services. The study and the chapter include results of a survey or questionnaire of users and staff of the evaluated website. User's acceptance to use e-services relates to the initial use when users trial the use of e- Services system and evaluate its effectiveness in meeting their objectives for visiting the e- Services system. For example, a student may use e-services system on a university website for emailing but its effective use can only be determined if such activities meet with the student's objectives. If the objectives are not met, the student is unlikely to accept e-services. Another area that the author focused on is to evaluate the gap between paper-based and web-based e-service system. Those are found due to information gap, design gap, communication, and fulfillment gap. The chapter also discussed the risk of asking the same people to compare and evaluate between the earlier and the new systems and what evaluators are expecting.

Izzat Alsmadi
Yarmouk University, Jordan

Acknowledgment

First of all, perfect thanks are due to our Lord for giving us the strength and power to have a life full of life, joy, happiness and challenges.

As the effort in this book is an integration for effort from several authors, I would like first to thank all contributing authors for their effort in both writing and reviewing chapters. Without their effort in taking such a significant time required to complete their work, the completion of this book would be impossible. We all have busy schedules and lots of work and family responsibilities. Thank you all for making this effort deliverable and useful to software engineering and testing practitioners.

Second, I would like also to thank all IGI Global publishing team members who assisted me throughout this process. In particular, I would like to thank Mr. Joel Gamon who assisted me in several administrative activities from the start to the end. In some stages bottlenecks may have risked the completion of the whole project without sincere assistant from such professionals.

I would like also to thank many of my graduate students, and friends in the academic fields for assisting me in processes such as marketing, reviewing, et cetera. Their help was greatly appreciated and I ask you all to excuse me for not being able to mention you one by one by names. Your help was and will always be appreciated.

I would like last to thank my dearest wife, kids, and family for giving me support and patience to complete this work. Thank you all.

Izzat Alsmadi
Yarmouk University, Jordan

Chapter 1
How Much Automation can be Done in Testing?

Izzat Alsmadi
Yarmouk University, Jordan

ABSTRACT

It is widely acknowledged that software testing stage is a stage in the software project that is time and resources' consuming. In addition, this stage comes late in the project, usually at the time where pressure of delivery is high. Those are some reasons why major research projects in testing focus on methods to automate one or more of activities in this stage. In this chapter, description of all sub stages in software testing is explained along with possible methods to automate activities in this sub stage. The focus in this chapter is on the user interface of the software as it is one of the major components that receives a large percentage of testing. A question always raised in testing is whether full test automation is possible and if that can be feasible, possible and applicable. While 100% test automation is theoretic and impractical, given all types of activities that may occur in testing, it is hoped that a maximum coverage in test automation will be visible soon.

INTRODUCTION

Part of software project development, it is very important to make sure, before product delivery, the software is working as expected without serious flaws or problems. Testing the software, like any other product, can be seen from several perspectives. It can be seen based on what we are testing. For example, each deliverable in the

DOI: 10.4018/978-1-4666-0089-8.ch001

software project (e.g. the requirements, design, code, documents, user interface, etc) should be tested. Moreover, in the code, which is the main deliverable, we may test the code based on the user and functional requirements or specification (i.e. black box testing). In this level, we are testing the code as a black box to make sure that all services expected from the program are: existed, working as expected and with no problem. On this perspective, we may need also to test the internal structure of the code (i.e. white box testing) based on the code structure or any other element. Testing can be also divided based on the sub stages or activities that occur in testing. For example, the testing stage includes the main activities: test case generation and design, test case execution and verification, building the testing database or oracle, coverage evaluation and assessment, results reporting and so on. Software testing tries to ensure that software products are not developed heuristically and optimistically. This software engineering stage ensures that the developed software is, ultimately and hopefully, error free. However, in reality, no process can guarantee that the developed software is 100% error free). In all cases, it is widely agreed that, this stage takes a large percent of the overall project resources.

Software test automation is the process of achieving one or more of software testing activities mentioned earlier programmatically or automatically with no user intervention (or with minimal user intervention). Software test automation is expected to cost more at the beginning while save more eventually. There are extra costs for test automation framework at start-up. However, once correctly implemented, it is widely accepted that test automation will decrease the cost as it reduces the required number of human testers and hence reduces the cost of testing. There are several repetitive tasks in testing that take a long time and that occur very often (e.g. regression testing, reporting, test cases' execution, etc.). For such activities, test automation is the best choice.

As explained at the beginning of this chapter, the focus of this chapter is in test automation for Graphical User Interfaces (GUIs). GUIs are getting more and more focus and roles in new applications. Earlier, the GUI has less important role and many program events can be executed with very simple Console commands. Developing rich GUIs that can handle complex types of application-user interactions became a trend in all new applications. A typical programming Integrated Development Environment (IDE) such as.NET, Eclipse or NetBeans includes lots of types of GUI components. Every time a new release is developed of those IDEs, one of the expected additions is new or richer GUI components. Such richness in GUI components add extra overhead to software testing where testing such components extensively require several different complex scenarios.

Challenges in GUI Test Automation

GUI test automation is a major challenge for test automation activities. Most of the current GUI test automation tools are partially automated and require the involvement of users or testers in several stages. Examples of some of the challenges that face GUI test automation is: dealing with continuously new controls or components, the dynamic behavior of the user interface, timing and synchronization problems, etc.

Test automation tools are still complex and expensive. They don't fully replace testers. They can be usually used to re-execute those repeated tasks. Companies consider taking the decision to buy, or not, a GUI test automation tool as a tough decision since they don't know how much time it will require upfront for setup. They also don't know how much of test automation tasks can be fully or partially automated. Software testers all agree that complete coverage in test automation is impractical as we also agree that complete coverage in manual testing is impractical too.

In record/play back test automation tools, we have to retest the application in case of any change in the functionalities or the GUI of the program. In many cases, this is seen as making such tools impractical especially as the program GUI is expected to be continuously evolved and changed.

GUI Test Automation Tools

There are several GUI test automation tools available in the market. Some of the larger vendors for such tools include: IBM Rational, Mercury, and Segue. Trying to build a GUI test automation tool is like trying to make a new operating system in that the available resources for the existing ones (i.e. in the market or the industry) are hard to compete with. However, GUI test automation has not reached a mature level were those tools can be implemented in all scenarios with no problems. User Interfaces evolves rapidly with richer and newer components. The automation processes in general use artificial intelligence algorithms to simulate user activities. The richness and complexity of this space make it possible for new research ideas to compete with long time existed test automation tools in the industry.

In the research field, there are several research papers about GUI testing using the data model (Ames and Jie, 2004, Nistorica 1998, Memon et al., 2003, Memon, 2004, Memon and Xie, 2005, and Sprenkle et al. 2005). The overall goals and approach for this work is very similar to their goals. The GUI testing framework described, as a GUI test automation structure, is generic and should be applied to any testing or GUI testing model. Since research projects in general have limited resources, each paper discusses a specific area of GUI test automation activities. Without having all components, it is very hard to use such ideas in the industry. There is a need for

3

using universal standards for the output formats in all testing activities. If each tool is producing several intermediate outputs (generated test cases, recorded scripts, log Files, etc), it will be impossible to use those tools or ideas in other research projects. Some papers follow a complex procedure in test case generation and do not consider any state reductions. Assuming that changing any property in any GUI object changes the GUI state is an assumption that generated a very large number of possible states (i.e. states' explosion problem) for even small applications. State reduction techniques are considered here to improve the effectiveness of the proposed track. There are also several papers that discuss techniques to improve test case generation with the goal of improving test coverage (Memon 2001, Memon 2002, Memon et al., 2003, Godase 2005, Sampath 2006, Xie 2006, Makedonov 2005, Memon 2008).

The majority of existed test automation tools are classified under the record/play back type or method of automation. In this method, the first time is always executed through a human. The tool records those activities to emulate them later on. Earlier versions of those tools were producing complex scripts that can be tediously complex and hard to debug or modify if required. Example of market tools in this method include: WinRunner, QuickTest pro, Segui silk, QARun, Rational Robot, JFCUnit, Abbot and Pounder. Capture/reply tools exist and have been used in the industry for years. This may make them currently, more reliable and practical as they have been tested and improved through several generations and improvements. However, there are several problems and issues in using record/play back tools. The need to reapply all test cases when the GUI changes, the complexity in editing the script code, and the lack of error handlings are examples of those issues. The reuse of test oracles is not very useful in the case of using a capture/replay tool.

An alternative to capture/replay tools, many recent test automation tools use the "data model" approach that uses reverse engineering methods to dynamically read the program code and generate, execute and verify test cases automatically based on that. We expect future software projects to be more GUI complex which will make the test automation data model more practical. Many researches and improvements need to be done for the suggested data model to be more practical and usable.

Methods for Generating Test Cases Automatically

Several papers are presented to suggest or implement software test automation. For example, some projects or papers described by Memon and his research fellows use planning from AI for software testing. After analyzing the application user interface to determine what operations are possible, they (i.e. the operations) become the operators in the planning problem. Next an initial and a goal state are determined for each case. Planning is used determine a path from the initial state to the goal state. This path becomes the test plan. However, since research projects in general have limited resources, each paper discusses a specific area of GUI test automation. Without having all components, it is very hard to use such ideas in the industry. There is a need for using universal standards for the output formats in all testing activities. If each tool is producing several intermediate outputs (generated test cases, recorded scripts, log files, etc), it will be impossible to use those tools or ideas in other research projects. Some papers follow a complex procedure in test case generation and do not consider any state reductions. Assuming that changing any property in any GUI object changes the GUI state is an assumption that generated a very large number of possible states for even small applications. State reduction techniques are considered here to improve the effectiveness of the track. We intended to follow the same GUI testing framework for our future work and expect the overall results to be more practical and easier to apply on actual projects.

(Mustafa et al 2007) paper focused on testing web based software. The paper proposed using economic feasibility based web testing as an alternative for model based testing due to the limitation of applying model based testing on the web. However, the challenge is in the automation of such approach in order to reduce its overall expenses.

In (Alsmadi and Magel 2007, and Ganadeep 2010), the authors used XML schema for GUI components regression testing. An application is developed to compare new and old test cases to differentiate between those similar and those which are new or different.

(Hanna et al 2011) studied web services robustness testing based on the platform. Besides robustness, there are several major criteria that are the focus web services testing. This includes performance, reliability and functionality.

Relative to GUI testing (Mao et al 2006) focused on GUI testing and selection based on user sessions (statistically) or usage to model the usage of the software. Usage paths are collected using Windows Navigation Networks (WNNs) based on transition probability. Those can be also collected automatically from the usage log.

(Xin et al 2010) paper mixed the using of user profile and Marcov chain for automatically deriving the testing model to improve the reliability of the software. Reliability testing is increasingly important for critical systems, particularly synchronous or reactive systems where even minor errors can be risky and expensive.

THE CAPTURE/PLAY-BACK TECHNIQUE AND TOOLS

Software testing has evolved over the years to incorporate tools for test automation. Most user interface test automation tools use the capture/play-back technique to record and replay test scripts.

We will demonstrate the basics of capture/play-back tools by using the IBM Rational Robot (from Stewart, 2008). The robot can capture and then replay user interactions with the GUI, a Java application or a Java applet. Figure 1 shows the interface for the Robot scripting application.

The user starts the recording process using the tool selection shown in Figure 1. The user performs some tasks which are recorded. Figure 2 shows an example of a recorded script. To re-execute the recorded actions on the application, you can select to run one or more recording from those displayed in the script interface (Figure 3). You can also edit the scripts to add or modify any line of code.

Rational Robot uses Virtual User (VU) script for performance testing or the GUI script for functional testing. VU has its own scripting language while GUI script uses the SQABasic scripting language. GUI scripts are used to replay the GUI activities that users record, while VU scripts are used to replay client/server requests the users record during performance testing sessions.

Depending on the tools used, there are several ways to verify the success of an executed script. In general, a user can define some rules or test points (i.e. assertions) to be checked during the execution process. The user defines the expected results at those assertion points (expected results can be difficult to describe in GUI testing).

Although many of the capture/play-back tools have been available for several years, they have some drawbacks. They are relatively expensive, writing and recording test scripts is labor intensive and error prone. They often use proprietary scripting languages that make the company developers incapable of editing or fixing their errors. They may require a long time to redo test scripts whenever a change occurs to the GUI as a result of a new release. They are not fully automated tools as they require a user to record the tests at the beginning and whenever a significant change occurs to the GUI functionalities or components.

Figure 1. Interface for IBM Rational Robot scripting tool (Stewart, 2008)

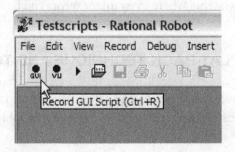

Figure 2. An example of a recorded script from IBM Rational Robot (Stewart, 2008)

```
Sub Main
    Dim Result As Integer

    'Initially Recorded: 7/3/2003  5:46:50 PM
    'Script Name: Notepad

    Window SetContext, "Class=Shell_TrayWnd", ""
    PushButton Click, "Text=start"

    Window SetContext, "Caption=Start Menu", ""
    ListView Click, "ObjectIndex=2;\;ItemText=Run...", "Coords=61,18"

    Window SetContext, "Caption=Run", ""
    InputKeys "Notepad"
    PushButton Click, "Text=OK"

    Window SetContext, "Caption=Untitled - Notepad", ""
    InputKeys "hello"
    MenuSelect "File->Exit"

    Window SetContext, "Caption=Notepad", ""
    PushButton Click, "Text=No"

End Sub
```

GUI Test Automation Using the Data Model Technique

Object oriented tools gather information at run time which make them always up-to-date, hence these tools do not require any rewriting of the test scripts. Programming languages such as Java and C# can be used in building the tools and writing the test cases. Several current market test automation tools started to include the data model technique in addition to the record/replay technique to offer both options for users or testers.

There are several papers presented on GUI test automation using the object data model. Some papers include a description of an overall data model framework. (Memon 2004,White et al 2001, and Bret 2004). The GUI testing framework described in some of those references is a general test automation structure that includes test case generation, selection, execution and verification. It can be applied to any testing or GUI testing model.

Other papers specifically discuss an area of the data-driven model such as studying test case generation and fault detection effectiveness (White et al 2001,Memon and Xie 2005,Xie 2006, Xie and Memon 2006), the advantage of using the data model for regression testing (White 1996,Ames and Jie 2004,Memon and Soffa 2003). Some of those papers describe a technique to generate test cases dynamically. The

Figure 3. Executing a test script using Rational TestManager (Wilber and Weishaar 2002)

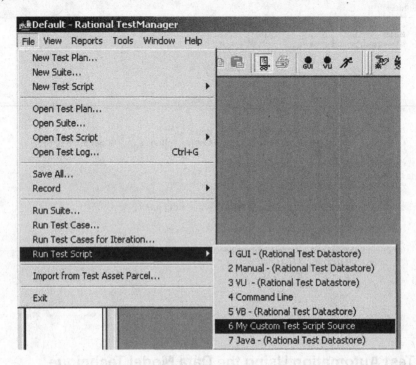

user has to specify the pre- and post-conditions for each test case. The algorithms generate test cases that fulfill those conditions.

Other papers explain specific areas of the testing process such as the process of parsing or ripping the GUI into a more easily analyzed format (Memon et al 2003). Critical paths are studied to reduce the overall cost of GUI testing (Ames and Jie 2004). Dynamic and run time behaviors in test automation are the subject of another related paper (Mitchell and Power 2004). The overall goals and approach for this work are similar to their goals; developing a data driven GUI test automation framework.

The GUI rippers described in (Memon 2001, Memon et al 2003, Memon and Xie 2005, Xie 2006) serialize everything and does not select certain criteria for the serialization. Serializing all GUI controls or objects with their entire properties makes the task cumbersome and error prone. GUI testing does not need all those properties.

The above data model approach requires user involvement and decisions in several parts of the test process. Some of the above research projects also follow a complex procedure for test case generation. Assuming that changing any property in any GUI control changes the GUI state is an unnecessary assumption that generates a very large number of possible states for even small applications.

Other approaches to GUI test automation involve partial test automation techniques (White and Almezen 2000, Steven 2000, Ames and Jie 2004), using some capture/play-back tools like WinRunner, QuickTest pro, Segui silk, QARun, Rational Robot, JFCUnit, Abbot and Pounder, to create unit tests for the GUI, and to execute and verify the results.

Some papers elaborated on problems with capture/play-back tools (Marick 1998, and Saket 2005). The need to reapply all test cases, editing the script code is complex, and the lack of error handlings are some examples of those issues. The reuse of test oracles is not very useful in the case of using a capture/play-back tool.

The standard industry practice of buying test tools for just the testers is unacceptable. The goal of automated tests is to be usable by everybody. Licenses for GUI test tools currently often run to up to $7,500 a seat (Bret 2004). It's hard enough for traditional organizations to find the budget to buy some licenses for their testers.

In the next part some other papers are presented. Those papers are related to the specific work of each module in the software testing sub stages. The following paragraphs present some of those papers.

Several approaches have been proposed for test case generation, including: random, path-oriented, goal-oriented, intelligent approaches (Memon et al 2003) and domain testing (which includes equivalence partitioning, boundary-value testing, and the category-partition methods) (Memon 2004).

Path oriented techniques generally use control flow information to identify a set of paths to be covered and generate the appropriate test cases to execute each identified path. These techniques can be classified as static or dynamic. Static techniques are often based on symbolic execution, whereas dynamic techniques obtain the necessary data by directly executing the application under test (Alsmadi and Magel 2007).

Goal-oriented techniques identify test cases covering a selected goal such as a statement or branch, irrespective of the path taken. Intelligent techniques of automated test case generation rely on complex computations to identify test cases. The real challenge to test generation is the generation of test cases that are capable of detecting faults in the AUT.

(Goga 2003) introduces an algorithm based on a probabilistic approach. It suggests combining test generation and test execution in one phase. (Tretmans 1996) studies test case generation algorithms for implementations that communicate via inputs and outputs, based on specifications using the Labeled Transition Systems (LTS). In the (MulSaw project 2006), the team used two complementary frameworks, TestEra and Korat for specification based test automation. To test a method, TestEra and Korat, automatically generate all non-isomorphic test cases from the method's pre-condition and check correctness using the method's post-condition as a test oracle. There are several papers published related to the MulSaw project.

(Clay 1999) presents an overview for model based software testing using UML. He suggests a framework for using the various UML diagrams in the testing process. As a model based software testing, prior to test case generation, (Alsmadi and Magel 2007) develop an XML model tree that represents the actual GUI which is serialized from the implementation. Test cases are then generated from the XML model.

(Turner and Robson 1993) suggest a new technique for the validation of Object Oriented Programming System (OOPS) which emphasizes the interaction between the features and the object's states. Each feature maps its starting or input state to its ensuing or output state affected by any stimuli. (Tse, Chan, and Chen 1994, and 1998) introduce normal forms for an axiom based test case selection strategy for OOPS's, and equivalent sequences of operations as an integration approach for object oriented test case generation.

(Orso and Silva 1998) introduce some of the challenges that object oriented technologies add to the process of software testing. Encapsulation and information hiding make it impossible for the tester to check what happens inside an object during testing. Due to data abstraction there is no visibility of the inside of objects making it impossible to examine their state. Encapsulation implies the contrary of visibility, which means that objects can be more difficult, or even impossible to test.

(Rajanna 2001) studies the impact and usefulness of automated software testing tools during the maintenance phase of a software product by citing the pragmatic experiences gained from the maintenance of a critical, active, and very large commercial software product. The experiment demonstrates that most of the error patterns reported during maintenance are due to inadequate test coverage, which is often the outcome of manual testing.

In the specific area of GUI test case generation, (Memon 2001) has several papers about automatically generating test cases from the GUI using an Artificial Intelligent (AI) planner. The process is not totally automatic and requires user intervention to set the current and goal states.

The AI planner finds the best way to reach the goal states given the current state. One issue with this research is that it does not address the problem of the huge number of states that a GUI in even a small application may have resulting in too many test cases. The idea of defining the GUI state as the collection state for all its controls, such that a change of a single property in one control leads to a new state is valid, but is the reason for producing the huge number of possible GUI states.

To solve the issue of dealing with a large number of possible GUI states, we suggest another alternative definition of a GUI state (Alsmadi and Magel 2007). We define the GUI state as the XML tree that is generated and representing the controls' structure and their selected properties. If the tree structure or any selected control property is changed, this is considered a GUI state change. The GUI state changes can be recognized by comparing the current XML file with the earlier one.

The automatic comparison and check of the overall GUI state (i.e. GUI structure) is not intended to be used for test case generation. It can be used to trigger the execution of regression testing in the same way a sensor triggers switching on, or off, an air condition system.

In one attempt related to the automatic generation of test cases, (Mcglade 2001) worked toward generating automatically feasible test cases from the source code.

In (Memon 2001), Planning Assisted Tester for grapHical Systems (PATHS) takes test goals from test designer as inputs and generates sequences of events automatically. These sequences of events or plans become test cases for the GUI. PATHS first performs an automated analysis of the hierarchical structure of the GUI to create hierarchical operators that are then used during the plan generation. The test designer describes the preconditions and effects of these planning operators, which subsequently, become the input to the planner. Each planning operator has two controls that represent a valid event sequence. For example, File_Save, File_SaveAs, Edit_Cut, and Edit_Copy are examples of planning operators. The test designer begins the generation of particular test cases by identifying a task, consisting of initial and goal states. The test designer then codes the initial and goal states or uses a tool that automatically produces the code (that is not developed yet). The process to define, in a generic way, the current and the goal states automatically, can be very challenging.

The previously described approach relies on an expert to manually generate the initial sequence of GUI events and, then uses genetic algorithm techniques to modify and extend the sequence. The test case generator is largely driven by the choice of tasks given to the planner.

Currently in PATHS, these tasks are chosen manually by the test designer. One suggestion that is suggested in (Memon 2001) is to maintain the pre- and post conditions for some standard critical events (like saving a file, copying text, changing control properties) in a library that can be reused. We will explain, later in the execution and verification chapter, some of the work done toward this goal in our research.

TEST AUTOMATION FRAMEWORK

In this section, we will summarize the software testing sub activities along with possible automation in each sub stage. Figure 4 represents a generic software testing framework (Makedonov 2005).

Figure 4. Generic software testing framework

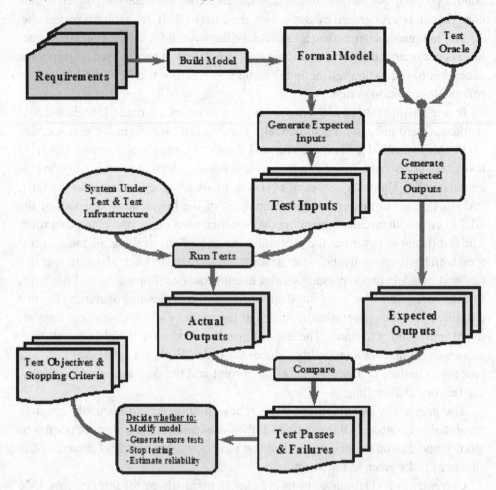

The framework contains the following components:

1. **Building the test model.** The input to this stage is the software requirements specification. At the beginning, requirements are written informally in natural language formats. However, in order to generate test cases automatically, there is a need to define the requirements formally. Although in many cases, the formality is accomplished using formal method tools and techniques, nevertheless, this is not usually a must. The idea is to formalize the definition and description of requirements to make them consistent and structured. This is necessary to be able to use or build a tool that can understand such structure and generate the test cases automatically based on that formal structure. As an alternative to the formal requirements, test cases can be generated automatically

from the actual application. This is actually what occurs in record/replay and data model tools where those tools use the actual application as an input for the generation of test cases. This can be more realistic as the test cases will be generated from the actual model and executed on it as well.

2. **Testing oracle or database.** This is the testing database that includes all test cases generated along with their expected results. In regression testing activity, which is a testing process that is triggered whenever the program passes a stage of evolution, all test cases are executed to make sure that the recent code modification did not cause any problem to the existed code.

3. **Test case generation (test case inputs and expected outputs).** As explained earlier, test cases can be automatically generated from the formal requirements or from the program itself. On the other hand, expected (correct) output for each test case can be defined based on requirements and the program itself.

4. **Test case execution.** This is the stage that gets the fame of being automated. The automatic generation of test cases on the code without the user interface can be relatively simple and is usually accomplished through code test automation tools such as JUnit and NUnit. However, executing test cases on the GUI and simulating the user interactions with the program can be far more complicated. The two most popular test automation methods (i.e. record/replay and the data model) are different on this based on the way they generate and execute the test cases (as described earlier).

5. **Test case results comparison and verification.** Results verification also differ in complexity, when comparing code verification compared with GUI test cases' verification. In many cases, the automatic test case verification for GUI test cases can be complicated due to the fact that it is difficult to "describe" the expected results for those test cases. For example, if we have a test case that change the look, color, components of the GUI, it will be hard for a programmer to instrument the code to automatically know what is the new GUI state after executing the test case.

Computer Assisted Testing or Test Automation?

Computer-assisted testing (CAT) includes the use of the computer to aid in the testing process. The assistance may be in the form of test case generation, test execution or delivery, scoring, record keeping, reporting results, providing feedback to examinees. It is a cost and time effective process as it replaces some of the tedious tasks usually done by testers. For some test processes, such as analyzing the source code for errors, designing test case generation algorithms, first state test evaluation, and debugging errors, it is better and more useful for a human to perform those tasks. For some other tasks such as: running and recording tests, rerunning regression tests, and generating test cases from algorithms, it is more time and cost effective to automate those tasks.

In short, GUI test automation does not mean replacing users totally by computers, it means reducing the involvement of users or humans in testing to the practical minimum. Full test automation that means no involvement of testers through all the process stages is not practical or feasible. The main goal of test automation is to reduce time and cost of testing as one of the major stages that consume resources in software development.

Automating black box testing requires generating test cases on the basis of a representative model of the system called the test model. This model gets its information from the specification or design. This is usually known as model-based test automation techniques. Automating white box testing requires generating test cases from the code or implementation.

It is useful and cost effective to start automating the testing activities that are repeated frequently. This makes it more cost effective to build or use a test automation tool in some testing activities such as regression testing. We also automate when the number of tests to execute is large. It will take a lot of testers' time to run those test cases and verify their results.

In some cases, testing is required to run automatically after work hours where some testers may not be available. Test automation can free the scarce resources of developers and testers to do some other tasks. We do not automate to get rid of testers; we automate to extend their capabilities.

In the following sections, we will present the software testing sub activities based on the model and research projects described in our previous published papers (Alsmadi and Magel 2007, Tubeishat et al 2010, Alsmadi and AlKabi 2011).

GUI Modeling

In the first activities described of the software testing framework, a formal format is required to generate the test cases automatically from. We defined a GUI test automation model in an XML format for that purpose (Alsmadi and Magel 2007). The tool analyses the GUI and extract its hierarchical tree of controls or objects. The decision to use XML File as a saving location is in the fact that XML Files support hierarchy. This hierarchy can be persisted from the XML File. We encoded a level code for each control. The Main Window is considered of level 0, and so on. A Notepad version is designed as a managed code in C# to be used for testing. For this version the total number of controls for the whole application came up to 1133. There may be some redundancy in this list as roots in each file are listed twice to preserve the hierarchy.

For test adequacy, each path of the GUI tree should be tested or listed at least once in the test cases. A complete test case is a case that starts from level 0 and select an object from level 1 and so on. This is with taking the hierarchical structure into consideration and selecting for example an object from level 2 that is within the reach of the selected object in level 1.

A partial test case can take two objects. Test case selection should also take in consideration the number of controls or objects in each level. For the above example, level 0 will take 55/1133 = 4.85% of the total test cases, level1 will take 522/1133 = 46.07% of the total, level2 will take 41/183= 27.36%, and level3 will take 246/1133 = 21.71% of the total.

We should decide whether we want to run a full test case which means a test case that start from level 0 and go back to level 0 (in the graph path, start from top, traverse to an end and then go back to the top), or partial test cases. The test case can take the full route from level 0 to the deepest level and then back on the same path (or another) to the same original point.

In this Notepad example, the limitation we should consider is that controls in levels 1 and up may not be accessible directly or randomly and they have to be accessed through their level 0 control. In addition, since we are pulling all controls together, the naming convention should be unique so that the object can be known, or otherwise we should use its full name.

To preserve the GUI hierarchical structure from the XML File, the application parses it to a tree view. Two different terminologies are used (encoded in the tree):

1. **Control-level:** This is the vertical level of the GUI control. The main GUI is considered the highest level control or control 0, then we keep adding 1 as we go down the hierarchy.
2. **Control-Unit:** This is the horizontal level of the control. For example, in Notepad, File menu, with all its sub unit are unit 1, Edit menu unit 2, Format, unit 3 and so on.

Generally, each "full" test case has to start from control-level zero and go back to this point. As an example, a test case will not be considered a valid test case if it moves from File to Edit to Format (i.e. the main menus). The test case has to move at least one level up or down. Each control is defined by where it is located horizontally and vertically. Checking for consistency in the graph should verify that there are no two objects that have the same control unit and level.

Figure 5 shows Notepad with the control unit and level for its GUI objects. This is a graph of the GUI objects showing the control level and unit for each object.

Getting the Event Flow Graph (EFG), or the GUI graph from the above tree is straightforward. A particular event will occur in the tree if moving within the same

Figure 5. Notepad control units and levels

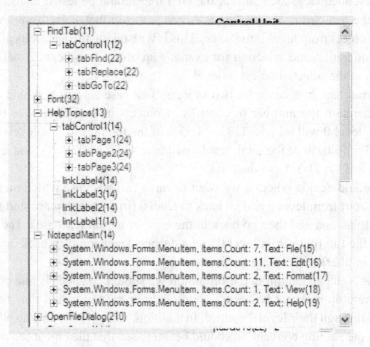

control unit number one control level down. For example, NotepadMain(14)-Edit(16) is a valid event since both have the same control unit number "1". Numbers in the above GUI components (i.e. NotepadMain (14), Edit (16)) represent encoding values that uniquely locate each control in the GUI graph.

We can pick the number of test cases to generate and the tool will generate full or partial test cases that observe the previous rules. Figure 6 shows an example of a full test case that the tool generates.

We used some abstraction removing those properties that are less relevant to the GUI state and testing to reduce the large number of possible states. In order to build a GUI test oracle, we have to study the effect of each single event. The test case result will be the combining results of all its individual events effects. For example If we have a test case as File-Save-Edit- copy – select test – paste, then the result of this test case has effects on two objects; File-Save has effect on a File. We should study the File state change, and not the whole GUI state change. Then Edit-Copy has an effect on the clipboard object, Paste will have the effect on the main editor object or state, adding the copied text.

Verifying the results of this test case will be through verifying the state change of the three objects affected; The File, the clipboard and the object editor. For such scenarios, we may need to ignore some intermediate events. Each application should have a table or tables like Table 1, to be checked for test oracles.

Figure 6. A full test case generated

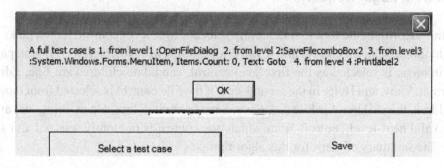

Test Case Generation

In test case generation, several Artificial Intelligent (AI) heuristically based algorithms are created for the automatic generation of test cases. We proposed and implemented those algorithms to ensure a certain degree or level of coverage in the generated test cases where such algorithms try to verify that generated test cases are not repeated or redundant. Those algorithms are heuristic as they are not based on mathematical formula or background. Those algorithms manually verify that randomly generated test cases are new or they will be eliminated. In one algorithm, all GUI paths are given an initial weight for test case selection and those weights are reduced every time an edge or path is selected. The following dynamically-created test generation algorithms are heuristics. The goal is to generate unique test cases that represent legal test scenarios in the GUI tree with the best branch coverage. This is guaranteed by creating a unique test scenario each time. Here is a list of some of the developed algorithms.

Table 1. A sample table for GUI events effects using Notepad menus

Control-event pair	Control originating the event	The object(s) Affected	Effect
File,save	File-Save	A File	The text from the object editor will be saved to the specified File
Edit,cut	Edit-Cut	Clipboard, object Editor	Moving a text-image to clipboard, clearing the original location
Edit,copy	Edit-Copy	Clipboard	Moving a text-image to clipboard, keep a copy in the original location.
Edit, paste	Edit- paste	Object editor	Copying a text/image to a destination

Random Legal Sequences

In this algorithm, the tool first randomly selects a first-level control. It then picks a child for the selected control and so on. For example, in a Notepad AUT, If Notepad main menu is selected as the first level control; candidate children are File, Edit, Format, View, and Help. In the second step, if the File control is selected from those children, the children for File (i.e. Save, SaveAs, Exit, Close, Open, Print, etc) are the valid next-level controls from which one control is randomly selected and so on. The summary of steps for this algorithm is:

- Select dynamically (i.e., the tool) the main entry control (or select any control of level 0).
- Find all the children for the control selected in one and randomly pick one child.
- Find all the children for the control selected in two and select one child control.
- Repeat three until no child is found for the selected control. The test scenario for this cycle is the sequence of controls from all previous steps.
- Repeat the above steps for the total number of the required test scenarios.

Random Less Previously Selected Controls

In this algorithm, controls are randomly selected as in the previous algorithm. The only difference is that if the current control is previously selected (e.g. in the test case just before this one), this control is excluded from the current selection. This causes the algorithm to always look for a different new control to pick. Figure 7 shows the pseudo code for this algorithm.

Excluding Previously Generated Scenarios

Rather than excluding the previously selected control as in the second algorithm, this algorithm excludes all previously generated test cases or scenarios and hence verifies the generation of a new unique test case every time. The scenario is generated and if the test suite already contains the new generated scenario, it will be excluded and the process to generate a new scenario starts again. In this scenario, the application may stop before reaching the number of required test cases (requested by the user) to generate if there are no more unique test scenarios to create. As explained earlier, the algorithm is given limited resources. It is expected to find the solution within

Figure 7. Pseudo code for the algorithm: "Random less previously selected controls"

```
WHILE numtestcase < testcase_required
SELECT control_root
DISPLAY control_root
WHILE control_root has new child
DISPLAY child
END WHILE
INCREMENT numtestcases
END WHILE
```

those resources or the algorithm stops and is considered to have failed (similar to the way ping command in networks works; given limited time to test reachability). The steps for this algorithm are:

- Select a first level control.
- Find all the children for the selected control in step one and randomly pick one child of that control.
- Find all the children for the control selected in step two and pick one child of that control.
- Repeat step three until no child is found for the selected control.

The test scenario for this cycle is the controls in sequence from all previous steps. Save the sequence of the test scenario to a Hashtable (e.g. a data structure).

- Check the scenarios that are existed in the Hashtable. If the current created scenario is in the Hashtable, exclude it from the selection and restart the selection process.
- Repeat the above steps for the total number of the required test scenarios unless a termination process is called. Figure 8 shows a sample output from the above algorithm.

As seen in the sample, some of the generated test cases are canceled as they were previously generated (from looking at the sequence of the test cases).

Weight Selection Algorithm

In this scenario, rather than giving the same probability of selection or weight for all candidate children of controls, as in all previous scenarios, in this algorithm any child that is selected in the current node causes its weight (i.e. probability of selection)

Figure 8. A sample of the unique-scenarios algorithm

```
1,NOTEPADMAIN,FORMAT,WORD WRAP,,,
3,NOTEPADMAIN,OPEN,OPENFILELABEL4,,,
5,NOTEPADMAIN,FORMAT,FONT,FONTLABEL1,,
7,NOTEPADMAIN,LABEL1,,,,
9,NOTEPADMAIN,BUTTON1,,,,
11,NOTEPADMAIN,HELPTOPICSFORM,HELPTOPICS,INDEX,LABEL3,
13,NOTEPADMAIN,OPEN,OPENFILELABEL8,,,
15,NOTEPADMAIN,FILE,OPEN,OPENFILELABEL9,,
17,NOTEPADMAIN,FIND,TABCONTROL1,TABFIND,FINDTABTXTFIND,
19,NOTEPADMAIN,FIND,TABCONTROL1,TABGOTO,GOTOTABTXTLINE,
21,NOTEPADMAIN,SAVE,SAVEFILEBUTTON1,,,
23,NOTEPADMAIN,SAVEAS,SAVEFILECOMBOBOX4
25,NOTEPADMAIN,FONT,FONTLISTBOX1,,,
27,NOTEPADMAIN,HELPTOPICSFORM,LINKLABEL2
29,NOTEPADMAIN,FIND,TABCONTROL1,TABREPLACE,REPLACETABLABEL3,
31,NOTEPADMAIN,HELP,ABOUT NOTEPAD,,,
33,NOTEPADMAIN,BUTTON2,ABOUT NOTEPAD,,,
35,NOTEPADMAIN,HELP,HELP TOPICS,,,
37,NOTEPADMAIN,BUTTON2,,,,
39,NOTEPADMAIN,BUTTON2,HELP TOPICS,,,
41,NOTEPADMAIN,LABEL1,HELP TOPICS,,,
43,NOTEPADMAIN,EDIT,GOTO,,,
45,NOTEPADMAIN,SAVEAS,SAVEFILELABEL2,,,
47,NOTEPADMAIN,FIND,TABCONTROL1,TABGOTO,GOTOTABLABEL4,
```

next time to be reduced by a certain percent. If the same control is selected again, its weight is reduced again and so on. The summary of steps for this algorithm is:

- Select the first level control.
- Select randomly a child for the control selected in step one. Give equal weights·for all children. Decrease weight for the selected one by a fixed value.
- Find all the children for the control selected in step two and randomly pick one child control. Give equal weights for all children and decrement the weight for the selected one by the same fixed value (this value can be the same for all levels, or each level can have a different value).
- Repeat step three until no child is found for the selected control.
- The test scenario for this cycle is the sequence of the selected controls from all the previous steps.
- Repeat the above steps for the total number of the required test scenarios unless a termination process is called. Keep the decreased weights from the earlier scenarios.

Figure 9. A sample of generated test cases

1,NOTEPADMAIN,FILE,NEW,TXTBODY,,
2,NOTEPADMAIN,FILE,SAVE AS,SAVEFILEBUTTON1,,,

The last two algorithms are designed to ensure branch coverage, all-paths testing (i.e. testing that experience all possible paths of an application. Paths usually represent different decisions in the code), and reduce redundancy in the generated test suite.

We define test suite effectiveness that can be calculated automatically in the tool in order to evaluate the above algorithms. Test suite effectiveness is defined as the total number of edges discovered to the actual total number of edges. Figure 9 shows test effectiveness for the four algorithms explained earlier.

To evaluate test generation efficiency in the generated test cases, the total number of arcs visited in the generated test cases is calculated to the total number of arcs or edges in the Application Under Test (AUT). File-Save, Edit-Copy, Format-Font are examples of arcs or edges. An algorithm is developed to count the total number of edges in the AUT by using the parent info for each control. (This is a simple approach of calculating test efficiency. More rigorous efficiency measuring techniques should be invistigated). Of those tested applications, about 95% of the application paths can be discovered and tested using 200-300 test cases.

Critical Path Testing and Test Case Prioritization

Critical paths are the paths that cause test execution to be slow, or the paths that have more probability of errors than the other testing paths. Here are some of the critical path examples:

- An external API or a command line interface accessing an application.
- Paths that occur in many tests (in a regression testing database)
- The most time consuming paths. Three algorithms are developed to find critical paths automatically in the AUT.

Critical Paths Using Node Weight

In this approach, each control is given a metric weight that represents the count of all its children. For example if the children of File are: Save, SaveAs, Close, Exit, Open, Page Setup, and Print, then its metric weight is seven (another alternative is to calculate all the children and grand children). For each generated scenario, the weight of that scenario is calculated as the sum of all the weights of its individual selected controls.

To achieve coverage with test reduction, the algorithm selects randomly one of those scenarios that share the same weight value as a representative for all of them. An experiment should be done to test whether those scenarios that have the same weight can be represented by one test case or not (i.e., from a coverage perspective).

Other alternative is to set a minimum weight required to select a test scenario and then generate all test scenarios that have a weight higher than the selected cut off. The two criteria that affect the critical path weight factor are the number of nodes that the path consists of and the weight of each node. This technique can help us dynamically define the longest or deepest paths in an application.

Critical Path Level Reduction through Selecting Representatives

This technique approaches test selection reduction through selecting representative test scenarios. Representatives are elected from the different categories, classes or areas to best represent the whole country. In this approach, the algorithm arbitrarily selects a test scenario. The selected scenario includes controls from the different levels. Starting from the lowest level control, the algorithm excludes from selection all those controls that share the same parent with the selected control. This reduction shouldn't exceed half of the tree depth. For example if the depth of the tree is four levels, the algorithm should exclude controls from levels three and four only.

We assume that three controls are the least required for a test scenario (such as Notepad – File – Exit). We continuously select five test scenarios using the same reduction process described above. The selection of the number five for test scenarios is heuristic. The idea is to select the least amount of test scenarios that can best represent the whole GUI.

Weight Controls from User Sessions

The previously described algorithms for critical paths' selection depend on statistics pulled from the implementation model. As an alternative, we can analyze several user captured sessions (e.g. from testers or users in beta testing) to automatically weight the GUI controls. User session data is the set of user actions performed on the AUT from entering the application until leaving it. We can analyze several user captured sessions (e.g. from testers or users in beta testing) to automatically weight the GUI controls or widgets. User session data is the set of user actions performed on the Application Under Test (AUT) from entering the application until leaving it.

We can classify a control, or a pair of controls, according to the number of times they are repeated in a user session. User sessions are likely to detect faults in the application that are not predictable in earlier testing phases. Another advantage of testing with user sessions is that testing is possible in the absence of specifications or in the presence of incorrect and incomplete specifications, which often occurs in software development.

The session logs all the controls that are executed in the different scenarios. A simple count or percentage is given to each control depending on how many times it is listed in those scenarios. The test scenarios should include all primary and major use cases for the AUT. The controls' weights (calculated from user sessions) can drive the test case generation and execution. Theoretically all controls should get the same weight in the generated test suite. However, in real scenarios this may not be true. We can use the weighing method for single controls or for a sequence of controls (result from a specific use case).

We may cluster the controls, or sequence of controls, according to their usage from user sessions into three levels; heavily used, medium and low. Depending on the availability of the resources for testing, we may choose one or two categories and generate test cases that cover those controls in the categories with a proportion to their weight or occurrence. The developed algorithm in this research is considered as a hybrid technique that uses some of the capture/ reply processes. In a capture/ reply tool, the same user session that is captured in the manual testing is executed. In this approach the controls' weights are extracted from the manual testing to guide test case generation and execution. The reason for considering this track rather than using capture/ reply test execution and validation is to avoid the dependency on the absolute location of the screen and controls that is required by capture/replay tools. Having a hybrid solution may give us the best of both and utilize the accumulative experience and knowledge in different technologies.

In order to record user events, we implemented in our C# application (Alsmadi 2008) the interface IMessageFilter that is used to capture messages between Window applications and components. In the AUT, each GUI control that is triggered by the user is logged to a file that represents the user sessions. The minimum information required is the control, its parent and the type of event. The user session file includes the controls triggered by the user in the same sequence. Such information is an abstract of the user session sequence. In many cases, the same control is repeated several time (due to the nature of logging the window messages), The implementation will get rid of all those controls repeated right after each other. The same information can be extracted from the events written to the event log.

Test Case Execution and Verification

For test verification, a log file is created to track the events that are executed in the tool during the execution process. In a simple example, Figure 9 shown below, two test cases are generated that write a text in Notepad and save it to a file. Those test cases are generated using the tool.

The first test case opens a new document and writes to it. As part of the default input values, we set for each control a default value to be inserted by the tool through execution. A textbox writes the word "test" or the number "0" whenever it is successfully called. A menu item is clicked, using its parent, whenever it is successfully called. For example, if Save is called as a control, File-Save as an event is triggered. We should have tables for valid and invalid inputs for each GUI control. The second test case opens the save File dialogue and clicks the OK or accept button (SaveFilebutton1), to save the document. Here is the corresponding log file output for the above test cases (Figure 10).

Since the test execution process is subjected to several environment factors, the verification process is divided into three levels.

1. In the first level the tool checks that every control in the test suite is successfully executed. This step is also divided into two parts. The first part is checking that all controls executed are existed in the test suite. This is to verify that the execution process itself does not cause any extra errors. The second part that ensures all controls in the test suites are executed tests the execution and its results. In the implementation of this level, some controls from the test sce-

Figure 10. Log file output of a sample test case

Control   Event   Date Time
File new   Menu Click   10/3/2008 11:51:23 AM File   new   Mouse Down 10/3/2008 11:51:23 AM File new Mouse Up 10/3/2008 11:51:23 AM
New   txtbody Menu Click   10/3/2008 11:51:23 AM New   txtbody Mouse Down   10/3/2008 11:51:23 AM New   txtbody Mouse Up   10/3/2008 11:51:23 AM TxtBody   Mouse Move 10/3/2008 11:51:23 AM TxtBody   Key Down   10/3/2008 11:51:23 AM TxtBody   Key UP 10/3/2008 11:51:23 AM
(Test) is written in the document   10/3/2008 11:51:23 AM (Test) is written in the document 10/3/2008 11:51:24 AM
SaveFilebutton1 Mouse Move 10/3/2008 11:51:24 AM SaveFilebutton1 Mouse Button Down 10/3/2008 11:51:24 AM SaveFilebutton1   Mouse Button Up   10/3/2008 11:51:24 AM   File SAVE AS Menu Click 10/3/2008 11:51:24 AM
File   SAVE AS Mouse Down 10/3/2008 11:51:24 AM
File   SAVE AS Mouse Up 10/3/2008 11:51:24 AM SaveFilebutton1 Mouse Move 10/3/2008 11:51:24 AM SaveFilebutton1 Mouse Button Down 10/3/2008 11:51:24 AM SaveFilebutton1 Mouse Button Up   10/3/2008 11:51:24 AM

narios were not executed. This is maybe the case of some dynamic execution or time synchronization issues where some controls are not available the time they are expected.

2. In the second level the tool checks that the number of controls matches between the two suites.

3. In the third level, the tool checks that the events are in the same sequence in both suites. The verification process is automated by comparing the test cases' file with the log file. Time stamp is important to verify the correct sequence of events. The controls in the test case suites are written to a sorted list and the execution sequence is also written to another sorted lists. To verify the results of the test execution, the two lists are compared with each other. Upon testing several applications, a small percent of controls generated in the test cases and not executed. Timing synchronization causes some controls to be unavailable or invisible within their execution time. Regular users "wait" for a new menu to be opened. This time varies depending on the application, the computer and the environment. Time synchronization and some other dynamic issues are part of the future research goals.

One approach for the GUI test oracle is to have event templates. For each test scenario listed, expected results are written in a way that can be automatically verified. This requires some level of abstraction where similar events are abstract into one event (like the saving process). This proposal does not mean exhaustively testing all probable events. By selecting critical events for automation and abstracting similar events we will get a valuable state reduction that makes the number of GUI states more practical in terms of testing.

CONCLUSION

In this chapter, different software test automation activities and approaches are investigated with the focus on the GUI part of the software. The majority of research papers and application in the software testing field focus on automating the testing activities as this can reduce the amount of effort required through manual testing. Consequently, this will reduce the time and cost of the overall software project. The chapter summarized the author previous work and research projects on that goal that include attempts to automate all software testing activities. A user interface XML model is dynamically generated to be the first automated step in the framework. This model is used as an input for other testing activities such as: test case generation, prioritization, metrics and comparison. The automatic execution of the generated test cases is then applied on the actual program. Test case verification is also implemented to compare the results of the automatic execution process with those expected.

Test automation is a process that needs to be continuously updated and evolved. This is as applications, GUI components and environments are themselves continuously updated and evolved.

REFERENCES

Alsmadi, I. (2008). The utilization of user sessions in testing. In *Proceedings of the Seventh IEEE/ACIS International Conference on Computer and Information Science* (ICIS 2008).

Alsmadi, I., & Al-Kabi, M. (2011). GUI structural metrics. *The International Arab Journal of Information Technology (IAJIT), 8*(2).

Alsmadi, I., & Magel, K. (2007). GUI path oriented test generation algorithms. *Proceedings of the Second IASTED International Conference on Human Computer Interaction*, March 14-16, 2007, Chamonix, France.

Alsmadi, I., & Magel, K. (2007b). *An object oriented framework for user interface test automation*. MICS07.

Ames, A., & Jie, H. (2004). *Critical paths for GUI regression testing*. University of California, Santa Cruz. Retrieved from http://www.cse.ucsc.edu/~sasha/ proj/ gui_testing.pdf

Godase, S. (2005). *An introduction to software automation*. Retrieved from http:// www.qthreads.com/articles/testing-/an_introduction_to_software_test_automation. html

Goga, N. (2003). *A probabilistic coverage for on-the-y test generation algorithms*. Retrieved from.

Hanna, S., & Abu Ali, A. (2011). Platform effect on Web services robustness testing. *Journal of Applied Sciences, 11*(2), 360–366. doi:10.3923/jas.2011.360.366

http://www.fmt.cs.utwente.nl/publications/Files/ 398_covprob.ps.gz

Makedonov, Y. (2005). *Managers guide to GUI test automation*. Software Test and Performance Conference 2005. Retrieved from http://www.softwaretestconsulting. com/Presentations_slides/Manager_sGuide_GUI_Test-Automation11wh.pdf

Mao, Y., Boqin, F., Zhenfang, H., & Li, F. (2006). Important usage paths selection for GUI software testing. *Information and Technology Journal, 5*(4), 648–654. doi:10.3923/itj.2006.648.654

Marick, B. (1998). When should a test be automated. In *Proceedings of the 11th International Software/Internet Quality Week. Software Research*, San Francisco, USA. Retrieved from http://www.testing.com/writings/automate.pdf

Mcglade, L. (2008). *Structural testing of Web-based scripting programs*. Retrieved from http://www.cra.org/Activities/craw/dmp/awards/2001/mcglade/final_paper.htm

Memon, A. (2001). *A comprehensive framework for testing graphical user interfaces*. Ph.D. thesis, Department of Computer Science, University of Pittsburgh, July 2001.

Memon, A. (2001). Hierarchical GUI test case generation using automated planning. *IEEE Transactions on Software Engineering, 27*(2), 144–155. doi:10.1109/32.908959

Memon, A. (2002). GUI testing: Pitfall and process. *Software Technologies, 35*(8), 87–88.

Memon, A. (2004). *Developing testing techniques for event-driven pervasive computing applications*. Department of Computer Science, University of Maryland.

Memon, A. (2008). Automatically repairing event sequence-based GUI test suites for regression testing. *ACM Transactions on Software Engineering and Methodology, 18*(2). doi:10.1145/1416563.1416564

Memon, A., Banerejee, I., & Nagarajan, A. (2003). GUI ripping: Reverse engineering of graphical user interfaces for testing. In *Proceedings of the 10th. Working Conference on Reverse Engineering* (WCRE'03), (pp. 1095-1350).

Memon, A., & Soffa, M. (2003). Regression testing of GUIs. In *Proceedings of ESEC/FSE'03*, September 2003.

Memon, A., & Xie, Q. (2005). Studying the fault detection effectiveness of GUI test cases for rapidly evolving software. *IEEE Transactions on Software Engineering, 31*(10), 884–896. doi:10.1109/TSE.2005.117

MIT Software design group. (2008). *Computer science and artificial intelligence laboratory*. Retrieved from http://sdg.csail.mit.edu/index.html

Mitchell, A., & Power, J. (2004). An approach to quantifying the run-time behavior of Java GUI applications. In *Proceedings of the Winter International Symposium on Information and Communication Technologies*, Cancun, Mexico, (pp. 1–6).

Mustafa, G., Ali Shah, A., Asif, K. H., & Ali, A. (2007). A strategy for testing of Web based software. *Information Technology Journal, 6*(1), 74–81. doi:10.3923/itj.2007.74.81

Nistorica, G. (2005). Automated GUI testing. O'Reilly Network. Retrieved from http://www.perl.com/pub/a/2005/08/11/win32guitest.html

Orso, A., & Silva, S. (1998). Open issues and research directions in object oriented testing. In *Proceedings of the 4th International Conference on "Achieving Quality in Software: Software Quality in the Communication Society" (AQUIS '98)*, Venice, Italy.

Pettichord, B. (2004). *Homebrew test automation*. ThoughtWorks. Retrieved from www.io.com/~wazmo/ papers/homebrew_test_automation_200409.pdf

Rajanna, V. (2001). Automated software testing tools and their impact on software maintenance. In *Proceedings of the 3rd Annual International Software Testing*, India. Retrieved from Softwaredioxide.com

Sengupta, G. J. (2010). Regression testing method based on XML schema for GUI components. *Journal of Software Engineering, 4*(2), 137–146. doi:10.3923/jse.2010.137.146

Sprenkle, S., Gibson, E., Sampath, S., & Pollock, L. (2005). Automated replay and failure detection for Web applications. *Proceedings of the 20th IEEE/ACM international Conference on Automated Software Engineering*, November 07-11, 2005, USA.

Sreedevi, S. (2006). *Cost effective techniques for user session based testing of Web applications*. PhD dissertation, University of Delaware. Retrieved from 128.4.133.74:8080/dspace/bitstream/123456789/168/1/-sampath.dissertation06.pdf

Stewart, F. (2008). *Practical use of Rational Robot in transactional monitoring*. IBM. Retrieved from http://www.ibm.com/developerworks/tivoli/library/tration-alrobot/index.html

Tretmans, J. (1996). Test generation with inputs, outputs, and quiescence. In *Proceedings of the Second International Workshop on Tools and Algorithms for Construction and Analysis of Systems, Passau, Germany, Lecture Notes in Computer Science*, 1055, (pp. 127–146).

Tse, T. H., Chan, F. T., & Chen, H. Y. (1994). An axiom-based test case selection strategy for object-oriented programs. *IFIP Conference Proceedings, Software Quality and Productivity: Theory, Practice and Training*, London, UK, (pp. 107–114).

Tse, T. H., Chan, F. T., & Chen, H. Y. (1998). In black and white: An integrated approach to object-oriented program testing. [TOSEM]. *ACM Transactions on Software Engineering and Methodology, 7*(3), 250–295. doi:10.1145/287000.287004

Tubeishat, M., Alsmadi, I., & Al-Kabi, M. (2010). Using XML for user interface documentation and differential evaluation. *Journal of Theoretical and Applied Information Technology, 21*(2).

Turner, C. D., & Robson, D. J. (1993). The state-based testing of object-oriented programs. In *Proceedings of the IEEE Conference on Software Maintenance* (CSM-93), Montreal, Canada, (pp. 302–310).

White, L., Al Mezen, H., & Alzeidi, N. (2001). User-based testing of GUI sequences and their interactions. In *Proceedings of the 12th International Symposium on Software Reliability Engineering* (ISSRE'01), Hong Kong, PRC, (p. 54).

White, L., & Almezen, H. (2000). Generating test cases from GUI responsibilities using complete interaction sequences. In *Proceedings of the International Symposium on Software Reliability Engineering (ISSRE'00),* San Jose, USA, (pp. 110-121).

Wilber, J., & Weishaar, G. (2002). *Executing visual test scripts with IBM Rational TestManager*. IBM. Retrieved from http://www.ibm.com/developerworks/rational/library/2962.html

Williams, C. (1999). Software testing and the UML. In *Proceedings of the International Symposium on Software Reliability Engineering* (ISSRE'99), Boca Raton, USA.

Xie, Q. (2006). Developing cost-effective model-based techniques for GUI testing. In *Proceedings of The International Conference of Software Engineering 2006* (ICSE'06).

Xin, W., Feng-Yan, H., & Zheng, Q. (2010). Software reliability testing data generation approach based on a mixture model. *Information Technology Journal, 9*(5), 1038–1043. doi:10.3923/itj.2010.1038.1043

Chapter 2
On the Application of Automated Software Testing Techniques to the Development and Maintenance of Speech Recognition Systems

Daniel Bolanos
University of Colorado at Boulder, USA

ABSTRACT

This chapter focuses on the description and analysis of an automated software testing approach followed during the development of a new generation automatic speech recognition system. Automatic speech recognition systems present a series of characteristics that distinguish them from other software systems and that make the elaboration of test-cases a truly complex task: the metrics used to measure their performance and accuracy, the nature of the input and output data that they receive and produce, the multiple data formats, their working mode, the high number of configuration parameters, et cetera.

This chapter provides practitioners in the field with a set of guidelines to help them through the process of elaborating an adequate automated testing framework to competently test automatic speech recognition systems. Through this chapter the testing process of such a system is analyzed from different angles, and different methods and techniques are proposed that are well suited for this task.

DOI: 10.4018/978-1-4666-0089-8.ch002

1. INTRODUCTION

Automatic speech processing is a multidisciplinary field dedicated to the analysis of speech signals. One of the main areas of speech processing is automatic speech recognition (ASR), which consists of extracting the linguistic information from a speech signal. ASR systems are extremely complex systems that must integrate a number of sources of information (acoustic, linguistic, speaker, environmental, information and others) and, in like manner, must process a massive amount of features in real time. Furthermore, given that the accuracy and reliability of state-of-the-art ASR systems are still lacking in many respects, new algorithms and techniques that apply to almost every module of these systems that are developed each year by researchers and published in the corresponding scientific literature. Thus, one must recognize that a speech recognition system is a truly complex software system, which implies that it is prone to development errors. Moreover, for it to stay competitive in terms of accuracy and real time performance, it is a system that needs to be constantly evolving in order to incorporate the latest advances in the field. The combination of these two factors makes automated software testing a must in order to guarantee that the developed system meets the high quality standards required for a product of its kind.

Automated software testing techniques provide the software developer with a comprehensive set of tools and techniques that ease the design and automation of all types of software tests (unit, integration, functional, etc.) across the life-cycle of a software system. The development of speech processing systems and, in particular, automated speech recognition systems requires a fairly extensive knowledge of a number of topics, such as signal processing, statistics, search algorithms, machine learning, phonetics, and linguistics. Thus, speech recognition developers are typically scientists who come from many different areas and who do not necessarily possess a strong background in software development and even less so in software engineering or automated software testing techniques. For this reason, a number of the speech recognition systems are made publicly available, a group which includes some of the most widely used systems in the research community, do not meet basic software engineering or software testing principles. This makes it difficult for practitioners to modify or adapt these systems with enough confidence and sometimes hinders or even prevents the incorporation of the latest techniques necessary to keep them up-to-date. Thus, it is sometimes the case that a system is not updated as rapidly as it should be (because there is no one confident enough to do so) and eventually the system becomes outdated. This creates the necessity of building a new system, practically from scratch, instead of updating a perfectly good existing system. What comes into play here is the bad principle of *if something works (reasonably well) do not touch it*, as opposed to the good principle of software testing: *make your changes confidently and run the necessary tests* (which include the regression and the newly developed test-cases.) We believe that following an adequate automated software testing methodology can overcome these issues and potentially facilitate a more rapid development of the field by providing researchers with clear guidelines for how to automate the testing process of ASR systems, so they can be updated safely and confidently.

This chapter focuses on the description and analysis of a software engineering and automated software testing approach followed during the development of a new generation speech recognition system, which will be released as an open source system in the near future to be used for the research community. The aim of the chapter is to provide practitioners in the field with a set of guidelines to help them through the process of elaborating an adequate automated testing framework to competently test ASR systems. ASR systems present a series of characteristics that distinguish them from other software systems and that make the elaboration of test-cases a truly complex task: the metrics used to measure their performance and accuracy, the nature of the input and output data that they receive and produce, the multiple formats in which this data can be stored and retrieved, their working mode (live, or batch mode), the configuration parameters (of which there are a large number and which greatly affect the recognition accuracy) etc. In addition, an ASR system comprises a number of modules that need to be integrated and tested seamlessly. For this reason, there are many issues upon which to shed light and much insight to be provided. Potential readers of this chapter could be anyone from speech processing specialists to software developers interested in this particular case-study.

This chapter is divided as follows: section two provides some background on the topic, in which preliminary work on software testing and automated speech recognition will be discussed. Section three introduces the speech recognition systems tested. Section four discusses the testing approach and methodology followed. Section five describe how unit testing has been utilized to test different parts of the system and how test cases have been designed to test each of the modules of the system: loading of the input data, generation of the output data (recognition hypotheses), and actual recognition process. Section six describes how to test the system as a whole (i.e. functional testing). Section seven describes how software management configuration tools have been used to manage the software elements, production code and test code and how to interact with them during the development cycle. Finally, we draw conclusion in section eight.

2. BACKGROUND

Due to the increasingly important role of software testing in software quality assurance, during recent years, the use of testing frameworks that assist the developer during the testing process, and particularly the use of those belonging to the xUnit family, have proven to be invaluable. The production of high-quality and bug-free software products and solutions has gained a crucial importance in the software development industry, with its focus on meeting the needs of its increasingly more demanding end-users. In the last few years, many software testing techniques and methodologies have emerged to address these challenges, some of them are influenced by Agile methodologies (Beck, 2001) and particularly by eXtreme Programming (XP) (Beck, 2000). These techniques provide us with a wide set of principles, practices and recommendations for all the tasks involved in the software testing process, from test case design to automation of functional tests. In this context, an overwhelming number of testing frameworks and tools have been developed and are available (many of them under open-source licenses) with the purpose of aiding the developer in testing every particular system aspect written in any programming language imaginable.

However, as the number of resources and techniques available continues to increase, so does, the complexity derived from the selection and integration of the most relevant software testing principles, techniques and tools into a convenient and effective software testing framework. In this respect, although it will contain some information about the tools utilized, this chapter is mainly focused on techniques and strategies that help in the development of effective automated tests in the context of a speech recognition system and in particular for a speech decoding system.

To our knowledge, very little work has been published in the literature on this topic. For example in (Harrington, 2008) a embedded speech recognition system that recognizes isolated words using Dynamic Time Warping (DTW) is developed and tested using different testing approaches like unit testing and component-wide integration tests. However, unlike the ASR system we developed, this system does not do continuous speech recognition[1] and it is based on a rather simple patter matching technique called DTW. Thus, the procedure to design the test cases and the testing techniques utilized are substantially different. Most of the times the word "testing" appears in the speech recognition literature in connection with testing the actual recognition accuracy of the ASR system, which is measured using standard metrics like the Word Error Rate. For example, Sphinx (Lee, 1990), one of the most popular speech recognition systems used for research, provides the user with a mechanism to run "regression tests", which in this case are tests that are run regularly to determine how Sphinx performs under a variety of tasks (ranging from small vocabulary to very large vocabulary tasks). These tests are useful to track the recognition accuracy over time of the system but have nothing to do with the kind of testing (i.e. software testing) that we are discussing in this chapter.

3. THE TESTED SYSTEM

During the last several months we have been working on the development of a new speech recognition system, in particular a speech decoding system[2]. This system incorporates some of the latest advances in the speech recognition field such as tree-structured state network compression, language model look ahead caching, preventive pruning during token expansion, graph based confidence estimation, etc. This system has been entirely developed using the C++ programming language (for efficiency reasons) and the Standard Template Library (STL) (Stepanov, 1995). The system is intended to be platform independent although currently it has only been tested on Linux machines.

Given the complexity of the system developed, we have put special emphasis on the testing process to make sure that every module of the system behaves as specified in the Software Requirements Specification (SRS). In addition, we plan to keep advancing the system in the near future to keep it state-of-the-art and to incorporate new features such as online environment and speaker adaptation methods. Thus, it is of the utmost importance for us to build a testing framework that can aid us with the regression tests and that can be easily extendable when new functionality is added to the system. The testing framework must also support a collaborative work model, given that several researchers will be contributing to the system implementation.

4. TESTING APPROACH AND METHODOLOGY

In this section the testing strategy and the testing techniques used to test the developed speech recognition system will be described. Both black box and white box testing paradigms were utilized to design the test cases used to test independent modules of the system in isolation (unit testing). However, only black box testing techniques were used to test the system as a whole. Unit tests were developed for each of the C++ classes that constitute the system. Once the system was completely implemented according to the Software Requirements Specification (SRS) and the unit test were returning positive results (which indicates a good degree of reliability at the component level), we proceed to integrate the C++ classes into the final system and carried out the functional tests to verify its completeness and correctness. Software elements related to production software and testing software are managed by the use of a centralized software repository. A single Ant (Loughran, 2000) script has been written that deploys the software and executes test cases from both unit and functional tests.

Software Tools Utilized

- **Unit testing:** The library used for unit testing is CxxTest (Volk, 2004), which is available under the GNU Lesser General Public License (Free Software Foundation, 2007). CxxTest is a portable library that uses either Perl or Python to run unit test of C++ classes.
- **System testing:** the same library CxxTest has been used for unit and system testing.
- **Software deployment and test cases execution:** Ant
- **Software Management Configuration:** SVN Subversion (Collabnet, 2000).

Consistent Reporting of Testing Errors

A C++ class has been developed which collects error messages generated by test cases that fail and dump the information in a single file. Every time a CxxTest assert fails, a message is generated that is specific to the test case where the failure has occurred, this message is sent to this class, which stores it in a unique file. This way, it is possible to run the whole series of test cases that exercise different verifications over different modules of the system and over the system as a whole and generate a unique testing report, which contains the test execution results.

5. UNIT TESTING

The first step when carrying out unit testing is to design the test cases. Black box and white box techniques are both suitable for this purpose. Black box consists of testing whether the output of a function or method, given certain inputs, conforms to its functional specification contained in the SRS. White box consists of analyzing the source code in order to guide the selection of test data. Test data must be appropriately selected to achieve adequate coverage over the code to test.

Perhaps one of the most challenging aspects of performing unit testing is to achieve the complete isolation of a class from its collaborative classes. Typically, an object makes use of other objects to carry out certain tasks beyond its own functionality. Obviously, the execution results, and also the test results, of methods belonging to that object will be, to a great degree, determined by the inner-state of the object. Usually it is very difficult to set up a domain state in such a way that it exposes the features to be tested. Even if it can be done, the written test will probably be quite complex and difficult to understand and maintain. We can avoid these problems using Mock Objects (Mackinnon, 2000) that are a substitute implementation to emulate or instrument another domain code (in particular the collaborative classes). They should be simpler than the real code, not duplicate its implementation, and allow the developer to set up private state to aid in testing. Mock Objects are very useful, but creating them by hand can be tedious so we have taken advantage of the mechanism that CxxUnit provides at this respect.

One of the most important factors impacting the quality of the testing process is the appropriate selection and design of the test cases that will be used to exercise the system during the testing process. In the case of a speech recognition system, the design of the test cases needs to be based on a fairly deep understanding of the internals of the ASR system. We believe that having sufficient experience in the field can make a significant difference in this respect, and that is one of the motivations for writing this chapter. For example, if we need to test a C++ class that generates a graph of words containing recognition hypotheses, it will be necessary to possess a profound understanding of the properties of the graph to write an appropriate and comprehensive set of test cases. While these properties can be easily enumerated in the SRS, some background in the field is necessary to correctly interpret and reflect them in an effective set of test cases. The quality of these test cases will profoundly determine the success of the software testing process.

This section covers in detail the process of testing in isolation the core C++ classes of the ASR system developed. These classes are the class that creates the decoding network and the class that implements the Token Passing algorithm. The testing process of the remaining classes of the system are not considered as relevant so they won't be described in this section.

5.1. Testing the Correctness of the Decoding Network

The decoding network is a graph that contains all the lexical units (typically words) that are in the recognition vocabulary. Each of the nodes in the network represents a HMM-state (the state of a left to right Hidden Markov Model) of a given triphone (which is the equivalent to a phone when context independent acoustic modeling is used) of a given lexical unit. Most of the decoding time is spent traversing the decoding network so testing it thoroughly is crucial. Some of the most important checks that we have performed to verify its correctness are listed below:

- There has to be one and only one word-identity node in between the root node or any fan-in node and any reachable word-end node.

- There has to be a word-identity node for each of the words in the active vocabulary and their corresponding alternative pronunciations in the pronunciation lexicon.
- All the nodes have to be connected and there can not be redundant transitions.
- Backward transitions can only occur at word-ends.
- All the emitting nodes (those that represent HMM-states) have to have a self-transition.
- It must be possible to transition from the end of any one word to the beginning of any other word in the active dictionary.
- Check the coherence between node-depth and node position within the network.

5.2 Testing the Token Expansion Process

As in most state-of-the-art speech decoding systems, the system we have built relies on the Token Passing Paradigm (Young, 1989) to carry out the search process, which is an efficient implementation of the time synchronous Viterbi Search (which is a dynamic programming algorithm). According to this paradigm, at the beginning of utterance, a number of tokens are placed in the root node of the decoding network, which is compiled beforehand, and propagated from left to right to explore the search space. Every time a token arrives at a word identity node, a new word is added to the partial hypothesis attached to the token. Once the whole utterance is processed, the hypothesis of the best scoring token will be the final recognition hypothesis.

A number of test cases have been implemented to verify that the token expansion process is done correctly. Given the complexity of steps in the process, a number of assert clauses have been used for verification purposes. Assert clauses can be placed at very specific locations inside a complex algorithm, are less intrusive and it is easy to configure the compiler so that they are passed over when generating the final system release. We list below a series of checks that were made to verify the correctness of the token-expansion process:

- Make sure that the best token at time t has a lower score than the best token at time t-1, otherwise it could mean that the acoustic models are broken, since the probability that a Gaussian Mixture Model (GMM) generates any feature vector is always positive (negative when log), has to be a, or a token was not actually expanded during the last iteration.
- Make sure that all the tokens have observed the same number of feature frames.

- Make sure that all the active nodes in the network actually contain at least one token.
- Etc.

In addition to those checks, an algorithm was specifically implemented to verify the correctness of the token-expansion process. The goal of this algorithm is to make sure that in the case that the best theoretical path according to the available acoustic and language models (and also the value of those configuration parameters that affect the search outcome, like the insertion penalty) corresponds to the string of words in the orthographic transcription of the utterance, it is actually found (and with the same associated global score) at the end of the search process[3]. The idea behind this algorithm is that at each time frame during the Viterbi search, all the paths with a score within the beam width survive.

The algorithm proceeds as follows:

1. Define a reasonable set of configuration parameters in order to minimize pruning errors.
2. For each utterance in the speech material available for testing purposes (which will typically be the training partition of the speech corpus):
   a. Decode it and get a hypothesis with its corresponding global and frame-level score and the time alignment information (information of starting and ending times for each of the lexical units in the path).
   b. For each utterance, perform a forced alignment against the orthographic transcription using the same language and acoustic models and the same insertion penalty values. Keep the frame-level and global score.
   c. Compare global scores resulting from steps (a) and (b). Here, there are three possibilities:
      i. If both scores are the same, check that the time alignment information in both paths is identical. If that is not the case, an error should be reported.
      ii. If the global score resulting from (b) is lower (recall that in automatic speech recognition log-likelihood values are taken to avoid problems with the dynamic range of floating point variables) than the global score in (a), it means that the recognition system has produced an incorrect hypothesis and has failed to output the string of words corresponding to the orthographic transcription (what the speaker actually said) of the utterance. This is most likely caused by inaccuracies in the acoustic or language modeling, and not due to implementation errors, and is therefore out of the scope in testing.

It is generally known that speech recognition systems never yield 100% accuracy, regardless of the task.

iii. On the other hand, if the score resulting from (a) is higher than the score obtained from (b), a recognition error has occurred that was prompted by one or two factors; a pruning error or an implementation error. Using the frame-level scores that were kept during steps (a) and (b), it is possible to determine the source of this error. If the frame-level score of the path resulting from (b) is always within the beam pruning width with respect to the frame-level score of the path resulting from (a), then the recognition error can not have been caused by a pruning error, but instead has occurred due to an implementation error, and in this case, an error is reported.

Note that if other types of beam pruning methods are used, like layer-dependent beam pruning or histogram-based pruning, additional verifications need to be carried out in step III to determine whether the recognition error is caused by a pruning error or by an implementation error. In layer-dependent beam pruning[4], tokens in specific layers of the decoding network are pruned using beams of different width, and typically narrower for the word-end layer. In this case, additional checks need to be made to make sure that the score in positions of the path obtained in (b) that correspond to those layers in the network is within the layer-specific beam relative to the best overall score at that frame. In histogram-based pruning, only the best N tokens survive at each iteration of the Viterbi search. This will require that additional checks be performed in step III to make sure that the frame-level score of the path obtained in (b) was not actually pruned off the search simply because it ranked above N. In this case, it becomes slightly more complicated, due to the actual characteristics of histogram-based pruning. In histogram-based pruning, the idea is to keep the N best scoring tokens and to avoid the computational complexity of sorting the whole set of tokens, which can be considerable. The computational complexity of histogram based pruning is $O(n)$, where n is the number of tokens resulting from a token expansion, while sorting the whole set of tokens would be about $O(\log(n))$, which makes a big difference for a large n. The implementation consists of building a histogram from the scores of all the tokens resulting from the expansion process and keeping the tokens that are in the higher bins (those where the tokes with higher scores are). Since this method keeps the best bins, which are those containing approximately N tokens in total, and not necessarily the best N tokens (note that tokens will be typically distributed unevenly across bins), it will be necessary to replicate the histogram-based pruning during step III, as opposed to merely checking whether the path resulting from (B) has a score which is the same or higher than the Nth path.

6. SYSTEM TESTING

System testing or functional testing is carried out once all the components of the system have been tested in isolation showing a good degree of reliability. System testing consists of testing a software system as a whole using its inputs and outputs. While white and black box techniques are used to select the data to use when performing unit test, only black box techniques are used for functional testing. This section is devoted to describe functional tests carried out over the developed ASR system.

6.1 Testing the Input Elements of the System in Isolation

A speech recognition system must be able to load the input data and verify that it is correct and coherent before initiating the actual recognition process. From the automatic testing perspective, it is thus necessary to build a set of test cases that verify whether the system is able to properly handle different parameter configurations; both admissible and non admissible. This section will serve to describe how to build a set of negative test cases that verify the response of the system to ill-formed parameter configurations. The execution of positive test cases will be covered later in this section. Negative test cases are those that exercise the response of a software system to "abnormal" conditions, like an input file that does not exist in disk or can not be opened, or a configuration parameter that is ill-formed. On the other hand, positive test cases exercise the response of a software system to "normal" conditions.

To begin, it is necessary to briefly describe the characteristics of the input data. The input elements of a speech recognition system when working in batch mode[5] can basically be divided into two main groups: configuration parameters, which are located in the configuration file, and command line parameters. Configuration parameters define the system's mode of operation (batch, live, etc) and fine-grained attributes such as the beam pruning widths, the feature extraction method, the language model scaling factor, the format of the output file, etc. On the other hand, command line parameters contain information about the data to be processed, such as the name of the raw audio file to be decoded, the name of the file containing voice activity detection cuts or the name of the hypothesis file that will be generated at the end of the recognition process.

6.1.1 Tests Related to Configuration Parameters

Configuration parameters are defined in the configuration file, which consists of a series of pairs attribute-value. The set of test cases designed to verify the system response to incorrect configuration parameters present the following structure:

- **Test case data:** a configuration file is created with a series of parameters corresponding to the goal of the test case.
- **Test case execution:** the speech recognition system is invoked with the configuration file (functional test).
- **Test case verifications:** several asserts are carried out to verify that the system behaved as expected. For example if wrong configuration parameters where given, the system has to report the corresponding error in the Log file. In addition, no hypothesis file should be generated because no actual recognition process should begin.

In order to test response of the recognition system to incorrect configuration parameters, two types of incorrect parameters have been found: unrecognized parameters (i.e. those that are not defined in the Software Requirements Specification) and those that receive a wrong value. A wrong value can be a value that is not of the right data type (for example a floating point parameter that receives a Boolean value), or a value that is outside the right range, for example, a negative language model scaling factor. The following negative test cases were designed to test the correctness and coherence of the configuration parameters:

- Define parameters that are not actual parameters of the system.
- Define parameters that have dependencies and omit the definition of those dependencies. Some parameters have dependencies, if the dependencies are not defined the system must report an error.
- Define parameters that are dependencies of parameters that are not defined or that do not have the required values. For example, the recognition system should report a configuration error if the parameter confidenceEstimation. graphPosteriors.confidenceMeasure, which indicates the confidence measure to be computed, is defined, and the parameter confidenceEstimation.best-Path, which determines whether confidence estimation will be carried out is not defined.
- Define parameters with the wrong data types (a type that is inconsistent with the Software Requirements Specification (SRS)).
- Define parameters which value is out of range.

6.1.2 Test Cases Related to Command Line Parameters

Command line parameters in our ASR system are basically the name of files that will serve as input for the decoding process (and thus are supposed to exist) or will be created during or at the end of the decoding process (such as the hypothesis file). Thus, a set of negative test cases was created to verify the behavior of the system to incorrect or inconsistent command line parameters. Some of these test cases are listed below:

- To invoke the decoder with the name of files that does not exist.
- To invoke the decoder with files for which the decoder does not have reading access.
- To invoke the decoder with files that are not in the right format according to the SRS. There are some limitations on this respect since the decoder works with files of raw audio that do not have a header and therefore it is not possible to check their correctness.

In addition to those negative test cases in which we verify whether the system behaves as expected when the input data is incomplete and/or incorrect, it is crucial to design a comprehensive set of positive test cases in which the behavior of the system is verified for "normal" conditions.

6.1.3 Testing the Coherence between the Configuration Parameters and the Command Line Parameters

Finally, it is necessary to check the coherence between the parameters defined in the configuration file and the command line options. For example, if the configuration parameter speechAcitivityDetection.offline receives the value false, indicating that no speech activity detection will be carried out during decoding and that speech activity detection cuts will be provided beforehand, the command line option -sad <speech activity detection file> has to be used when invoking the speech decoder. On the other hand, if speechAcitivityDetection.offline receives the value true, the command line option -sad cannot be provided. Checking the coherence between configuration parameters and command line parameters can be easily done through the design of a comprehensive set of negative test cases, in which the decoder will be invoked with incoherent input and will be checked so as to determine if it is able to handle this input properly (in the case of our decoder, by generating a new entry with the appropriate informative message in the log file).

6.2 Testing the System's Output

The output of a speech recognition system consists of a hypothesis (or series of alternative hypotheses) about what the speaker said. The hypothesis is essentially a string of lexical units with their corresponding timing information and confidence annotation. Given that the metrics to evaluate the accuracy of speech recognition systems, such as the Word Error Rate (WER), are applied to the hypothesis generated, it is of the utmost importance that it is verified for correctness. When it comes to designing the appropriate set of test-cases that will be needed to verify the output correctness, a number of verifications should immediately be apparent for the average developer. For example, it is clear that any lexical unit in the hypothesis will need to be accompanied by its corresponding acoustic and language score values and that the value of those scores must be negative (because are log-likelihoods). It is also clear that a confidence estimate expressed as a probabilistic value (a posterior probability) can only receive values within the $[0,1]$ interval. However, there are other non-trivial aspects that may go unnoticed by those who are unfamiliar with speech recognition systems and, thus, may escape the testing process. It is particularly important to verify the coherence between the hypotheses generated (and they can be generated in multiple forms) and the configuration parameters (and their values) used during the decoding process that ultimately produced the hypotheses. For example, if we design the decoding network so that a given *special* lexical unit (for example, the silence, which is typically denoted as <SIL>) is not allowed to appear multiple times in a row, then we need to design a test-case that specifically checks that there are not two consecutive <SIL> symbols in any of the hypotheses generated. To give another example: if we set a beam width of X for the likelihood based beam pruning, then we should not observe multiple paths in the graph of hypotheses that have absolute scores which are separated by more than X (since the one with the lower score should have been pruned off the recognition). Note that, depending on how the recombination of edges in the graph is performed, the scenario just mentioned could actually take place. This also must be taken into consideration when designing the test cases.

The output of a speech recognition system can take two forms; the "best single path", and the "graphs of lexical units", which are typically graphs of words.

- **Best single path:** in the Maximum A Posteriori approach (MAP), the best single path is the string of lexical units (typically words) with the highest posterior probability given the acoustic and language models used during decoding.
- **Word graphs:** also known as lattices, these are directed acyclic graphs of lexical units. They are a compact representation of multiple recognition hypotheses and are composed of edges and nodes. Each edge is typically used to store a lexical unit (in most of the cases a word or a special symbol like silence <SIL>), its starting and ending time in the utterance, its left and right context (if cross-word context-dependent acoustic modeling is used), its acoustic and language model score, its posterior probability, etc. Nodes connect edges in the graph and represent transitions between lexical units in the hypotheses.

The following list shows the necessary checks that need to be covered by test-cases:

- Make sure that every edge in the graph (except the initial and terminal edges used to denote the beginning and end of sentence respectively) is linked forward and backward to at least another edge in the graph.
- Make sure that there are no cycles or back transitions in the graph.
- Make sure that the time alignment information is coherent across edges and transitions between edges.
- Make sure that there are not any unconnected regions in the graph. An error during the creation of the graph may result in the creation of two or more independent connected regions.
- Make sure that the global score of any path in the graph is not better than that of the best single path (since otherwise, it would be the actual "best single path"). This can be carried out by applying the Dijkstra algorithm in order to find the best scoring path of the graph, which, obviously, can be no other than the "best single path".
- Make sure that all the paths in the graph have the same length, in terms of the number of feature vectors to which they are aligned.

6.3. Testing the Systems Application Programming Interface (API)

Speech recognition systems, when used for speech research purposes, typically work in batch mode as standalone applications. In this case, the system receives the configuration parameters and the input data (a list containing series of speech utterances to decode) from the configuration file and the command line respectively. However, in many other scenarios, speech recognition systems are required to work as a library that provides functionality to an upper level application layer. For example if a speech recognition system is recognizing live audio in an automatic attendant application, the audio needs to be fed into the recognition process in real time so that the hypotheses are generated in real time as well. This library offers a set of function calls that allow for the performance of different operations on the decoder, such as initialization, feeding raw audio, retrieving partial/global hypotheses and so on. This set of functions constitutes the decoder API and its properly testing is a major goal in the testing process.

Function calls contained in this API perform equivalent operation to those that can be performed in batch mode. Thus, equivalent test cases to those described earlier to test the input and output of the system were written. One of the few exceptions is the functionality to retrieve partial hypotheses (which are not necessary in batch mode). This functionally however can be tested equivalently to the one of global hypotheses.

6.4 Observations

Finally it is worth to note that the speech corpora used for testing purposes must have full phonetic coverage respect to the set of acoustic models used, otherwise some of the models in the acoustic inventory might never be used and some software defects might go unnoticed. In modern ASR systems triphone acoustic models are used that capture the contextual information of speech at the phone level. However, the set of triphones used during decoding can be just a subset of those resulting from the training process. The reason is that some words in vocabulary are used during training may never appear in the test partition.

7. INCORPORATING SOFTWARE MANAGEMENT CONFIGURATION TOOLS (SMC TOOLS) INTO THE TESTING PROCESS

Nowadays, Software Management Configuration (SMC) tools are essential for the tracking of the evolution of software systems under development. SMC tools also represent the basic support for the collaborative work model of every software development team. The version control system that we chose was SVN Subversion (Collabnet, 2000). This tool was originally created to replace CVS (Concurrent Version System) and presents some advantages over it; Among them, its simplicity of use.

In Linux, interaction with SVN can be easily carried out from the command line. In Windows systems, the interaction can be done by means of a Windows client named TortoiseSVN (Onken, 2001), which is integrated into the Windows Explorer contextual menu. The repository can also be accessed for reading purposes through a standard Web browser using Apache authentication. Working with the repository is straightforward and can be done using only a few commands (import, checkout, commit, etc).

We wrote a script that is used at the beginning of the work cycle to automatically load the latest configuration of the recognition system (including the software testing elements) from the repository to the local file system. At the end of the work cycle, the same script allows the changes made to the software to be committed to the repository. Like any other software system, only software configuration elements that are subject to change across the software life cycle are kept in the repository. The following list shows those elements:

- Speech recognition source code (production code).
- Testing code (to execute the test cases and to report error found).
- Test cases data.
- Test cases code
- Test cases execution script.
- Configuration file of the speech recognition.
- Software deployment scripts.
- Etc.

8. CONCLUSION

Through the course of this chapter, we have described a software testing framework that was successfully used during the development of a speech recognition system, in particular a speech decoder system. In this framework, different testing strategies and techniques have been integrated to automatically verify the correctness and coherence of different software components from multiple angles: unit testing (black box and white box), functional testing, etc. This framework was designed to provide the software developer with an automated format by which to test the system during the whole development cycle and, even more important in a system of its kind, during the software maintenance life cycle. A speech recognition system is a system that needs to stay up-to-date and thus needs to be constantly updated by incorporating new research contributions.

- A comprehensive description has been provided of test cases that were designed to test different components of the speech recognition system, from the configuration file to the token expansion implementation.
- Strategies to test the internals of a speech recognition system have been provided.
- A mechanism to execute the automated test cases designed from a single script has been described.
- A mechanism to report testing errors in a consistent fashion has been described.
- How to take advantage of Software Management Configuration tools during the development process to aid and support the testing process of an ASR system has been described.

To summarize, a testing framework has been described that will assist speech researchers and software developers in the difficult task of keeping a speech recognition system up-to-date without compromising its reliability and overall accuracy.

REFERENCES

Beck, K. (2000). *Extreme programming explained: Embrace change*. Addison Wesley.

Beck, K., et al. (2001). *Manifesto for agile software development*. Retrieved from http://agilemanifesto.org/

Collabnet. (2000). *SVN: An open source software revision control.*

Free Software Foundation. (2007). *GNU lesser general public license*. Retrieved from http://www.gnu.org/copyleft/lesser.html

Harrington, N., & Schardl, T. B. (December 10, 2008). *Speech recognition in hardware: For use as a novel* input device.

Lee, K., Hon, H., & Reddy, R. (1990). Sphinx, an open source continuous speech recognition system. Retrieved from http://cmusphinx.sourceforge.net/sphinx4/

Loughran, S. (2000). *Apache Ant*. Retrieved from http://ant.apache.org/

Mackinnon, T., Freeman, S., & Craig, P. (2000). *Endo-testing: Unit testing with mock objects*. eXtreme Programming and Flexible Processes in Software Engineering – XP2000.

Onken, L., & Kueng, S. (2001). *Tortoise, a SVN client for Windows*. Retrieved from http://tortoisesvn.tigris.org/

Stepanov, A., & Lee, M. (1995). *The standard template library*. HP Laboratories Technical Report 95-11(R.1).

Volk, E. (2004). *CxxTest: A JUnit/CppUnit/xUnit-like framework for C/C++*. Retrieved from http://cxxtest.sourceforge.net/guide.html

Young, S. J., Russell, N. H., & Thornton, J. H. S. (1989). *Token passing: A simple conceptual model for connected speech recognition systems. Tech. Rep.* CUED.

ENDNOTES

[1] Continuous speech recognition works with unsegmented speech data so during recognition, alignment and classification are carried out simultaneously. On the other hand isolated speech recognition starts with known speech boundaries (the starting and end of word) so it is a much simpler task.

2   A speech recognition system can be roughly divided into a speech trainer and a speech decoder. The speech trainer uses transcribed speech material to train acoustic models (this process is a offline process) while a speech decoder uses the acoustic models trained and other sources of information like language models, to extract lexical information from unseen speech segments contained in digital audio.

3   Note, however, that sometimes the best path is pruned off the search because at some time frame its score lies outside the beam width. This event is not caused by an error in the implementation of the token-expansion mechanism but because of a pruning error. Pruning errors are not implementation errors but are due to the use of pruning beams that are too narrow. Note that this same algorithm can be utilized to find the percentage of recognition errors that are not caused by inaccuracies of the acoustic or language models but because of pruning errors. It can also be used to portray the correlation between the beam width used for pruning tokens and the recognition errors (Word Error Rate) without performing multiple decoding processes.

4   Layer dependent pruning is implemented in most state-of the art speech recognition systems, in which the decoding network is divided in at least two parts: the WE-layer and the rest. Recent implementations of speech recognition systems like (ref) and the one under discussion in this article presents a decoding network organized in multiple layers for improved real-time performance.

5   Testing aspects related to the live working mode will be discussed in following sections.

Chapter 3
Runtime Verification of Distributed Programs

Eslam Al Maghayreh
Yarmouk University, Jordan

ABSTRACT

Ensuring the correctness of a distributed program is not an easy task. Testing and formal methods can play a significant role in this regard. However, testing does not allow for formal specification of the properties to be checked. On the other hand, formal methods verify that a model of a distributed system satisfies certain properties that are formally specified. However, formal methods do not guarantee that a particular implementation of the system under consideration will also satisfy all of the necessary properties. Runtime verification tries to combine some of the advantages of testing and some of the advantages of formal methods. Runtime verification works on a particular implementation of the system and at the same time it allows us to specify the properties of interest formally. In this chapter we have talked about runtime verification of distributed programs. The main components of a runtime verification framework have been presented and discussed in some details. The reasons that make runtime verification of distributed programs a difficult task have been discussed. A summarization of some of the techniques presented in the literature to simplify runtime verification of distributed programs has also been presented.

INTRODUCTION

Runtime verification is a technique that combines formal verification and traditional testing. The main components of a runtime verification framework are shown in Figure 1. The observed behavior (in terms of log traces) of a program can be monitored and verified dynamically to make sure that given requirements (properties)

DOI: 10.4018/978-1-4666-0089-8.ch003

Figure 1. The main components of a runtime verification framework

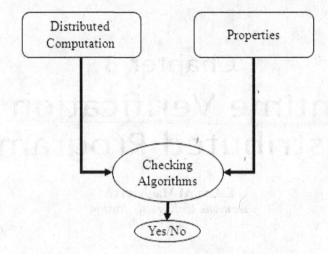

are satisfied. Such requirements are typically specified by a formalism which can express temporal constraints, such as LTL-formulae (Linear Temporal Logic).

Testing is an ad hoc technique that does not allow for formal specification and verification of the properties that the program needs to satisfy. Formal methods work on an abstract model of the program. Consequently, even if a program has been formally verified, we still cannot be sure of the correctness of a particular implementation. However, for highly dependable systems, it is important to analyze the particular implementation.

Runtime verification is more practical than other verification methods such as model checking and testing. Runtime verification verifies the implementation of the system directly rather than verifying a model of the system as done in model checking. It is also based on formal logics and provides formalism, which is lacked in testing. Figure 2 demonstrates that runtime verification combines the benefits of traditional testing techniques and formal method.

In the literature, the following four reasons were mentioned in order to argue for runtime verification:

1. If you check the model of your system you cannot be confident on the implementation since correctness of the model does not imply correctness of the implementation.
2. Some information is available only at runtime or is convenient to be checked at runtime.
3. Behavior may depend heavily on the environment of the target system; then it is not possible to obtain the information necessary to test the system.

Figure 2. Runtime verification combines the advantages of formal methods and traditional testing

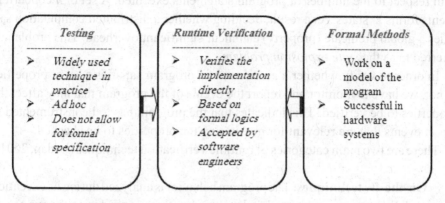

4.   Runtime verification allows for formal specification and verification or testing of the properties that a system has to satisfy. Traditional testing techniques such as unit testing are ad hoc and informal. It is only a partial proof of correctness in that it does not guarantee that the system will operate as expected under untested inputs.

In terms of its ability to guarantee software correctness, runtime verification is weaker than formal methods but stronger than testing. Testing can only guarantee the correctness of a limited set of inputs at implementation time. As a result, undiscovered faults may result in failures at runtime. Formal methods are stronger than runtime verification but are hard to be understood and applied properly by software engineers, for this reason runtime verification are sometimes referred to as light weight formal methods and hence it has a better chance of being accepted and used by software engineers.

Distributed programs are particularly vulnerable to software faults. These programs often contain bugs, which are very difficult to detect without automatic verification. Verification of distributed programs and software fault-tolerance are important ways to ensure the reliability of distributed systems. Detecting a fault in an execution of a distributed system is a fundamental problem that arises during the verification process. A programmer upon observing a certain distributed computation for bugs can check whether the observed computation satisfies some expected property. The idea of checking whether a distributed program run satisfies an expected property (also referred to as runtime verification) has recently been attracting a lot of attention for analyzing execution traces.

The execution of a distributed program involves the concurrent advancement of multiple processes that work together to perform the necessary functions. Due to concurrency, the number of global states of an execution can grow exponentially with respect to the number of program statements executed. A set of n concurrent events forms 2^n states. As a result, deciding whether a distributed computation satisfies a global predicate (property) can incur significant overhead. This problem is referred to as the *state explosion problem*.

In order to verify whether a given run of a program satisfies a set of properties or not, we have to monitor and report the events of the program that may affect the properties to be verified. This indicates that the program has to be instrumented to report events that are relevant for monitoring the properties to be checked.

There are two main categories of runtime verification techniques (Ladan, 2001):

1. **On-the-fly techniques:** The program behavior is analyzed during its execution such that errors are detected and reported as they occur during the run.
2. **Offline techniques:** These techniques collect a log of events that occur during a program's execution and post-process the log to detect errors. The main disadvantage of these techniques is that execution logs can be very large for parallel and distributed programs.

The rest of this chapter is organized as follows: Section 2 presents a model of a distributed program run. Section 3 explores some of the logics used to formally specify the properties that a programmer may need to check. Section 4 presents the main approaches used to verify distributed programs. Section 5 briefly describes the difficulty of checking global properties of distributed programs. Sections 6, 7 and 8 are dedicated to review a variety of strategies for ameliorating the state explosion problem that have been explored in the literature. These strategies include: exploiting the structure of the property, atomicity and program slicing. Section 9 give a brief description of POTA which is one of the tools that can be used for runtime verification of distributed programs.

A MODEL OF A RUN OF A DISTRIBUTED PROGRAM

One of the important issues in reasoning about a distributed program is the model used for a distributed program run (distributed computation). In this section, we will present a distributed system model and a model for capturing the behavior of a distributed program.

We assume a loosely-coupled message-passing distributed program without any shared memory or global clock. It consists of n processes denoted by $P_1, P_2, ..., P_n$ and a set of unidirectional channels. A channel connects two processes. The delay incurred in sending a message through a channel is arbitrary but finite. The state of a channel at any point is defined to be the sequence of messages sent along that channel but not received.

Definition 1. *An event marks the execution of a statement. It can be an internal computational event or an external message event.*

Lamport (Lamport, 1978) has argued that, in a true distributed system, events can only be partially ordered. Events are related by either their execution order in a process or message send/receive relations across processes. The traditional happened-before relation ($\rightarrow$) between events applies to all events executed (Lamport, 1978).

Definition 2. *A run of a distributed program is an event structure $\langle E, \rightarrow \rangle$ formed by the set of events executed (E) and the happened-before relation ($\rightarrow$) among these events.*

A run of a distributed program can be viewed in terms of a two dimensional space time diagram. Space is represented in the vertical direction and time in the horizontal direction. Circles are used to depict events. Transmission of a message is represented by a directed edge linking the send event with the corresponding receive event. The space time diagram shown in Figure 3 depicts a distributed computation involving three processes.

In a space time diagram, the events within a single process are totally ordered. $a \rightarrow b$ if and only if there is a directed path from event a to event b. The happened before relation is only a partial order on the set of events. Thus two events a and b may not be related by the happened before relation, in this case we say that a and b are ***concurrent*** (denoted by $a \| b$). For example, in Figure 3, $b \| f$ because $\neg(b \rightarrow f)$ and $\neg(f \rightarrow b)$.

Figure 3. An example of an event structure that represents a run of a distributed program consisting of three processes

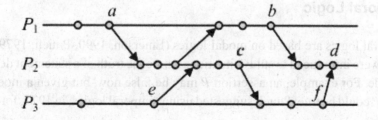

Definition 3. *A consistent cut C of an event structure* $\langle E, \rightarrow \rangle$ *is a finite subset* $C \subseteq E$ *such that if* $e \in C \wedge e' \rightarrow e$ *then* $e' C \in$.

For each consistent cut C, there is a corresponding *global state* of the program represented by the values of the program variables and channels states attained upon completion of the events in C. For simplicity of presentation, we do not distinguish between a consistent cut and the global state associated with it.

The set of global states of a given distributed computation endowed with set union and intersection operations form a distributive lattice, referred to as the *state lattice* (Mattern, 1989). Based on this state lattice, one can check if the run satisfies the required properties in program testing and debugging.

Figure 4 shows the state lattice L corresponding to the event structure shown in Figure 3. Each state is identified by the most recent event executed in each process. For example, $\langle a,c,f \rangle$ is the state reached after executing event a in P_1, event c in P_2 and event f in P_3. Only a subset of the events in Figure 3 and a subset of the states in Figure 4 are labeled for future reference.

SPECIFICATION OF THE PROPERTIES TO BE VERIFIED

Propositional and first order logics can be used to express properties of states (Alagar & Periyasamy, 1998). Each formula represents a set of states that satisfy it. These formulas are considered static in the sense that they represent a collection of states, but not the dynamic evolution among them during program execution.

Modal logics (Hughes & Cresswell, 1996) extend propositional and first order logics by allowing the description of the relation between different states during the execution. This is more suitable for specifying properties of distributed systems, where we are not only interested in the relation between the values at the beginning and at the end of the execution, but also other properties related to the sequence of states during the execution. In the following subsection we will give a brief introduction to temporal logic which is based on modal logics and has been widely used to specify properties of distributed programs.

Temporal Logic

Temporal logics are based on modal logics (Emerson, 1990, Pnueli, 1979). Modal logics were introduced to study situations where the truth of a statement depends on its mode. For example, an assertion P may be false now, but given a mode future, future P could be true. Pnueli suggested using temporal logics, in 1977, for formally

Figure 4. The state lattice (L) associated with the event structure shown in Figure 3

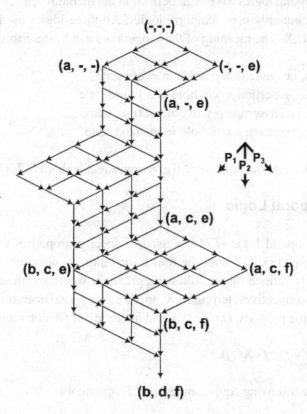

specifying behavioral properties of systems (Pnueli, 1977, 1979). This view has been confirmed by the extensive use of temporal logics in the last two decades.

Temporal logic formulas consist of the usual atomic propositional logic formulas (non-temporal part), plus temporal operators. The non-temporal part specifies the basic properties of states. The temporal operators specify temporal properties. Non-temporal properties can be checked on each state based on the values of the variables in that state, whereas verifying temporal properties requires the investigation of state paths.

We will use the term atomic properties to refer to the basic properties of states (non-temporal part). Given a transition system $T=(S,I,R)$ where S is a set of states, $I \subseteq S$ is a set of initial states, and $R \subseteq S \times S$ is a transition relation, we define AP to be the set of atomic properties of the system. We assume that we have a procedure $L: S \times AP \rightarrow \{true, false\}$ such that given a property $p \in AP$ and a state $s \in S$, procedure L can decide if $s \vDash p$, i.e., $s \vDash p$ *iff* $L(s,p) = true$.

Various temporal logics have been defined in the literature. *LTL*, *CTL* and *CTL** are the most commonly used temporal logics. All these logics use four temporal operators **G,F,U,X**. The meaning of these operators can be described as follows:

G*p*: Globally *p*, i.e., assertion *p* holds in every state.
F*p*: Future *p*, i.e., assertion *p* will hold in a future state.
*p***U***q*: *p* Until *q*, i.e., assertion *p* will hold until *q* holds.
X*p*: Next *p*, i.e., assertion *p* will hold in the next state.

In the following subsections we will give some details about *LTL*, *CTL* and *CTL**.

Linear Temporal Logic

Linear time temporal logic (*LTL*) is used to specify properties of interleaving sequences (i.e., paths). *LTL* uses the four basic temporal operators G,F,U,X. The syntax of *LTL* is defined by the following grammar where terminals ¬, ∧, and ∨ and are logical connectives; terminals X, and U are temporal operators; terminal *ap* denotes an atomic property, (*ap* ∈ *AP*); and nonterminal *f* denotes an *LTL* formula:

$$f ::= ap \mid f \wedge f \mid f \vee f \mid \neg f \mid \mathbf{X}f \mid f\mathbf{U}f$$

We have the following equivalences for *LTL* operators,

F*p*≡*true***U***p*

G*p*≡¬(*true***U**¬*p*)

Based on the above equivalences, any *LTL* property can be expressed using only symbols from the set {¬, ∨, **X,U**) ∪ *AP*.

More details about *LTL* property can be found in (Pnu, 1979).

Computation Tree Logic (*CTL*)

Computation tree logic *CTL* is a branching time logic; meaning that the computation starting from a state is viewed as a tree where each branch corresponds to a path (Eme, 1990). The truth of a temporal formula in *CTL* is defined on states. A temporal formula is true for a state if all the paths or some of the paths originating from that state satisfy a condition.

CTL temporal operators are pairs of symbols. They talk about what can happen from the current state. The first member of the pair is one of the path quantifiers **A** or **E**. Path quantifier **A** means "for all paths", whereas **E** means "there exists a path". The second member of the pair is one of the basic temporal operators **G,F,U,X**.

The syntax of *CTL* is defined by the following grammar, where terminals ¬, ∧, and ∨ are logical connectives; terminals **EX,EU** and **AU** are temporal operators; terminal *ap* denotes an atomic property, ($ap \in AP$); *f* denotes a *CTL* formula:

$$f ::= ap \mid f \wedge f \mid f \vee f \mid \neg f \mid \mathbf{EX}f \mid f\mathbf{EU}f \mid f\mathbf{AU}f$$

We have the following equivalences for *CTL* operators,

$$\mathbf{EF}p \equiv true\mathbf{EU}p$$

$$\mathbf{EG}p \equiv \neg(true\mathbf{AU}\neg p)$$

$$\mathbf{AF}p \equiv true\mathbf{AU}p$$

$$\mathbf{AG}p \equiv \neg(true\mathbf{EU}\neg p)$$

$$\mathbf{AX}p \equiv \neg\mathbf{EX}\neg p$$

The semantics of *CTL* is defined in Figure 5. Based on the rules given in this table, we can decide if a state in a transition system satisfies a *CTL* formula. The semantics of the temporal operators **EF,AF,EG** and **AG** follow from the equivalences given above and the rules given in Figure 5.

CTL*

*CTL** combines *LTL* and *CTL* into a single framework. There are two types of formulas in *CTL**: path formulas and state formulas. A path formula is true or false for paths (all *LTL* formulas are path formulas). A state formula is true or false for states (all *CTL* formulas are state formulas). The truth set of a state formula is a set of states, whereas the truth set of a path formula is a set of paths. All the formulas in *AP* are state formulas. Every state formula can be considered as a path formula with the interpretation that the truth of the formula depends only on the first state of the path.

The formulas $\mathbf{G}p, \mathbf{F}p, p\mathbf{U}q$, and $\mathbf{X}p$ are all path formulas. The path quantifiers **A** and **E** can be used to generate state formulas from path formulas. Given a path formula p, $\mathbf{A}p$ and $\mathbf{E}p$ are two state formulas. $\mathbf{A}p$ is true in a state, if and only if, for all paths originating from that state, p is true. $\mathbf{E}p$ is true on a state, if and only if, there exists a path originating from that state where p is true. For example, given

Figure 5. CTL semantics

$s \models p$	iff	$L(s,p) = true$ where $p \in AP$
$s \models \neg p$	iff	not $s \models p$
$s \models p \wedge q$	iff	$s \models p$ and $s \models q$
$s \models p \vee q$	iff	$s \models p$ or $s \models q$
$s_0 \models EX\ p$	iff	there exists a path $(s_0, s_1, s_2, ...)$, such that $s_1 \models p$.
$s_0 \models AX\ p$	iff	for all paths $(s_0, s_1, s_2, ...)$, $s_1 \models p$
$s_0 \models p\ EU\ q$	iff	there exists a path $(s_0, s_1, s_2, ...)$, such that there exists an i, $s_i \models q$ and for all $j < i, s_j \models p$.
$s_0 \models p\ AU\ q$	iff	for all paths $(s_0, s_1, s_2, ...)$, there exists an i, $s_i \models q$ and for all $j < i, s_j \models p$.

an atomic property p, Fp will be true for a path if there exists a state on the path that satisfies p. More details about *CTL** can be found in (Berard et al., 2001).

PROPERTY CHECKING APPROACHES

The first approach to check the satisfaction of a global property in a distributed computation is based on the global snapshot algorithm by Chandy and Lamport (Chandy & Lamport, 1985, Bougé, 1987, Spezialetti & Kearns, 1986). Their approach requires repeated computation of consistent global snapshots until a snapshot is found in which the desired property (predicate) is satisfied. This approach works only for stable properties, i.e., properties that do not turn false once they become true. The Chandy and Lamport approach may fail to detect a non-stable property because it may turn true only between two successive snapshots.

The second approach to check the satisfaction of a global property in a given distributed computation was proposed by Cooper and Marzullo (Cooper & Marzullo, 1991). Their approach is based on the construction of the state lattice (Cooper & Marzullo, 1991, Jegou, Medina, & Nourine, 1995) and can be used for the detection of *possibly*: ϕ and *definitely*: ϕ. The predicate possibly: ϕ is true if ϕ is true for any global state in the lattice. The predicate *definitely*: ϕ is true if, for all paths from the initial global state to the final global state, ϕ is true in some global state along that path. Though this approach can be used to detect both stable and unstable properties, the detection may be prohibitively expensive. This approach requires exploring

$O(m^n)$ global states in the worst case, where n is the number of processes and m is the number of relevant local states in each process. The third approach avoids the construction of the state lattice by exploiting the structure of the property to identify a subset of the global states such that if the property is true, it must be true in one of the states from this subset. This approach can be used to develop more efficient algorithms, but it is less general than the second approach. For example, (Garg & Waldecker, 1994, 1996) present algorithms of complexity $O(n^2 m^n)$ to detect *possibly*: ϕ and *definitely*: ϕ when ϕ is a conjunction of local properties (a local property is a property of a single process). (Chase & Garg, 1995, Tomlinson & Garg, 1993) present efficient algorithms that use this approach to detect $\sum x_i < C$ where the x_i are variables on different processes and C is constant.

PROBLEMS IN CHECKING GLOBAL PROPERTIES

Many of the problems in distributed programs can be reduced to the problem of observing a distributed computation to check whether it satisfies a given property or not. Termination detection and deadlock detection are some examples (Garg, 2002).

The difficulties of observing a distributed computation to check the satisfaction of a given property are due to the following characteristics of a distributed program (Garg, 2002):

1. The lack of a common clock, which implies that the events in a given distributed computation can only be partially ordered.
2. The lack of shared memory, which indicates that the evaluation of a global property will incur message overhead to collect the necessary information to evaluate it.
3. The existence of multiple processes that are running concurrently, which implies that the number of global states that needs to be considered in property checking will be exponential in the number of processes.

In general, the problem of detecting a global property in a given distributed program computation is NP-complete (Chase & Garg, 1998). A significant part of this chapter will be mainly dedicated to explore some of the work presented in the literature to efficiently check the satisfaction of a property in a given distributed computation. These include, restricting the class of the properties to be checked, atomicity and slicing.

CLASSES OF PROPERTIES

In this section we will describe four classes of properties for which efficient detection algorithms have been developed.

Stable Properties

A stable property remains true once it becomes true. Termination detection is an example of stable property detection. Stability depends on the system; some properties are stable in some systems but not stable in others. The global snapshot algorithm by Chandy and Lamport (Chandy & Lamport, 1985) can be used to check the satisfaction of a stable property in a given distributed computation.

The value of an unstable property may change from time to time. There is very little value in using a snapshot algorithm to detect a non-stable property—the property may have held even if it is not detected. Many researchers have described algorithms to detect stable and unstable properties (Garg & Waldecker, 1996, 1994, Schwarz & Mattern, 1994, Garg & Waldecker, 1992, Haban & Weigel, 1988).

Observer Independent Properties

Charron-Bost, Delporte-Gallet, & Fauconnier (1995) present a class of properties that they call observer independent. This class includes all properties such that (*Possibly*: ϕ) ≡ (*Definitely*: ϕ). A disjunction of local properties is an observer independent property. Any stable property is also observer independent, the proof of this fact can be found in (Charron-Bost et al., 1995).

The name "observer independent" originates from the notion of a set of observers where each observes a different sequential execution of the distributed program. Each observer can determine if ϕ becomes true in any of the global states observed by him. If property ϕ is observer independent, then all observers will agree on whether ϕ ever became true.

Observer independent properties can be detected efficiently because we need to traverse only a single path of the state lattice to detect an observer independent property ϕ. If ϕ is true for any global state in the path, then *Possibly*: ϕ is clearly true. On the other hand, if ϕ is false along that path, we know that *Definitely*: ϕ is also false. Since (*Possibly*: ϕ) ≡ (*Definitely*: ϕ) for observer independent properties, we conclude that *Possibly*: ϕ is also false for the lattice.

Linear Properties

A linear property is based on the notion of a "forbidden" state.

Let s be a local state, X and Y be two global states. X^s denotes the cut formed by advancing X to the successor of s. A local state is a forbidden state with respect to a property ϕ if its inclusion in any global state X implies that ϕ is not satisfied at X. This can be defined formally as follows (Chase & Garg, 1998):

$$forb_\phi\ (s, X) \equiv \forall\ Y: X \subseteq Y: \phi(Y) \Rightarrow X^s \subseteq Y$$

This means that if ϕ is false in X and s is the forbidden state, then ϕ will remain false until a successor to s is reached.

Conjunctive properties are linear. An efficient algorithm to detect conjunctive properties can be found in (Garg, 2002). Some properties are linear in some systems but not in others. For example, the property $x_1 + x_1 \le c$, where x_1 and x_2 are two variables belonging to different processes and c is a constant, is linear in systems where x_1 or x_2 is monotonically increasing.

Regular Properties

Let L be the state lattice of a distributed computation. A property ϕ is regular if and only if for any two global states G and H,

$$\phi(G) \wedge \phi(H) \Rightarrow \phi(G \cap H) \wedge \phi(G \cup H)$$

That is, a global property is a regular property if the set of global states satisfying the predicate forms a sublattice of the lattice of global states. A regular predicate is also linear and hence easy to detect.

The property ϕ = "There is no outstanding message in the channel" is an example of a regular property. This property holds on a global state X if for each send event in X the corresponding receive event is also in X. Suppose ϕ holds on X and Y ($\phi(X) \wedge \phi(Y)$), it is easy to show that it holds in $(X \cup Y)$. To show that ϕ holds in $(X \cap Y)$, consider a send event $s \in (X \cap Y)$. Let r be the corresponding receive event. $\phi(X)$ implies that $r \in X$ and $\phi(Y)$ implies that $r \in Y$. Thus $r \in (X \cap Y)$. Consequently, $\phi(X \cap Y)$ and hence ϕ is a regular predicate (Garg, 2002).

ATOMICITY

In the previous section we have described some of the property classes for which efficient checking algorithms can be found. However, if the property that we want to check does not belong to any of these classes (general property), the checking will incur significant overhead due to the exponential number of states that needs to be considered. The notion of atomicity can be exploited to reduce the number of states where a given property needs to be checked.

Lamport has developed a theorem in atomicity to simplify verification of distributed systems (Lamport, 1990). Lamport adopted the common approach of formally defining an execution of a distributed algorithm to be a sequence of atomic actions. At the lowest level of abstraction each event result from executing any statement in the distributed program can be considered an atomic action. Reducing the number of atomic actions makes reasoning about a concurrent program easier because there are fewer interleavings to consider. This is the main goal of Lamport's theorem.

According to this theorem, a sequence of statements in a distributed program can be grouped together and be treated as an atom under some stated conditions. Informally, an atom may receive information from other processes, followed by at most one externally visible event (for instance, altering a variable relevant to some global property), before sending information to other processes. This theorem allows a distributed program to be abstracted into a reduced distributed program with more general and possibly larger atoms. As a result, the cost of program verification can also be reduced.

Formally, consider a distributed algorithm A in which each process executes a sequence of non-atomic operations. Each operation removes a set of messages from the process's input buffers, performs some computation, and sends a set of messages to other processes. According to this theorem, the reduced version A' of algorithm A is one in which an entire operation is a single atomic action and message transmission is instantaneous; this means that a message appears in the receiver's input buffer when the message is sent. In this case, algorithm A' will not have any computation state in which a process is in the middle of an operation or a message is in transit. Hence, algorithm A' is simpler than algorithm A and it is easier to reason about A' than about A. In his work, Lamport defined six conditions and proved that if these conditions are satisfied, then A satisfies a correctness property ϕ if and only if A' satisfies ϕ.

PROGRAM SLICING

The concept of slicing arose from research on dataflow analysis and static program analysis (Weiser, 1984). The main goal of introducing this concept was to facilitate the debugging and understanding of sequential imperative programs. A slice of a program P with respect to a criterion C (usually a program point) is a set of statements of P, which are relevant to the computations performed in C. It has been extended in various ways to deal with more complex program constructs, e.g., arrays, pointers, and concurrency. Moreover, the concept of slicing has been extended to more modern formalisms, including Z specifications (Wu & Yi, 2004), and hierarchical state machines (Heimdahl & Whalen, 1997). In general, the basic idea behind program slicing is to remove details of the program that are not relevant to the analysis in hand. For example, if we wish to verify some property, slicing can be applied to eliminate parts of the program that do not affect that property.

Computation slicing was introduced in (Li, Rilling, & Goswami, 2004, Sen & Garg, 2003a, Garg & Mittal, 2001, Mittal & Garg, 2001) as an abstraction technique for analyzing distributed computations (finite execution traces). A computation slice, defined with respect to a global property, is the computation with the least number of global states that contains all global states of the original computation for which the property evaluates to true. This is in contrast to traditional slicing techniques, which either work at the program level or do slicing with respect to variables. Computation slicing can be used to eliminate the irrelevant global states of the original computation, and keep only the states that are relevant for our purpose. In (Mittal & Garg, 2001), Mittal and Garg proved that a slice exists for all global predicates. However, it is, in general, NP-complete to compute the slice. They developed efficient algorithms to compute slices for special classes of predicates.

PARTIAL ORDER TRACE ANALYZER

In this section we will give a brief introduction to Partial Order Trace Analyzer (POTA) which is a tool that can be used for runtime verification of distributed programs (computations) (Sen, 2004; Sen & Garg, 2003b).

The properties to be checked using POTA have to be specified using the specification language (RCTL+) which is a subset of temporal logic CTL. POTA contains the implementation of a number of efficient verification algorithms.

The tool has been implemented using the Java programming language. POTA takes as an input a program and a specification. The specification is given in a text file and then parsed. The program is instrumented using the instrumentor module and then executed. A trace of the program is collected while the program is running.

The trace is then given to the analyzer module as an input. The analyzer module implements the slicing and property checking algorithms. The POTA tool also involves a translator module that enables the use of a model checker on the program trace rather than on the program itself.

The purpose of the instrumentor module is to inject code at the appropriate places in the program to be verified. The main goal of the instrumented code is to output the relevant events (communication events or any event that may affect one of the properties to be checked) and a vector clock that is updated for each relevant event.

Upon executing the instrumented program, a log file is generated for each process. The contents of each log file is a sequence of (event, vector clock) pairs that a process generates. Each pair in the sequence is also appended by the values of the variables that the event in the pair manipulates. The log files of all of the processes in the distributed program are then merged to obtain a partial order representation of the execution trace.

The translator module takes as an input a trace of the program and translates it into Promela (input language of SPIN). The analyzer module contains the computation slicing and property checking algorithms (Sen, 2004).

REFERENCES

Alagar, V. S., & Periyasamy, K. (1998). *Specification of software systems*. New York, NY: Springer-Verlag, Inc.

Berard, B., Bidoit, M., Finkel, A., Laroussinie, F., Petit, A., & Petrucci, L. (2001). *Systems and software verification: Model-checking techniques and tools*. New York, NY: Springer.

Bougé, L. (1987). Repeated snapshots in distributed systems with synchronous communications and their implementation in CSP. *Theoretical Computer Science, 49*, 145–169. doi:10.1016/0304-3975(87)90005-3

Chandy, K. M., & Lamport, L. (1985). Distributed snapshots: Determining global states of distributed systems. *ACM Transactions on Computer Systems, 3*(1), 63–75. doi:10.1145/214451.214456

Charron-Bost, B., Delporte-Gallet, C., & Fauconnier, H. (1995). Local and temporal predicates in distributed systems. *ACM Transactions Programming Language Systems, 17*(1), 157–179. doi:10.1145/200994.201005

Chase, C. M., & Garg, V. K. (1995). Efficient detection of restricted classes of global predicates. In *WDAG '95: Proceedings of the 9th International Workshop on Distributed Algorithms* (pp. 303–317). Springer-Verlag.

Chase, C. M., & Garg, V. K. (1998). Detection of global predicates: Techniques and their limitations. *Distributed Computing, 11*(4), 191–201. doi:10.1007/s004460050049

Cooper, R., & Marzullo, K. (1991). Consistent detection of global predicates. *SIGPLAN Notices, 26*(12), 167–174. doi:10.1145/127695.122774

Emerson, E. A. (1990). *Temporal and modal logic.* Cambridge, MA: MIT Press.

Garg, V. K. (2002). *Elements of distributed computing.* New York, NY: John Wiley & Sons, Inc.

Garg, V. K., & Mittal, N. (2001). On slicing a distributed computation. In *ICDCS '01: Proceedings of the the 21st International Conference on Distributed Computing Systems* (p. 322).

Garg, V. K., & Waldecker, B. (1992). Detection of unstable predicates in distributed programs. In *Proceedings of the 12th Conference on Foundations of Software Technology and Theoretical Computer Science* (pp. 253–264). London, UK: Springer-Verlag.

Garg, V. K., & Waldecker, B. (1994). Detection of weak unstable predicates in distributed programs. *IEEE Transactions on Parallel and Distributed Systems, 5*(3), 299–307. doi:10.1109/71.277788

Garg, V. K., & Waldecker, B. (1996). Detection of strong unstable predicates in distributed programs. *IEEE Transactions on Parallel and Distributed Systems, 7*(12), 1323–1333. doi:10.1109/71.553309

Haban, D., & Weigel, W. (1988). Global events and global breakpoints in distributed systems. In *Proceedings of the Twenty-First Annual Hawaii International Conference on Software Track* (pp. 166–175). Los Alamitos, CA.

Heimdahl, M. P. E., & Whalen, M. W. (1997). Reduction and slicing of hierarchical state machines. In *ESEC '97/FSE-5: Proceedings of the 6th European Conference held jointly with the 5th ACM SIGSOFT International Symposium on Foundations of Software Engineering* (pp. 450–467). New York, NY: Springer-Verlag, Inc.

Hughes, G., & Cresswell, M. (1996). *A new introduction to modal logic.* London, UK: Routledge. doi:10.4324/9780203290644

Hurfin, M., Plouzeau, N., & Raynal, M. (1993). Detecting atomic sequences of predicates in distributed computations. In *Workshop on Parallel and Distributed Debugging* (pp. 32-42).

Jegou, R., Medina, R., & Nourine, L. (1995). Linear space algorithm for on-line detection of global predicates. In Desel, J. (Ed.), *Structures in Concurrency Theory, Proceedings of the International Workshop on Structures in Concurrency Theory (STRICT)*, Berlin, 11–13 May 1995 (pp. 175–189).

Ladan, M. A. (2001). A survey and a taxonomy of approaches for testing parallel and distributed programs. In *AICCSA '01: Proceedings of the ACS/IEEE International Conference on Computer Systems and Applications* (pp. 273-279).

Lamport, L. (1978). Time, clocks, and the ordering of events in a distributed system. *Communications of the ACM, 21*(7), 558–565. doi:10.1145/359545.359563

Lamport, L. (1990). A theorem on atomicity in distributed algorithms. *Distributed Computing, 4*(2), 59–68. doi:10.1007/BF01786631

Li, H. F., Rilling, J., & Goswami, D. (2004). Granularity-driven dynamic predicate slicing algorithms for message passing systems. *Automated Software Engineering, 11*(1), 63–89. doi:10.1023/B:AUSE.0000008668.12782.6c

Mattern, F. (1989, October). Virtual time and global states of distributed systems. In *Proceedings of the International Workshop on Parallel and Distributed Algorithms* (pp. 215–226). Château de Bonas, France.

Mittal, N., & Garg, V. K. (2001). Computation slicing: Techniques and theory. In *DISC '01: Proceedings of the 15th International Conference on Distributed Computing* (pp. 78–92). London, UK: Springer-Verlag.

Pnueli, A. (1977). The temporal logic of programs. In *FOCS: Proceedings of the 18th IEEE Symposium on Foundation of Computer Science* (pp. 46-57).

Pnueli, A. (1979). The temporal semantics of concurrent programs. In *Proceedings of the International Symposium on Semantics of Concurrent Computation* (pp. 1-20).

Schwarz, R., & Mattern, F. (1994). Detecting causal relationships in distributed computations: In search of the holy grail. *Distributed Computing, 7*(3), 149–174. doi:10.1007/BF02277859

Sen, A. (2004). *Techniques for formal verification of concurrent and distributed program traces.* PhD thesis, University of Texas at Austin.

Sen, A., & Garg, V. K. (2002). Detecting temporal logic predicates on the happened-before model. In *IPDPS '02: Proceedings of the 16th International Parallel and Distributed Processing Symposium* (p. 116).

Sen, A., & Garg, V. K. (2003a). *Detecting temporal logic predicates in distributed programs using computation slicing* (pp. 171–183). OPODIS.

Sen, A., & Garg, V. K. (2003b). Partial order trace analyzer (pota) for distributed programs. In *In Runtime Verification 2003, volume 89 of ENTCS*.

Spezialetti, M., & Kearns, P. (1986). *Efficient distributed snapshots* (pp. 382–388). ICDCS.

Tarafdar, A., & Garg, V. K. (1998). *Predicate control for active debugging of distributed programs* (pp. 763–769). IPPS/SPDP.

Tomlinson, A. I., & Garg, V. K. (1993). Detecting relational global predicates in distributed systems. In *Workshop on Parallel and Distributed Debugging* (pp. 21-31).

Weiser, M. (1984). Program slicing. *IEEE Transactions on Software Engineering*, *10*(4), 352–357. doi:10.1109/TSE.1984.5010248

Wu, F., & Yi, T. (2004). Slicing Z specifications. *SIGPLAN Notice*, *39*(8), 39–48. doi:10.1145/1026474.1026481

Chapter 4
On the Improvement of Cost–Effectiveness:
A Case of Regression Testing

Seifedine Kadry
American University of the Middle East, Kuwait

ABSTRACT

System maintenance is a general term required to keep a system running properly. The system could be a computer system, mechanical system, or other system. The maintenance in this sense is related to the deterioration of the system due to its usage and age. This context of maintenance does not apply to software, where the deterioration due to the usage and age don't make sense. Conventionally, the maintenance of software is concerned with modifications related to software system. These modifications come from the user needs, error correction, improvement of performance, adapt to a changed environment, and optimization.

INTRODUCTION

Software development companies spend more time on maintenance of existing software than on development of new software, and according to earlier studies software maintenance accounts for 40-70% (Figure 1) of its total life-cycle costs.

Due to the testing process of software, the maintenance phase is undoubtedly the most costly and crucial phase in the software development life cycle. In this chapter we study in detail two well known testing techniques: Regression Test

DOI: 10.4018/978-1-4666-0089-8.ch004

Figure 1. Costs of software development stages (Bell, 2005)

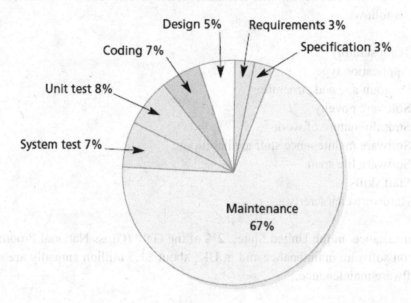

Selection and Automation test, in addition to the development of a new technique to ameliorate the cost-effectiveness of the regression testing. The proposed technique is applied to an insurance system in the SNA-Soft Company, the evaluation and a comparison with other techniques is given.

NEED FOR MAINTENANCE AND COST

As software systems age, it becomes more and more difficult to satisfy user requirements and to keep them 'up and running' without maintenance.

Maintenance is applicable to software developed using any software life cycle model (waterfall, spiral, etc). Maintenance must be performed in order to:

- Interface with other systems
- Correct faults
- Migrate legacy software
- Implement enhancements
- Adapt programs so that different hardware, software, system features, and telecommunications facilities can be used
- Improve the design
- Retire software

Some of the technical and non-technical factors affecting software maintenance costs, as follows:

- Team stability
- Application type
- Program age and structure
- Software novelty
- Stressful nature of work
- Software maintenance staff availability
- Software life span
- Staff skills
- Hardware characteristics

For instance, in the United States, 2% of the GNP (Gross National Product) is spent on software maintenance and in UK; about $1.5 million annually are spent on software maintenance.

TYPES OF SOFTWARE MAINTENANCE

E.B. Swanson initially identified three categories of maintenance: corrective, adaptive, and perfective. Later on, one additional category is added by Lientz and Swanson (1981): Preventive maintenance. The distribution of maintenance activities is shown in Figure 2.

Corrective maintenance is any maintenance activity to fix the bugs that has occurred or after delivery (Takang and Grubb, 1996), while adaptive maintenance keeps the software program working in a changed or changing environment such as the hardware or the operating system (Coenen and Bench-Capon, 1993). Perfective maintenance is every change to software to increase its performance or to enhance its user interface and its maintainability (van Vliet, 2000). The goal of preventive maintenance is to keep the software functioning correctly at any time.

TESTING AND VERIFICATION

After any modifications or maintenance, the verification step is very critical. Verification is the general term for techniques that aim to assure that software fully satisfies all the expected requirements without any "bugs". Testing is a widely used technique for verification, but note that testing is just one technique amongst several others. Currently the dominant technique used for verification is testing. And

Figure 2. Maintenance type's percentage (Jain, 2005)

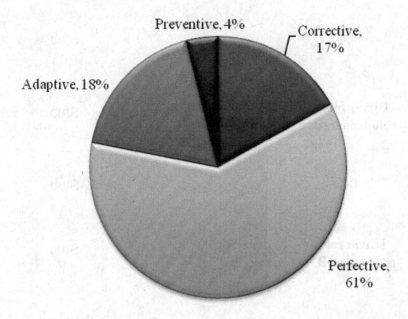

testing typically consumes an enormous proportion (sometimes as much as 50%) of the effort of developing a system. Microsoft employs teams of programmers (who write programs) and completely separate teams of testers (who test them). At Microsoft there are as many people involved in testing as there are in programming. Arguably, verification is a major problem and we need good techniques to tackle it. Often, towards the end of a project, the difficult decision has to be made between continuing the testing or delivering the software to the customers.

TESTING LEVELS

Unit testing: Most software consists of a number of components, each the size of a small program. How do we test each component? One answer is to create an environment to test each component in isolation (Figure 3). This is termed unit testing. A driver component makes method calls on the component under test. Any methods that the component uses are simulated as stubs. These stubs are rudimentary replacements for missing methods.

System testing: Thus far we have only considered unit testing – testing an individual software component, a method or a class. We have implicitly assumed that such a component is fairly small. This is the first step in the verification of software

Figure 3. Unit test environment

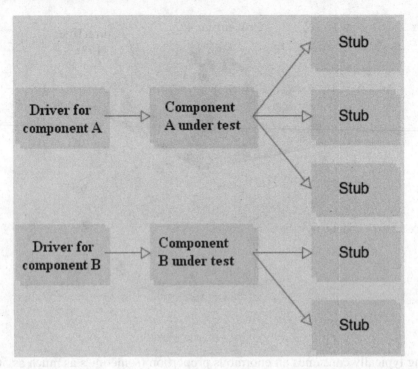

systems, which typically consist of tens or hundreds of individual components. The task of testing complete systems is called system or integration testing. Suppose that we have designed and code all the components for a system. How can we test these components and how can we test the complete system?

Here are three different approaches to system testing:

- **Big Bang:** bring all the components together, without prior testing, and test the complete system
- **Improved big bang:** test each component individually (unit testing), bring them all together and test the complete system
- **Incremental:** build the system piece by piece, testing the partial system at each stage.

The first approach – big bang or monolithic testing – is a recipe for disaster. There is no easy way of knowing which component is the cause of a fault, and there is an enormous debugging task. The second approach is slightly better because when the components are brought together, we have some confidence in them individually.

Now any faults are likely to be caused by the interactions between the components. Here again, there is a major problem of locating faults.

An alternative is to use some form of incremental testing. In this approach, first one component of the system is tested, then a second component is linked with the first and the system tested (Figure 4). Any fault is likely to be localized either in the newly incorporated component or in the interface between the two. We continue like this, adding just one component at a time. At each stage, any fault that presents itself is likely to be caused by the new component, or by its interface to the system. Thus fault finding is made considerably easier.

TESTING TECHNIQUES

Code can be tested at many different levels with different techniques: do individual statements execute according to specification, do procedures provide expected output for given input, and does the program as a whole perform in a particular way? Within this are many issues to be borne in mind. For example, it is possible to execute each statement without touching upon certain conditions. However, test cases should try to take account of all possible conditions and combinations of conditions, with special emphasis on boundary conditions and values where behavior is often erroneous. In the following sections, we discussed some of the techniques used in software testing.

Black Box or Functional Testing

Knowing that exhaustive testing is infeasible, the black box approach to testing is to devise sample data that is representative of all possible data. We then run the program, input the data and see what happens. This type of testing is termed black box testing because no knowledge of the workings of the program is used as part of the testing – we only consider inputs and outputs. The program is thought of as being enclosed within a black box. Black box testing is also known as functional testing because it uses only knowledge of the function of the program (not how it works). Ideally, testing proceeds by writing down the test data and the expected outcome of the test before testing takes place. This is called a test specification or schedule. Then you run the program, input the data and examine the outputs for discrepancies between the predicted outcome and the actual outcome. Test data should also check whether exceptions are handled by the program in accordance with its specification.

Figure 4. Incremental system testing

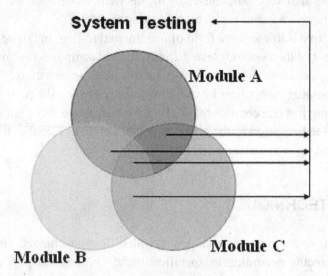

White Box or Structural Testing

This form of testing makes use of knowledge of how the program works – the structure of the program – as the basis for devising test data. In white box testing every statement in the program is executed at some time during the testing. This is equivalent to ensuring that every path (every sequence of instructions) through the program is executed at some time during testing. This includes null paths, so an "if statement" without an else has two paths and every loop has two paths. Testing should also include any exception handling carried out by the program.

DEBUGGING THE CODE

Some debuggers allow the user to step through a program, executing just one instruction at a time. Each time you execute one instruction you can see which path of execution has been taken. You can also see (or watch) the values of variables. It is rather like an automated structured walkthrough. In this form of testing, you concentrate on the variables and closely check their values as they are changed by the program to verify that they have been changed correctly. A debugger is usually used for debugging (locating a bug); here it is used for testing (establishing the existence of a bug).

TEST PROFILER

In a large system or program it can be difficult to ensure that the test data is adequate. One way to try to test whether it does indeed cause all statements to be executed is to use a profiler. A profiler is a software package that monitors the testing by inserting probes into the software under test. When testing takes place, the profiler can expose which pieces of the code are not executed and therefore reveal the weakness in the data. Another approach to investigating the test data is called mutation testing. In this technique, artificial bugs are inserted into the program. An example would be to change a + into a –. The test is run and if the bugs are not revealed, then the test data is obviously inadequate. The test data is modified until the artificial bugs are exposed.

BETA TESTING

In beta testing, a preliminary version of a software product is released to a selected market, the customer or client, knowing that it has bugs. Users are asked to report on faults so that the product can be improved for its proper release date. Beta testing gets its name from the second letter of the Greek alphabet. Its name therefore conveys the idea that it is the second major act of testing, following on after testing within the developing organization. Once Beta testing is complete and the bugs are fixed, the software is released.

TEST AUTOMATION

It is good practice to automate testing so that tests can be reapplied at the touch of a button. This is extra work in the beginning but often saves time overall. The following reasons lead the software companies to apply a test automation process on software:

- **Manual mistakes:** may occur due to human interference. In this direction, the execution of test automation reduces the wrong entering information by the tester.
- **Parallel execution:** the computer is multitask, it can run many tests in parallel hence the process can be done faster with less resources.
- **No Interruption:** there is no need to interrupt the execution of automated test, contrary to manually executed cycle.

- **Easy Result Analysis:** the analysis result phase comes after the execution of automated test. Also, this phase can be automated based on previous test analysis result, which is easier to do it manually.

Although the automation process seems to have more benefits than disadvantages, it is always good to be aware of the problems that may be encountered. The anxiety of having everything automated is higher because the tester wants to feel comfortable by running all the tests several times, avoiding bug insertions when the code changes (Oliveira et al., 2006). Some tests, even during reruns, may never find a bug and have no significant prospect of doing so. Hence automating everything may not be the best decision. To avoid these kinds of mistakes and have a cost-effective automation process, there are some tradeoffs that need to be well-understood before deciding whether a particular test should be automated.

To improve the automation test, the viability method (ATVM) is developed (Oliveira et al., 2006). Some questions were proposed whose answers will be analyzed and judged properly to decide if a test should be automate it or not in order to improve its cost-effectiveness, as illustrated in Table 1.

The Decision Tree (Figure 5) Learning Algorithm is based on the answer to the above questions (Table 1) of 500 automated test cases. The building process and verification of the decision tree is automatic. Usually, the size of the tree is small therefore the traversing cost is negligible but the tree needs to be traversed everytime a software component gets modified to make sure that the decision of whether to automate it has not changed.

The tree represents the ways that can be followed by answering the questions presented in Table 1. The numbers in the grey circles are the Identifiers for the questions that they are related to. The 'Y' and 'N' represent the end of the tree and mean 'Yes' or 'No', respectively. They are the indicators of cost-effectiveness.

All the proposed questions have a discrete number of answers: 'High', 'Medium' or 'Low', which are represented in the tree by the letters 'H', 'M' and 'L'. Note that, depending on the answer of each specific question, the tree takes you different ways. Going through the tree from the top to the end via the answered questions, an indicator of 'Yes' or 'No' will be obtained, showing if a test case is viable or not for automation. It is important to notice that not all the questions need to be answered for a test case. For example: if the answer given to the question number 2 is 'L', question number 4 will never be answered. Also, it is worth clarifying that there is no correct answer for these questions. However, the more you know about the tests being analyzed, the better the chances will be for success.

Example: customer registration in SNA-Soft system. In this example, we illustrate how to apply the above decision tree for a test case.

Table 1. Indicator questions for test automation

Identifier	Topics	Related Questions
1	Frequency	How many times is this test supposed to be executed?
2	Reuse	Can this test or parts of it be reused in other tests?
3	Relevance	How would you describe the importance of this test case?
4	Automation effort	Does this test take a lot of effort to be deployed?
5	Resources	How many members of your team should be allocated or how expensive is the equipment needed during this test's manual execution?
6	Manual Complexity	Is this test difficult to be executed manually? Does it have any embedded confidential information?
7	Automation Tool	How would you describe the reliability of the automation tool to be used?
8	Porting	How portable is this test?
9	Execution effort	Does this require a lot of effort to be executed manually?

Starting with the first question on the tree, "How many times is this test supposed to be executed?", if this operation has few executions, the answer is 'Low'. This answer takes you to the right side of the tree, leading to the second question, "Can this test or parts of it be reused in other tests?" Let's suppose that the code used to automate this test has little chance of being reused. Thus, the answer to Question

Figure 5. Decision tree

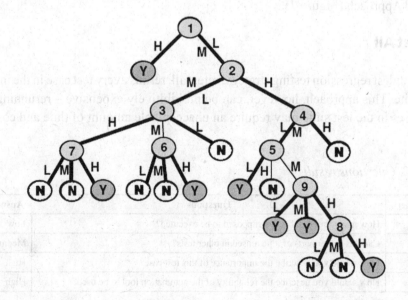

2 is 'Medium'. Now the Decision Tree takes us to the left side of the tree, to the next question, "How would you describe the importance of this test case?" Making a transaction on a bank website is an important task to be tested, so the answer is 'High'. The left side is taken, which leads to the last question, "How would you describe the reliability of the automation tool to be used?" As the test has very high relevance, the tool to be used must be quite reliable to ensure that this test is in fact being well executed. Therefore, the answer to this question is 'High'. The summary of the results reached with this example is presented in Table 2.

By answering the questions 1, 2, 3 and 7, following the decision tree (the black lines, Figure 6), the user would have a positive response, which would mark this test as a good candidate for automation. Note that it is not necessary to answer all the questions. Depending on the answers that are given, the tree can conduct the user to answer only some of the questions.

REGRESSION TESTING

Regression testing is defined as "the process of retesting the modified parts of the software and ensuring that no new errors have been introduced into previously tested code". Let P be a program, let P' be a modified version of P, and let T be a test suite for P. Regression testing consists of reusing T on P', and determining where the new test cases are needed to effectively test code or functionality added to or changed in producing P'. There is various regression testing techniques (Duggal and Suri, 2008): Retest all, Regression Test Selection, Test Case Prioritization and Hybrid Approach (Figure 7).

Retest All

The simplest regression testing strategy, retest all, reruns every test case in the initial test suite. This approach, however, can be prohibitively expensive – rerunning all test cases in the test suite may require an unacceptable amount of time and cost.

Table 2. Questions result

Identifier	Questions	Answers
1	How many times is this test supposed to be executed?	Low
2	Can this test or parts of it be reused in other tests?	Medium
3	How would you describe the importance of this test case?	High
7	How would you describe the reliability of the automation tool to be used?	High

Test Case Prioritization

This technique of regression testing prioritize the test cases so as to increase a test suite's rate of fault detection that is how quickly a test suite detects faults in the modified program to increase reliability. This is of two types: (1) General prioritization which attempts to select an order of the test case that will be effective on average subsequent versions of software. (2)Version specific prioritization which is concerned with particular version of the software.

Hybrid Approach

The fourth regression technique is the Hybrid Approach of both Regression Test Selection and Test Case Prioritization. There are number of researchers working on this approach and they have proposed many algorithms for it.

Regression Test Selection

Due to expensive nature of "retest all" technique, Regression Test Selection (RTS) is performed. In this technique instead of rerunning the whole test suite we select

Figure 6. Decision tree of the questions result

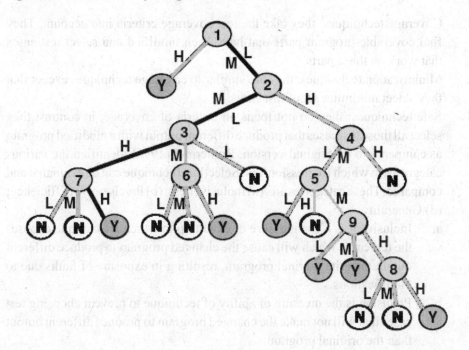

Figure 7. Regression testing techniques

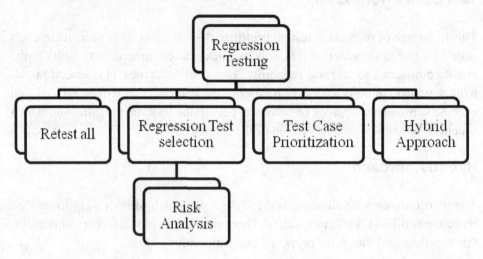

a part of test suite to rerun if the cost of selecting a part of test suite is less than the cost of running the tests that RTS allows us to omit. RTS divides the existing test suite into (1) Reusable test cases; (2) Re-testable test cases; (3) Obsolete test cases. In addition to this classification RTS may create new test cases that test the program for areas which are not covered by the existing test cases. RTS techniques are broadly classified into three categories.

1. Coverage techniques: they take the test coverage criteria into account. They find coverable program parts that have been modified and select test cases that work on these parts.
2. Minimization techniques: they are similar to coverage techniques except that they select minimum set of test cases.
3. Safe techniques: they do not focus on criteria of coverage; in contrast they select all those test cases that produce different output with a modified program as compared to its original version. Rothermel (1996) identified the various categories in which Regression Test Selection Technique can be evaluated and compared. These categories are: (a) Inclusiveness; (b) Precision; (c) Efficiency; (d) Generality.
   a. Inclusiveness is the measure of extent up to which a technique chooses the test cases which will cause the changed program to produce different output than the original program, resulting in exposure of faults due to modifications.
   b. Precision is the measure of ability of technique to prevent choosing test cases that will not make the changed program to produce different output than the original program.

c.   Efficiency measures the practicality (computational cost) of a technique.
d.   Generality is the measure of ability of a technique to handle complex modifications, realistic language constructs and realistic testing applications.

REGRESSION TEST SELECTION BASED ON RISK ANALYSIS

This section is based on the study of Chen and Probert (2003). Risk is anything that threatens the successful achievement of a project's goals. Specifically, a risk is an event that has some probability of happening, and that if it occurs, will result in some loss. The tester's job is to reveal high-priority problems in the product. Traditional testers have always used risk-based testing, but in an ad hoc fashion based on their personal judgment. Using risk metrics to quantitatively measure the quality of a test suite seems perfectly reasonable and is our approach.

Amland (2000) presented a simple risk model with only two elements of Risk Exposure. We use this model in our research. It takes into account both:

1.   The probability of a fault being present. Myers (1979) reports that as the number of detected errors increases, the probability that more undetected errors exist also in-creases. If one component has defects that are detected by full testing, it is very likely that we can find more defects in this component by regression testing (the more defects detected, the more defects we can expect). Thus, components with detected defects should be covered more carefully by regression tests.
2.   The cost (consequence or impact) of a fault in the corresponding function if it occurs in operation. It is a well-known, observed fact that most commercial software contains bugs at delivery time. Companies begin a project with the knowledge that they will choose, because of schedule pressures, to ship software that contains known bugs (Bach, 1998). However, when the budget is limited, we strive to detect the most critical defects first.

The mathematical formula to calculate Risk Exposure is RE (f) = P (f) × C (f), where RE (f) is the Risk Exposure of function f, P (f) is the probability of a fault occurring in function f and C (f) is the cost if a fault is executed in function f in operational mode. In this context, we calculate first the Risk Exposure for each test case (RE (t)). Then we choose test cases based on RE (t). To illustrate this formula we present a real example based on our SNA-Soft product. The evaluation of risk exposure involves 4 steps:

Step 1. Assess the cost for each test case

Cost means the cost of the requirements attributes that this test case covers. Cost C is categorized on a one to five scale, where one is low and five is high. Two kinds of costs will be taken into consideration:

- The consequences of a fault as seen by the customer, that is, losing market share because of faults.
- The consequences of a fault as seen by the vendor, that is, high software maintenance cost because of faults.

Table 3 shows the costs for some test cases in our case study, i.e. SNA-Soft insurance software.

Step 2. Derive severity probability for each test case

After running the full test suite, we can sum up the number of defects uncovered by each test case. Learning from real in-house testing, we find that the severity of defects (how important or serious the defect is) is very important for software quality. Considering this aspect, we modify the simple risk model that we mentioned previously. The probability element in the original risk model is changed to severity probability, which combines the average severity of defects with the probability. Based on multiplying the Number of Defects N by the Average Severity of Defects S (N×S), we can estimate the severity probability for each test case.

Severity probability falls into a zero to five scales, where zero is low and five is high. For the test cases without any defect, P (t) is equal to zero. For the rest of the test cases, P (t) for the top 20% of the test cases with the highest estimate N×S will be five, and P (t) for the bottom 20% of the test cases will be one. Table 4 displays P (t) for some of the test cases in our case study.

Table 3. Cost of test cases

Test Case (ct)	Cost C(ct)	Description
1000	5	Update the balance after payment
1010	5	Write changes to the log file
1020	4	Add new product to the customer profile
1030	3	Send email to the customer of the modifications
...	...	...

Step 3. Calculate Risk Exposure for each test case

Combining Table 3 and Table 4, we can calculate Risk Exposure RE (t) for each test case as shown in Table 5. To improve or focus the results, we can also add weights to test cases that we need to give preference to, for example, we might like to choose more test cases for some corporate flag-ship features, such as database features.

Step 4. Select Safety Tests

To get "good enough quality," our regression test suite should achieve some coverage target. This coverage target has to be set up depending on the available time and budget. Intuitively, we do not want to choose low-risk test cases, we choose test cases that have the highest value of RE (t).

THE PROPOSED TECHNIQUE

The main goal to use regression test selection based on risk analysis or automation test is to improve the cost-effectiveness of the test. Both of these techniques are expensive in resources sense. The new proposed technique is to combine these two techniques to obtain more improvement on the test cost-effectiveness by optimizing the number of cases that should be automated and the number of cases that should we calculate their risk exposures. The flowchart of the proposed technique is given by (Figure 8).

The process begin by selecting a test case, then to automate it or to calculate its risk exposure based on the result of the decision tree, then repeat the same process to finish all test cases.

Table 4. Severity probability of test cases

Test Case (ct)	Number of Defects (N)	Average severity of Defects (S)	NxS	P(t)
1000	1	2	2	2
1010	1	3	3	2
1020	2	3	6	4
1030	0	0	0	0
...	...	...		

Table 5. Risk exposure of test cases

Test Case (ct)	Cost C(ct)	Number of Defects (N)	Average severity of Defects (S)	NxS	P(t)	RE(t)
1000	5	1	2	2	2	10
1010	5	1	3	3	2	10
1020	4	2	3	6	4	16
1030	3	0	0	0	0	0
...	...	...	...			

Figure 8. Proposed technique flowchart

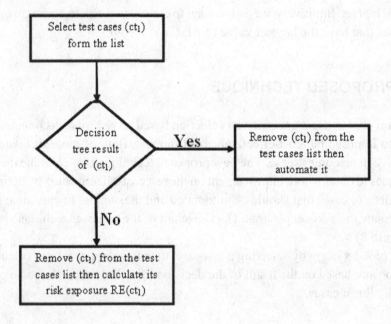

EVALUATION

To determine the influences on the cost-effectiveness of regression testing our evaluation methodology is based on three factors: Execution time complexity, number of errors detected, implementation time. Therefore the three techniques: Regression test selection based on risk analysis (TSRA), Test automation based on viability method (ATVM) and the proposed technique (PT) are evaluated based on these factors. The environment test is always the insurance software by SNA-Soft Company. This software is devoted to providing and managing all insurance products globally and it includes 20 modules. During the evaluation, we choose three different

Figure 9. Execution time factor

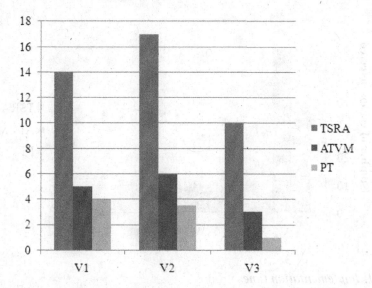

versions of the software. Each version is updates of the previous one, some errors are always expected. The threshold of TSRA was 70% of the total test cases with highest risk exposures. The following figure shows the execution time of the three methodologies. The average execution time of: TSRA is 13.6 hours, ATVM is 4.3 hours and PT is 2.6 hours. ATVM is more cost-effective of TSRA but PT is more cost-effective of both (Figure 9).

The difference in the results between different software versions was mainly caused by the bugs that were detected. When a bug was detected, we analyzed and tried to reproduce it by re-running the detecting test suite. These actions generally increased testing effort with all three methods. With TSRA, updating, calculating risk-exposures and selecting test suites required extra time. Figure 10 shows the number of errors detected with each method. Software version 3 did not contain any detected errors.

The TSRA missed some errors because it was set to reduce the number of tests effectively; it covers only 70% of the overall test coverage. The number of unde-tected errors in the proposed technique (PT) is less than the number of undetected errors using TSRA because some of the test cases are automated and others ran based on the their risk exposure. ATVM detected all errors.

Figure 11 shows the implementation time (design and implementation) of the three methods. The most consuming time in the implementation phase is the design and the implementation of a script to automate the test cases. Figure 11 reveals that

Figure 10. Number of errors factor

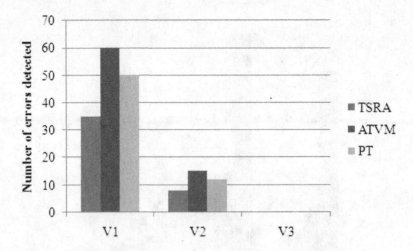

Figure 11. Implementation time

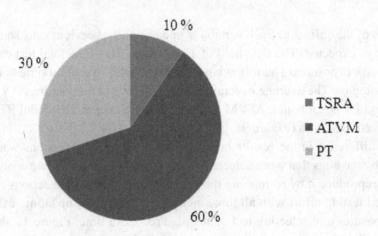

60% of the overall effort consumed in implementing ATVM, 30% for the proposed technique and only 10% for TSRA.

Based on the previous comparisons, the proposed technique could be utilized in larger scale as a method for improving the cost-effectiveness of regression testing. It's a compromise between TSRA and ATVM.

CONCLUSION

The objective of this chapter is to propose and evaluate a new technique to improve the cost-effectiveness of the regression testing. An evaluation between the proposed technique and two well known techniques: Automated test using viability method and Test selection based on Risk Analysis is given. The evaluation is based on three factors: execution time, number of detected errors and the implementation time. We recommend using the proposed technique as a compromise technique between TSRA and ATVM.

REFERENCES

Amland, S. (2000). Risk based testing and metrics: Risk analysis fundamentals and metrics for software testing including a financial application case study. *Journal of Systems and Software, 53*, 287–295. doi:10.1016/S0164-1212(00)00019-4

Bach, J. (1998). Good enough quality: Beyond the buzzword. *IEEE Computer, August*, (pp. 96-98).

Bell, D. (2005). *Software engineering for students: A programming approach* (4th ed.). Prentice Hall International.

Chen, Y., & Probert, R. (2003). *A risk-based regression test selection strategy.* Fast Abstract ISSRE 2003.

Coenen, F., & Bench-Capon, T. (1993). *Maintenance of knowledge-based systems: Theory, techniques and tools.* Cornwall, UK: Hartnolls Ltd, Bodmin.

Duggal, G., & Suri, B. (2008). *Understanding regression testing techniques.* COIT 2008, India.

Jain, N. (2005). *Agile maintenance.* Retrieved from www.thoughtworks.com

Lientz, B. P., & Swanson, E. (1981). Problems in application software maintenance. *Communications of the ACM, 24*(11), 763–769. doi:10.1145/358790.358796

Myers, G. L. (1979). *The art of software testing.* Wiley-Interscience.

Oliveira, J. C., Gouveia, C. C., & Filho, R. Q. (2006). *A way of improving test automation cost-effectiveness. CAST 2006.* Indianapolis: EUA.

Rothermel, R. (1996). *Efficient effective regression testing using safe test selection techniques.* Ph.D Thesis, Clemson University, May, 1996.

Takang, A. A., & Grubb, P. A. (1996). *Software maintenance concepts and practice.* London, UK: Thompson Computer Press.

Chapter 5

A Case Study on Testing for Software Security:
Static Code Analysis of a File Reader Program Developed in Java

Natarajan Meghanathan
Jackson State University, USA

Alexander Roy Geoghegan
L-3 Communications, USA

ABSTRACT

The high-level contribution of this book chapter is to illustrate how to conduct static code analysis of a software program and mitigate the vulnerabilities associated with the program. The automated tools used to test for software security are the Source Code Analyzer and Audit Workbench, developed by Fortify, Inc. The first two sections of the chapter are comprised of (i) An introduction to Static Code Analysis and its usefulness in testing for Software Security and (ii) An introduction to the Source Code Analyzer and the Audit Workbench tools and how to use them to conduct static code analysis. The authors then present a detailed case study of static code analysis conducted on a File Reader program (developed in Java) using these automated tools. The specific software vulnerabilities that are discovered, analyzed, and mitigated include: (i) Denial of Service, (ii) System Information Leak, (iii) Unreleased Resource (in the context of Streams), and (iv) Path Manipulation. The authors discuss the potential risk in having each of these vulnerabilities in a software program and provide the solutions (and the Java code) to mitigate these vulnerabilities. The proposed solutions for each of these four vulnerabilities are more generic and could be used to correct such vulnerabilities in software developed in any other programming language.

DOI: 10.4018/978-1-4666-0089-8.ch005

INTRODUCTION

Static Code Analysis is the process of examining a piece of code without actually executing it (McGraw, 2006). This allows the analyst to see everything that the code does and to consider the program as a whole, rather than just as a sequence of individual lines. Static Code Analysis (also invariably referred to as 'Source Code Analysis') is important from a software security standpoint. There are a number of issues which must be evaluated when performing a security analysis on a piece of code. Answering these questions (a sample is given below) can prove to be time-consuming for an analyst. Providing the right answers to these questions also requires a comprehensive knowledge of possible exploits and their solutions.

- What is the basic design of this application?
- What are the different technologies involved in this application?
- Who would want to attack this application?
- What would any attacker hope to gain by attacking the application?
- What is the risk associated with a successful attack?
- (and perhaps most importantly) How are the developers protecting this application?

In addition to an analysis of these security issues, a properly-performed static code analysis must also consist of (Graff & Van Wyk, 2003):

- **Type checking:** this is usually done by the compiler and refers to the process of examining a program's variables and parameters to ensure that a variable is not assigned to an incompatible type (Wysopal et. al, 2006);
- **Style checking:** this consists of examining the format of the code, such as indentation and the use of comments, to ensure readability;
- **Program verification:** this step consists of comparing a block of code with its task specification to ensure that the code is correct and generates the correct results (Howard & Lipner, 2006);
- **Property checking:** this step seeks to ensure that particular sequences of instructions do not occur, such as accessing a memory location after it has been released or prematurely releasing all of a program's allocated memory (Graff & Van Wyk, 2003);
- **Bug finding:** this step involves scanning the code for patterns of commands to identify where a programmer may have inadvertently left out some intended code (Graff & Van Wyk, 2003);
- and of course, the *security review*

Security review is one of the most important parts of a static code analysis. If a program is insecure and causes sensitive data to be released, it could have catastrophic consequences for the program's developers. Several key security problems that should be addressed during a security review (Wysopal et. al, 2006) are those related to input handling, errors and exceptions, and buffer/integer overflow.

- **Input Handling:** The simplest rule to follow when handling any type of input is "never trust the input" (Howard et. al, 2009). This applies not only to values passed from a user via a graphical user interface or command-line interface, but also applies to files being read from a disk, database values, system variables, and data from configuration files. While it is more probable for users to provide faulty data than the system, it is still a dangerous possibility and must be handled appropriately.
- **Errors and Exceptions:** Whenever a section of code throws or has the potential to throw an exception, it must be handled appropriately. Proper handling of errors and exceptions is critical and one should not simply ignore them. It should be the goal of the developer to identify the situations which cause such errors and exceptions to be thrown and take steps to avoid those situations.
- **Buffer/Integer Overflow:** Buffer overflow and integer overflow occur whenever data is added to a buffer or the value of an integer is changed without properly considering the size of the buffer or integer. In languages like C or C++ which are "not memory-safe", this can lead to serious security vulnerabilities, such as buffer overflow attacks (Howard et. al, 2009). While "memory-safe" languages like Java or C# try to catch buffer/integer overflow issues at compilation, the issues may not be ignored. It is still possible that an operation will cause a buffer/integer to overflow resulting in an error or exception. One should always check the size/value of buffers/integers before performing any operations on them to ensure that they will not overflow.

The following are the learning objectives of this book chapter with regards to static code analysis and testing for software security:

1. Explain the basics of static code analysis and its different sub-categories.
2. Use an automated tool to conduct static code analysis of a software program.
3. Understand the risk associated with the Denial of Service vulnerability and propose solution to mitigate it.
4. Understand the risk associated with the System Information Leak vulnerability and propose solution to mitigate it.

5. Understand the risk associated with the Unreleased Resource vulnerability in the context of streams and propose solution to mitigate it.
6. Understand the risk associated with the Path Manipulation vulnerability and propose one or more solutions to mitigate it.

Introduction to the Fortify Source Code Analysis (SCA) Suite

The Fortify Source Code Analyzer, SCA, can be used to perform a static code analysis on C/C++ or Java code and can be run in Windows, Linux, or Mac environments (Chest & West, 2008). The Fortify SCA can analyze individual files or entire projects. The analyzer follows a set of rules which are included in a rulepack, and users may use generic rulepacks or create their own custom sets of rules. The analyzer can create reports in HTML format for easy viewing, as well as reports which may be viewed with the Audit Workbench utility that is included in the Fortify suite of tools. The Audit Workbench allows users to fine-tune the results of a static code analysis and limit the displayed results to those in which they are interested. The Workbench also includes an editor which will highlight the troublesome-code and allow users to make changes to the code within the application. For each generic issue flagged by the analyzer, the Audit Workbench provides a description of the problem and how the problem may be averted.

Issues Identified by the Fortify SCA

With a generic rulepack, the SCA will identify four categories of issues: (i) semantic, (ii) dataflow, (iii) control flow, and structural issues.

Semantic issues include those such as system information leaks, present whenever information specific to the program's internal workings may be inadvertently provided to a user. The simplest example of this type of semantic issue is the use of the *printStackTrace*() method in Java's Exception class. This method outputs the call stack at the point at which the exception occurred and provides a user with information about the program's structure, including method names. While use of the *printStackTrace*() method is handy during debugging, it is not advisable to leave such code in a finished product.

Dataflow issues include those through which data can cause unwanted effects on a program's execution. For example, if a line of text were accepted from a user or a method of another class as an SQL query and executed directly onto the database without first checking the data for code which may perpetrate an SQL-injection attack (Whittaker, 2002). This highlights the need for proper input handling.

Control flow issues are those related to an improper series of commands. An example of a control flow issue would be if a resource were allocated but never

Figure 1. Audit workbench AuditGuide

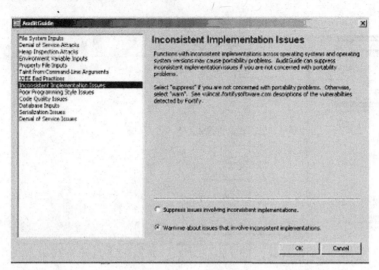

released. Another example of a control flow issue would be if a program attempted to access a resource that had already been released.

Structural issues can relate to bugs within the code that do not necessarily affect the performance of an application, but are still not advisable. An example of a structural issue is to hard-code a password into a program. If this is done, anyone who can gain access to the code can also gain access to the password.

Audit Workbench

While the source analyzer tool is a command-line tool, the Audit Workbench utility offers a graphical user-interface which makes it easy for users to view the results of a static code analysis on a set of source code files and correct the issues raised during the source code analysis. The Audit Workbench's input is a report generated by the source analyzer. The Audit Workbench's AuditGuide allows a user to control what types of warnings and issues are displayed during an audit. Each type of issue can be either turned on or off according to a user's needs. Figure 1 is a screenshot of the Audit Workbench's AuditGuide and shows the list of available warning types and a dialog box for turning each one on or off.

When an audit's settings have been selected, the Workbench displays the results of the audit. The interface displays a list of the issues that have been flagged and groups these issues according to their severity (hot, warning, or info). The original source code file is also displayed so that a user can immediately access the offending code by selecting an issue in the Issues Panel. For each issue that is shown, the

Figure 2. Audit workbench screenshot displaying details of a specific security issue identified

Workbench displays a panel providing background information about the issue and suggestions for resolving the issue. Figure 2 shows a screenshot of the Audit Workbench user-interface. The figure shows an open audit in which several issues have been flagged (1 hot, 3 warning and 7 info-level). The user has selected one of the Warning issues and the Workbench has loaded the source code file and selected the offending code within the file. Displayed in the panel at the bottom is the explanation of the Path Manipulation issue (the issue the user has selected). The Audit Workbench also gives the user the ability to generate reports on an audit in any of a number of formats (.doc,.html,.xml, and more).

CASE STUDY: SOURCE CODE ANALYSIS ON A FILE READER PROGRAM DEVELOPED IN JAVA

The objective of the File Reader program: testFileRead.java is to read the contents of a text file (name input by the user as a command line argument) on a line-by-line basis and output the lines as read. Figure 3 shows the original source code for the program. A run of the Fortify *Sourceanalyzer* utility on the testFileRead.java program generates (see Figure 4) the following vulnerabilities: 3 medium and 3 low.

When we forward the results to an Audit Workbench compatible.fpr file (see Figure 5) and open the log file in Audit Workbench (see Figure 6), we see the 6

Figure 3. Original source code for the File Reader program

```
1     import java.io.*;
2     class testFileRead{
3
5       public static void main(String[ ] args) throws IOException{
6
7       try{
8
9         FileReader fr = new FileReader(args[0]);
10        BufferedReader br = new BufferedReader(fr);
11
12        String line = null;
13
14        while ( (line = br.readLine( ) ) != null){
15          System.out.println(line);
16        }
17
18
19        br.close( );
20        fr.close( );
21
22
23      }// try block
24      catch(IOException ie){
25        ie.printStackTrace( );
26        }
27      }
28  }
```

vulnerabilities displayed in Figure 4 as Warnings (3) and Info (3). After we start Audit Workbench, we will have to load the appropriate.fpr file and we can also turn off the particular vulnerabilities we are not interested to find/ know about in our code by clicking "Continue to AuditGuide >>". Alternatively, if we are interested to know about all possible vulnerabilities that may exist in our code, we can select the "Skip AuditGuide" button. It is important to make sure the Java program compiles without any error before using the Fortify tools.

We will now show how to fix the following Warnings (Vulnerabilities) displayed by the Fortify Audit Workbench tool: (i) Denial of Service, (ii) System Information Leak, (iii) Unreleased Resource: Streams and (iv) Path Manipulation.

Denial of Service Vulnerability

A 'Denial of Service' vulnerability is the one using which an attacker can cause the program to crash or make it unavailable to legitimate users (Graff & Van Wyk, 2003).

Figure 4. Warnings generated for the original source code in Figure 3 – testFileRead. java

```
C:\res\CCLI-2010\Modules-Meghanathan\Static-Code-Analysis-Examples\Ex1_FileReade
r>sourceanalyzer testFileRead.java

[C:\res\CCLI-2010\Modules-Meghanathan\Static-Code-Analysis-Examples\Ex1_FileRead
er]

[F014B0E28C8E6288784927FC772618FE : low : Denial of Service : semantic ]
testFileRead.java(14) : BufferedReader.readLine()

[EDD1323454D69423D2DD7D4D187D22B7 : medium : System Information Leak : semantic
]
testFileRead.java(25) : Throwable.printStackTrace()

[78FA82368471A9D617111E250114E445 : medium : Path Manipulation : dataflow ]
testFileRead.java(9) :  ->new FileReader(0)
     testFileRead.java(5) :  ->testFileRead.main(0)

[865F144B2D584D3CB7CEDB696F19A416 : medium : Unreleased Resource : Streams : con
trolflow ]
     testFileRead.java(9) : start -> loaded : fr.new FileReader(...)
     testFileRead.java(10) : loaded -> loaded : fr.new BufferedReader(..., fr, ..
.)
     testFileRead.java(14) : loaded -> end_of_scope : #end_scope(fr) (exception t
hrown)
[423D552C35C67B4A8F045E1C079B74FB : low : J2EE Bad Practices : Leftover Debug Co
de : structural ]
     testFileRead.java(5)

[ADBD437811B82372BC593D8FB94B74B6 : low : Poor Logging Practice : Use of a Syste
m Output Stream : structural ]
     testFileRead.java(15)

C:\res\CCLI-2010\Modules-Meghanathan\Static-Code-Analysis-Examples\Ex1_FileReade
r>
```

Line 14 in the testFileRead.java code (see highlighted in Figure 7) has a Denial of Service Vulnerability. The *readLine*() method invoked on the *BufferedReader* object may be used by the attacker to read an unbounded amount of input. There is no limit on the number of characters that may be buffered and read as a line. An attacker can take advantage of this code to cause an *OutOfMemoryException* or to consume a large amount of memory so that the program spends more time performing garbage collection or runs out of memory during some subsequent operation.

Solution: The solution is to validate the user input to ensure that it will not cause inappropriate resource utilization. In the context of our program, we will limit the number of characters per line that can be read and buffered; it could be 200 or even

Figure 5. Logging the warnings for the testFileRead.java file to res_testFileRead_org. fpr file

```
C:\res\CCLI-2010\Modules-Meghanathan\Static-Code-Analysis-Examples\Ex1_FileReade
r>sourceanalyzer testFileRead.java -f res_testFileRead_org.fpr

C:\res\CCLI-2010\Modules-Meghanathan\Static-Code-Analysis-Examples\Ex1_FileReade
r>auditworkbench
```

Figure 6. Vulnerabilities (warnings and info) pointed out by Audit Workbench for code in Figure 3

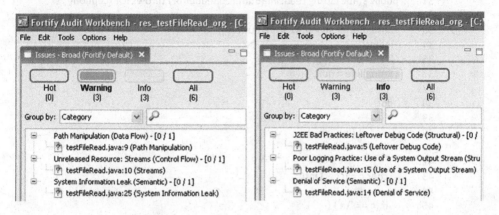

1000 characters long (defined through the static variable STR_MAX_LEN in the code of Figure 9); but there needs to be an upper limit to avoid the code from being misused. We create a new *readLine*() static method (refer Figure 8) in our testRead-File class and call it from our main program to read every line of the file through the BufferedReader (see Figure 9). We will call this version of the program as testFileRead_fixed_v1.java. Running the Fortify SCA generates the following new reduced set of vulnerabilities (Figure 10).

System Information Leak Vulnerability

The "System Information Leak" vulnerability refers to revealing system data or debugging information that may help an adversary to learn about the system and form a plan of attack (Whittaker, 2002). In our code, the *printStackTrace*() method (see Figure 11) called on the object of class 'IOException' in line 27 of the testFileRead_fixed_v1.java program has the potential to leak out sensitive information about the entire application program, the operating system it is running under and the amount of care the developers and administrators have put into configuring the

Figure 7. Segment of the testFileRead.java code with the denial of service vulnerability

```
Group by: Category
    J2EE Bad Practices: Leftover Debug Code (Structural) - [0 /         9    FileReader fr = new FileReader(args[0]);
        testFileRead.java:5 (Leftover Debug Code)              10    BufferedReader br = new BufferedReader(fr);
    Poor Logging Practice: Use of a System Output Stream (Stru    11
        testFileRead.java:15 (Use of a System Output Stream)   12    String line = null;
    Denial of Service (Semantic) - [0 / 1]                     13
        testFileRead.java:14 (Denial of Service)               14    while ( (line = br.readLine() ) != null){
                                                               15        System.out.println(line);
                                                               16    }
```

Figure 8. A newly added readLine() static method to the testReadFile.java program

```
31      public static  String readLine(BufferedReader br) throws IOException{
32
33      StringBuffer sb = new StringBuffer( );
34      int intC;
35      intC = br.read( );
36      String line = null;
37
38      do{
39
40          if (intC == -1)
41              return null;
42
43          char c = (char) intC;
44
45          if (c == '\n') {
46              break;
47          }
48          if (sb.length( ) >=  testFileRead.MAX_STR_LEN) {
49              Throw new IOException("input too long");
50          }
51          sb.append(c);
52      } while ( (((intC = br.read( )) != -1) );
53
54      line = sb.toString( );
55
56      return line;
57
58      }
```

program. Depending upon the system configuration, the leaked out information may be dumped to a console, written to a log file or exposed to a remote user.

Solution: Developers have to take extreme care while deciding what type of error messages should be displayed by their program, even for the purpose of debugging the program to diagnose problems, which may arise for testing pre- and post-release. It is always better to turn off detailed error information and preferably include very brief messages, keeping security in mind. For example, even an "Access Denied" message can reveal that a specific file or user exists on the system and it is just they do not have the requested access to a particular resource (Howard et. al, 2009). Debugging traces can sometimes appear in non-obvious places such as embedded comments in HTML for an error page. In our code, we merely print an error message for the particular exception occurred in the *catch* block without explicitly printing the entire system stack trace. The results generated from analyzing the testFileRead_fixed_v2.java code with Sourceanalyzer is shown in Figure 13.

Figure 9. testFileRead_fixed_v1.java with the denial of service vulnerability fixed

```
1    import java.io.*;
2
3    class testFileRead{
4
5            Static int MAX_STR_LEN = 200;
6
7        public static void main(String[ ] args) throws IOException{
8
9        try{
10
11        FileReader fr = new FileReader(args[0]);
12        BufferedReader br = new BufferedReader(fr);
13
14        String line = null;
15
16        while ( (line = readLine(br)) != null){
17            System.out.println(line);
18            line = null;
19        }
20
21        br.close( );
22        fr.close( );
23
24        }
25    catch(IOException ie){
26        ie.printStackTrace( );
27        }
28    }
```

Unreleased Resource (Streams) Vulnerability

The Unreleased Resource vulnerability occurs when the program is coded in such a way that it can potentially fail to release a system resource (Howard et. al, 2009). In our file reader program, we have vulnerability with the *File Reader* and the associated *Buffered Reader* streams being unreleased because of some abrupt termination of the program. If there is any exception returned from the *readLine*() method call in Line 16 of the testFileRead_fixed_v2.java program, then the control immediately switches from the *try* block to the *catch* block and the two streams 'fr' of *FileReader* and 'br' of *BufferedReader* will never be released until the operating system explicitly forces the release of these resources upon the termination of the program. From a security standpoint, if an attacker can intentionally trigger a resource leak, the attacker might be able to launch a denial of service attack by depleting the resource pool.

Figure 10. Fortify Sourceanalyzer results on testFileRead_fixed_v1.java

```
C:\res\CCLI-2010\Modules-Meghanathan\Static-Code-Analysis-Examples\Ex1_FileReade
r>sourceanalyzer testFileRead_fixed_v1.java

[C:\res\CCLI-2010\Modules-Meghanathan\Static-Code-Analysis-Examples\Ex1_FileRead
er]
[EDD1323454D69423D2DD7D4D187D22B7 : medium : System Information Leak : semantic
]
testFileRead_fixed_v1.java(26) : Throwable.printStackTrace()

[78FA82368471A9D617111E250114E445 : medium : Path Manipulation : dataflow ]
testFileRead_fixed_v1.java(11) :  ->new FileReader(0)
     testFileRead_fixed_v1.java(7) :   ->testFileRead.main(0)

[865F144B2D584D3CB7CEDB696F19A416 : medium : Unreleased Resource : Streams : con
trolflow ]
     testFileRead_fixed_v1.java(11) : start -> loaded : fr.new FileReader(...)
     testFileRead_fixed_v1.java(12) : loaded -> loaded : fr.new BufferedReader(..
., fr, ...)
     testFileRead_fixed_v1.java(16) : loaded -> end_of_scope : #end_scope(fr) (ex
ception thrown)

[423D552C35C67B4A8F045E1C079B74FB : low : J2EE Bad Practices : Leftover Debug Co
de : structural ]
     testFileRead_fixed_v1.java(7)

[ADBD437811B82372BC593D8FB94B74B6 : low : Poor Logging Practice : Use of a Syste
m Output Stream : structural ]
     testFileRead_fixed_v1.java(17)

C:\res\CCLI-2010\Modules-Meghanathan\Static-Code-Analysis-Examples\Ex1_FileReade
r>
```

Solution: A solution to the "Unreleased Resource" vulnerability is to add a *finally* { … } block after the *try* {…} *catch* {…} blocks and release all the resources that were used by the code in the corresponding *try* block. Note that in order to do so, the variables associated with the resources have to be declared outside and before the *try* block so that they can be accessed inside the *finally* block. In our case, we have to declare the *FileReader* object 'fr' and the *BufferedReader* object 'br' outside the *try* block and close them explicitly in the *finally* block. The modified code

Figure 11. Segment of the testFileRead_fixed_v1.java code with the vulnerability to leak system information due to the printStackTrace() method call of the Exception class

Figure 12. Segment of the testFileRead_fixed_v2.java code with the vulnerability to leak system information fixed by removing the call to the printStackTrace() method of the Exception class

```
1    import java.io.*;
2
3    class testFileRead{
4
5           static int MAX_STR_LEN = 200;
6
7        public static void main(String[ ] args) throws IOException{
8
9        try{
10
11        FileReader fr = new FileReader(args[0]);
12        BufferedReader br = new BufferedReader(fr);
13
14        String line = null;
15
16        while ( (line = readLine(br)) != null){
17              System.out.println(line);
18              line = null;
19        }
20
21        br.close( );
22        fr.close( );
23
24    }
25    catch(IOException ie){
26              System.out.println("IOException occurred ");
27    }
28 }
```

segment (testFileRead_fixed_v3.java) is shown in Figure 14. The results generated from analyzing the testFileRead_fixed_v2.java code with Sourceanalyzer is shown in Figure 15.

Path Manipulation Vulnerability

Path Manipulation vulnerability occurs when a user input is allowed to control paths used in file system operations (Graff & Van Wyk, 2003). This may enable an attacker to access or modify otherwise protected system resources. In our file reader program, the name of the file we would like to read is passed as a command-line argument (args[0]) and we directly insert this as the parameter for the *FileReader* constructor in line 11 (Figure 16). Path manipulation vulnerability is very risky

Figure 13. Fortify Sourceanalyzer results on testFileRead_fixed_v2.java (Note the system information leak vulnerability is no longer listed – the code has been fixed)

```
C:\res\CCLI-2010\Modules-Meghanathan\Static-Code-Analysis-Examples\Ex1_FileReade
r>sourceanalyzer testFileRead_fixed_v2.java

[C:\res\CCLI-2010\Modules-Meghanathan\Static-Code-Analysis-Examples\Ex1_FileRead
er]

[78FA82368471A9D617111E250114E445 : medium : Path Manipulation : dataflow ]
testFileRead_fixed_v2.java(11) :  ->new FileReader(0)
    testFileRead_fixed_v2.java(7) :  ->testFileRead.main(0)

[865F144B2D584D3CB7CEDB696F19A416 : medium : Unreleased Resource : Streams : con
trolflow ]
    testFileRead_fixed_v2.java(11) : start -> loaded : fr.new FileReader(...)
    testFileRead_fixed_v2.java(12) : loaded -> loaded : fr.new BufferedReader(..
.., fr, ...)
    testFileRead_fixed_v2.java(16) : loaded -> end_of_scope : #end_scope(fr) (ex
ception thrown)

[423D552C35C67B4A8F045EiC079B74FB : low : J2EE Bad Practices : Leftover Debug Co
de : structural ]
    testFileRead_fixed_v2.java(7)

[ADBD437811B82372BC593D8FB94B74B6 : low : Poor Logging Practice : Use of a Syste
m Output Stream : structural ]
    testFileRead_fixed_v2.java(17)

[ADBD437811B82372BC593D8FB94B74B7 : low : Poor Logging Practice : Use of a Syste
m Output Stream : structural ]
    testFileRead_fixed_v2.java(26)

C:\res\CCLI-2010\Modules-Meghanathan\Static-Code-Analysis-Examples\Ex1_FileReade
r>
```

and should be preferably avoided in a code. For example, if the program runs with elevated privileges, directly embedding a file name or a path for the file name in our program to access the system resources, it could be cleverly exploited by a malicious user who may pass an unexpected value for the argument and the consequences of executing the program with that argument may turn out to be fatal.

Solutions: Some of the solutions to prevent Path manipulation (Graff & Van Wyk, 2003): (i) One solution is to provide a list of valid values the user can enter for the arguments/ variables in question and the user cannot choose anything beyond those values. For example, in the File Reader program, we could present the user the list of files that could be read and the user has to select one among them. (ii) Another solution is to have a White list of allowable characters in the user input for the argument/ variable in question. For example, if a user is allowed to read only a text file, the last four characters of the user input should be ".txt" and nothing else. (iii) Another solution is to have a Black list of characters that are not allowed in the user input for the argument/ variable in question. For example, if the user is not permitted to read a file that is in a directory other than the one in which the file reader program is running, then the input should not have any '/' character to indicate a path for the file to be read. Solutions (ii) and (iii) have been implemented through the *sanitize()* method, the code of which is illustrated in Figure 18.

Figure 14. Segment of the testFileRead_fixed_v3.java code with the unreleased resource vulnerability fixed by adding a finally block to the try/catch blocks and releasing all resources through the finally block

```
6
7        public static void main(String[ ] args) throws IOException{
8
9          FileReader fr = null;
10         BufferedReader br = null;
11
12         try{
13
14           fr = new FileReader(args[0]);
15           br = new BufferedReader(fr);
16           String line = null;
17
18           while ( (line = readLine(br)) != null){
19               System.out.println(line);
20               line = null;
21           }
22
23         }// try block
24         catch(IOException ie){
25               System.out.println("IOException occurred ");
26         }
27
28         finally{
29           if (br != null)
30               br.close( );
31           if (fr != null)
32               fr.close( );
33         }
```

A SUMMARIZED OVERVIEW OF THE VULNERABILITIES AND THE SOLUTIONS

The Denial of Service vulnerability was identified with the file reader program when the code was originally developed to read the contents of a file – line by line; an attacker could misuse this feature by passing a file that has a significantly long line, amounting to potentially millions of characters. Such a line could overflow the memory as the characters read from the line are stored in a memory buffer that is not processed until the entire line is completely read. To mitigate this vulnerability, we present the idea of imposing a maximum limit on the number of characters read from a line in a file. Enforcing an upper bound on the number of characters that can

Figure 15. Fortify Sourceanalyzer results on testFileRead_fixed_v3.java (Note the Unreleased Resource Vulnerability is no longer listed – we have removed success-fully fixed the code!!)

```
C:\res\CCLI-2010\Modules-Meghanathan\Static-Code-Analysis-Examples\Ex1_FileReade
r>sourceanalyzer testFileRead_fixed_v3.java

[C:\res\CCLI-2010\Modules-Meghanathan\Static-Code-Analysis-Examples\Ex1_FileRead
er]

[78FA82368471A9D617111E250114E445 : medium : Path Manipulation : dataflow ]
testFileRead_fixed_v3.java(14) :   ->new FileReader(0)
     testFileRead_fixed_v3.java(7) :   ->testFileRead.main(0)

[423D552C35C67B4A8F045E1C079B74FB : low : J2EE Bad Practices : Leftover Debug Co
de : structural ]
     testFileRead_fixed_v3.java(7)

[ADBD437811B82372BC593D8FB94B74B6 : low : Poor Logging Practice : Use of a Syste
m Output Stream : structural ]
     testFileRead_fixed_v3.java(20)

[ADBD437811B82372BC593D8FB94B74B7 : low : Poor Logging Practice : Use of a Syste
m Output Stream : structural ]
     testFileRead_fixed_v3.java(26)

C:\res\CCLI-2010\Modules-Meghanathan\Static-Code-Analysis-Examples\Ex1_FileReade
r>_
```

be stored in the memory buffer before it is processed helps to avoid a situation where the memory could get filled and no other application could be run on the system.

The System Information Leak vulnerability arises when the program tries to display more information about the structure of the code and the sequence of method calls, in order to facilitate the developer to debug incase of any erroneous behavior/ output. Often such print statements are left in the code even after deployment in the consumer market. This leads to attackers attempting to pass carefully chosen input values that can generate these error messages that can be used to infer the structure of the program. There is always a tradeoff between the amount of information displayed through the error messages and the ease associated with debugging the error and fixing the problem. However, if developers are prudent enough to remove the revealing error messages used during development (pre-release) and include only generic error messages during deployment (post-release), the above vulnerability could be effectively handled.

Figure 16. Segment of the testFileRead_fixed_v3.java code with the path manipulation vulnerability

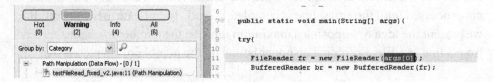

Figure 17. Segment of the testFileRead_fixed_v4.java code with the path manipulation vulnerability fixed by obtaining the user input using a Scanner object and sanitizing the input

```
28      try{
29
30      Scanner sc = new Scanner(System.in);
31      String filename = sc.next( );
32
33      if (sanitize(filename) != -1){
34
35       fr = new FileReader(filename);
36       br = new BufferedReader(fr);
37       String line = null;
38
39          while ( (line = readLine(br)) != null){
40              System.out.println(line);
41              line = null;
42          }
43
44      } // sanitized successfully if block
45
46      }// try block
47
48      catch(IOException ie){
49              System.out.println("IOException occurred ");
50      }
51
52      Finally{
53
54       if (br != null)
55              br.close( );
```

Figure 18. Code for the Sanitize() method to validate the filename input by the user

```
8       public static int sanitize(String filename){
9
10      if (filename.indexOf( (int) '/') != -1){
11      System.out.println(" invalid argument... You cannot read from a directory other than the current one");
12          return -1;
13      }
14
15      if ( !filename.endsWith(".txt") ){
16          System.out.println(" you can read only a text file with a .txt extension..");
17          return -1;
18      }
19
20      Return 0;
21      }
```

Figure 19. Fortify Sourceanalyzer results on testFileRead_fixed_v4.java (Note the path manipulation vulnerability is no longer listed – the code has been fixed)

```
C:\res\CCLI-2010\Modules-Meghanathan\Static-Code-Analysis-Examples\Ex1_FileReade
r>sourceanalyzer testFileRead_fixed_v4.java

[C:\res\CCLI-2010\Modules-Meghanathan\Static-Code-Analysis-Examples\Ex1_FileRead
er]

[4054EDD073EBA8B87AA199FE5A3355FD : low : Poor Logging Practice : Use of a Syste
m Output Stream : structural ]
    testFileRead_fixed_v4.java(11)

[4054EDD073EBA8B87AA199FE5A3355FE : low : Poor Logging Practice : Use of a Syste
m Output Stream : structural ]
    testFileRead_fixed_v4.java(16)

[A14D94C53A7A04B7DA3A391EBBD73E12 : low : Poor Logging Practice : Use of a Syste
m Output Stream : structural ]
    testFileRead_fixed_v4.java(40)

[A14D94C53A7A04B7DA3A391EBBD73E13 : low : Poor Logging Practice : Use of a Syste
m Output Stream : structural ]
    testFileRead_fixed_v4.java(49)

C:\res\CCLI-2010\Modules-Meghanathan\Static-Code-Analysis-Examples\Ex1_FileReade
r>
```

Figure 20. Fortify Sourceanalyzer results on testFileRead_fixed_v4.java viewed from Audit Workbench

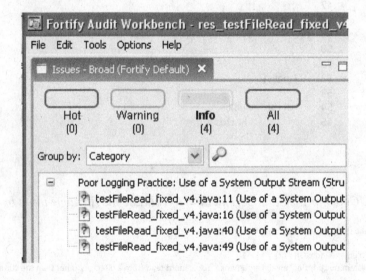

The Unreleased Resource vulnerability arises when the developer basically forgets to release the resources after their intended use and no longer needed in the software program. In the context of the file reader program, the stream objects instantiated to read the file have to be released either after the contents of the file have been completely read or an unanticipated error during the execution of the program forces the read module to prematurely end. In the latter case, try-catch blocks are typically used to process the errors and once the control leaves the catch block, the program continues to normally execute the code following the try-catch block and behave as if nothing happened before. Care should be taken to release the resources that were allocated inside the try block – since there can be more than one catch block depending on the specific exceptions that are to be captured, it would not be proper to put statements pertaining to the release of the allocated resources in each of these catch blocks. Instead, we suggest the option of exploiting the finally block (that is not mandatory for use with try-catch blocks) and insert there all the statements pertaining to resource release.

The Path Manipulation vulnerability arises when the inputs entered by the user are directly passed and executed in the program, without validating the correctness and appropriateness of the input values. It becomes more critical if the user values are directly embedded into path statements that read a critical system resource (say a file) and executes them with elevated privileges (higher than that of the user who passed the input). We present solutions to handle this vulnerability and illustrate the use of a Sanitizing module that can be used to filter the input by scanning for a blacklist of non-allowable characters and the path requested in the input.

CONCLUSION

Software security is a rapidly growing field and is most sought after in both industry and academics. With the development of automated tools such as Fortify Source Code Analyzer, it becomes more tenable for a software developer to fix, in-house, the vulnerabilities associated with the software prior to its release and reduce the number of patches that need to be applied to the software after its release. This book chapter presented a case study of a file reader program (developed in Java) on how to analyze the source code of an application using an automated tool, to capture the inherent vulnerabilities present in the code and to mitigate one or more of these vulnerabilities. We discussed the use of an automated tool called the Source Code Analyzer (SCA), developed by Fortify, Inc., and illustrated the use of its command line and graphical user interface (Audit Workbench) options to present and ana- lyze the vulnerabilities identified in a software program. The SCA could be used in a variety of platforms and several object-oriented programming languages. The four vulnerabilities that are specifically discussed in length and mitigated in the case study include the Denial of Service vulnerability, System Information Leak vulnerability, Unreleased Resource (streams) vulnerability and the Path Manipula- tion vulnerability. Even though our code is written in Java, the solutions proposed and implemented here for each of these four vulnerabilities are more generic and can be appropriately modified and applied in other object-oriented programming language environments.

FUTURE RESEARCH DIRECTIONS

Software security is getting more prominence and is considered as an essential artifact of a software development lifecycle (SDLC). By considering software security, starting from the stage of 'Requirements Analysis,' all the way to the 'Testing' stages of a SDLC, one can significantly enhance cyber security and reduce the number of attacks when the software is being in use (i.e., post-release). The book chapter focuses more on the static code analysis of software program. A natural extension of our work would be to conduct a run-time code analysis of software programs and compare the two approaches with respect to the potential vulnerabilities identified and the ease of fixing and again analyzing the presence of these vulnerabilities. In this pursuit, we will also be studying the various tools (like the Fortify SCA) that are available among the Software Development community for both static code analysis and run-time code analysis and analyze the pros and cons of some of the commonly used tools. In the case of run-time code analysis, we will also develop test-cases that can be used to capture the different vulnerabilities associated with the software. With the Fortify SCA, we also plan to study some simple C++ programs, like that of the file reader program in this case study, and identify/analyze vulnerabilities that are either characteristic of the language (such as the Buffer Overflow attacks) or also seen in other contemporary programming languages like Java.

ACKNOWLEDGMENT

The work leading to this book chapter was funded through the U. S. National Science Foundation (NSF) CCLI/TUES grant (DUE-0941959) on "Incorporating Systems Security and Software Security in Senior Projects." The views and conclusions contained in this chapter are those of the authors and do not represent the official policies, either expressed or implied, of the funding agency.

REFERENCES

Chess, B., & West, J. (2008). *Secure programming with static analysis*. Boston, MA: Addison-Wesley.

Graff, M. G., & Van Wyk, K. R. (2003). *Secure coding: Principles and practices.* Sebastopol, CA: O'Reilly Media.

Howard, M., Leblanc, D., & Viega, J. (2009). *24 deadly sins of software security: Programming flaws and how to fix them.* New York City, NY: McGraw-Hill.

Howard, M., & Lipner, S. (2006). *The security development lifecycle: SDL: A process for developing demonstrably more secure software.* Sebastopol, CA: O'Reilly Media.

McGraw, G. (2006). *Software security: Building security in.* Boston, MA: Addison-Wesley.

Whittaker, J. A. (2002). *How to break software.* Boston, MA: Addison-Wesley.

Wysopal, C., Nelson, L., Dai Zovi, D., & Dustin, E. (2006). *The art of software security testing: Identifying software security flaws.* Boston, MA: Addison-Wesley.

ADDITIONAL READING

Antoniol, G. (2009). Search Based Software Testing for Software Security: Breaking Code to Make it Safer. In *Proceedings of the International Conference on Verification and Validation Workshops* (pp. 87-100). Denver, CO, USA: IEEE.

Antunes, N., & Vieira, M. (2009). Comparing the Effectiveness of Penetration Testing and Static Code Analysis on the Detection of SQL Injection Vulnerabilities in Web Services. In *Proceedings of the 15th IEEE Pacific Rim International Symposium on Dependable Computing* (pp. 301-306). Shanghai, China.

Baca, D. (2010). Identifying Security Relevant Warnings from Static Code Analysis Tools through Code Tainting. In *Proceedings of the International Conference on Availability, Reliability and Security* (pp. 386-390). Krakow, Poland: IEEE.

Baca, D., Petersen, K., Carlsson, B., & Lundberg, L. (2009). Static Code Analysis to Detect Software Security Vulnerabilities – Does Experience Matter? In *Proceedings of the International Conference on Availability, Reliability and Security* (pp. 804-810). Fukuoka, Japan: IEEE.

Caseley, P. R., & Hadley, M. J. (2006). Assessing the Effectiveness of Static Code Analysis. In *Proceedings of the 1st Institution of Engineering and Technology International Conference on System Safety* (pp. 227-237). London, UK: IET.

Chelf, B., & Ebert, C. (2009). Ensuring the Integrity of Embedded Software with Static Code Analysis. *IEEE Software, 26*(3), 96–99. doi:10.1109/MS.2009.65

Choi, Y., Kim, H., & Lee, D. (2007). Tag-Aware Text File Fuzz Testing for Security of a Software System. In *Proceedings of the International Conference on Convergence Information Technology* (pp. 2254-2259). Nice, France.

Hanna, A., Ling, H., Furlong, J., & Yang, Z. (2008). Targeting Security Vulnerabilities: From Specification to Detection. In *Proceedings of the 8th International Conference on Quality Software* (pp. 97-102), Oxford, UK.

He, K., Feng, Z., & Li, X. (2008). An Attack Scenario based Approach for Software Security Testing at Design Stage. In *Proceedings of the International Symposium on Computer Science and Computational Technology* (pp. 782-787). Shanghai, China: IEEE.

Holzer, M., & Rupp, M. (2006). Static Code Analysis of Functional Descriptions in SystemC. In *Proceedings of the 3rd International Workshop on Electronic Design, Test and Applications* (pp. 242-248). Kuala Lumpur, Malaysia: IEEE.

Huang, S., Hui, Z., Wang, L., & Liu, X. (2010). A Case Study of Software Security Test based on Defects Threat Tree Modeling. In *Proceedings of the International Conference on Multimedia Information Networking and Security* (pp. 362-365). Nanjing, China: IEEE.

Hui, Z., Huang, S., Hu, B., & Yao, Y. (2010). Software Security Testing based on Typical SSD: A Case Study. In *Proceedings of the 3rd International Conference on Advanced Computer Theory and Engineering* (pp. 312-316). Chengdu, China: IEEE.

Kim, D., Kim, I., Oh, J., & Cho, H. (2009). Lightweight Static Analysis to Detect Polymorphic Exploit Code with Static Analysis Resistant Technique. In *Proceedings of the International Conference on Communications* (pp. 1-6). Dresden, Germany: IEEE.

Kim, H., Choi, Y., & Lee, D. (2008). Practical Security Testing using File Fuzzing. In *Proceedings of the 10th International Conference on Advanced Communication Technology* (pp. 1304-1307). Phoenix Park, Korea: IEEE.

Louridas, P. (2006). Static Code Analysis. *IEEE Software, 23*(4), 58–61. doi:10.1109/MS.2006.114

Mantere, M., Uusitalo, I., & Roning, J. (2009). Comparison of Static Code Analysis Tools. In *Proceedings of the 3rd International Conference on Emerging Security Information, Systems and Technologies* (pp. 15-22). Athens, Greece: IARIA.

Mcheick, H., Dhiab, H., Dbouk, M., & Mcheik, R. (2010). Detecting Type Errors and Secure Coding in C/C++ Applications. In *Proceedings of the International Conference on Computer Systems and Applications* (pp. 1-9). Hammamet, Tunisia: IEEE/ACS.

Nordio, M., Bavera, F., Medel, R., Aguirre, J., & Baum, G. A Framework for Execution of Secure Mobile Code based on Static Analysis. In *Proceedings of the 24th International Conference of the Chilean Computer Science Society* (pp. 59-66). Arica, Chile.

Novak, J., Krajnc, A., & Zontar, R. (2010). Taxonomy of Static Code Analysis Tools. In *Proceedings of the 33rd International Convention on Information and Communication Technology, Electronics and Microelectronics* (pp. 418-422). Opatija, Croatia: IEEE.

Plosch, R., Gruber, H., Hentschel, A., Pomberger, G., & Schiffer, S. (2008). On the Relation between External Software Quality and Static Code Analysis. In *Proceedings of the 32nd Annual Software Engineering Workshop* (pp. 169-174). Kassandra, Greece: IEEE.

Plosch, R., Gruber, H., Korner, C., & Saft, M. (2010). A Method for Continuous Code Quality Management using Static Analysis. In *Proceedings of the 7th International Conference on the Quality of Information and Communications Technology* (pp. 370-375). Porto, Portugal: IEEE.

Potter, B., & McGraw, G. (2004). Software Security Testing. *IEEE Security and Privacy, 2*(5), 81–85. doi:10.1109/MSP.2004.84

Song, H., Liang, W., Changyou, Z., & Hong, Y. (2010). A Software Security Testing Method based on Typical Defects. In *Proceedings of the International Conference on Computer Application and System Modeling* (vol. 5, pp. 150-153). Taiyuan, China.

Stytz, M. R., & Banks, S. B. (2006). Dynamic Software Security Testing. *IEEE Security and Privacy, 4*(3), 77–79. doi:10.1109/MSP.2006.64

Tondel, I. A., Jaatun, M. G., & Jensen, J. (2008). Learning from Software Security Testing. In *Proceedings of the International Conference on Software Testing Verification and Validation Workshop* (pp. 286-294). Lillehammer, Norway: IEEE.

Tonella, P., & Potrich, A. (2002). Static and Dynamic C++ Code Analysis for the Recovery of the Object Diagram. In *Proceedings of the International Conference on Software Maintenance* (pp. 54-63). Montreal, Canada: IEEE.

Wang, A. J. A. (2004). Security Testing in Software Engineering Courses. In *Proceedings of the 34th Annual Conference on Frontiers in Education* (vol. 2, pp. 13-18). Savannah, GA, USA: IEEE.

Wang, X., Jhi, Y.-C., Zhu, S., & Liu, P. (2008). STILL: Exploit Code Detection via Static Taint and Initialization Analyses. In *Proceedings of the Annual Computer Security Applications Conference* (pp. 289-298). Anaheim, CA, USA.

KEY TERMS AND DEFINITIONS

Attack: A sequence of actions that when executed will exploit the vulnerability in a code and cause the software to fail and/or behave in an unexpected and often undesirable manner.

Denial of Service: An attack that will lead to the software becoming unavailable for use for legitimate users.

Path Manipulation: A vulnerability that arises when the inputs entered by the user are directly passed and executed in the program, without validating the correctness and appropriateness of the input values.

Sanitize: The process of scanning through input values (either from the user, system or the run-time environment) to analyze and verify for the correctness and appropriateness of usage before actually being executed as part of a program.

Static Code Analysis: The process of examining a piece of code without actually executing it. Static Code Analysis is also referred to as Source Code Analysis.

System Information Leak: A vulnerability that when exploited will lead to the disclosure of the program structure, critical system information and other sensitive details of the software and its application environment.

Unreleased Resource: A vulnerability that arises when the developer basically forgets to release the resources after their intended use and no longer needed in the software program.

Vulnerability: An inherent flaw in the code that when exploited will cause the software to fail and/or behave in an unexpected and often undesirable manner.

Chapter 6
Test Case Prioritization using Cuckoo Search

Praveen Ranjan Srivastava
Birla Institute of Technology and Science Pilani, India

D. V. Pavan Kumar Reddy
Birla Institute of Technology and Science Pilani, India

M. Srikanth Reddy
Birla Institute of Technology and Science Pilani, India

Ch. V. B. Ramaraju
Birla Institute of Technology and Science Pilani, India

I. Ch. Manikanta Nath
Birla Institute of Technology and Science Pilani, India

ABSTRACT

Test Case prioritization consists of proper organization and scheduling of the test cases in a specific sequence. Regression testing is an important issue and concept during software maintenance process, but due to scarcity of resources re-execution of all test cases, is not possible during regression testing. Hence in version or re-vision specific regression testing, it is more important to execute those test cases that are beneficial. In this chapter, a new prioritization technique is proposed for version specific regression testing using Cuckoo Search Algorithm. This technique prioritizes the test cases based on lines of code where the code is modified.

DOI: 10.4018/978-1-4666-0089-8.ch006

INTRODUCTION

In software development, the ethics behind Software Engineering is very important and essential. Software development and management is depend upon series of phase known as software development life cycle (SDLC), in this life cycle Software Testing (Pressman R S,2005) involves identifying the conditions where software deviates from its normal behaviour or exhibit different activity in contrast to its specification. Software testing has a major role in software development lifecycle (SDLC) to develop the high quality software product. At least, software testing consumes 50% of the development cost. Testing is the process of checking whether the developed project conforms to the expected output by finding errors in the program, and also to reveal inadequacies (Mathur Aditya P, 2007).

Regression testing (Srivastava Praveen Ranjan et al, 2008) (Singh Yogesh et al, 2010) is conducted to ensure that changes in software are correct and have not affected the unchanged portions of the software. Test suites that are already available from earlier versions of software can be expensive to execute completely. Hence test case prioritization (Horgan J R and S London, 1992) is one of the techniques for reducing cost related to regression testing.

Test case prioritization (Srivastava Praveen Ranjan, 2008) helps software testing by decreasing the effort and time based on some criterion such as code coverage. It has been identified that one of the software engineering areas with a more suitable and realistic use of artificial intelligence techniques is software testing (McMinn Phil, 2004) and those techniques are known as metaheuristic approaches (Srivastava Praveen Ranjan, 2008). A recently developed metaheuristic optimisation algorithm, Cuckoo Search (Yang X S and Deb S, 2009), is being used under this study for prioritization of different test cases in a test suite. In the later sections of this chapter, the use of Cuckoo search algorithm in test case optimization is discussed. The background work includes drawbacks of some of the existing methods of test case optimization is discussed in section 2. In next concept of cuckoo search is discussed. Test case prioritization using cuckoo search has been discussed in detail under the section proposed strategy. A simple implementation of the approach is given in the section case study.

BACKGROUND WORK

An early representation of test prioritization was reported by Horgan and London (Horgan J R and S London, 1992) in an industrial strength tool, this tool is used for variety of control flow and data flow based coverage criteria. Coverage based (Aggrawal K K et al,2004) technique for test case prioritization, where prioritization is based on the original test suite and modified version, however they do not combine code coverage information with function coverage. (Elbaum Sebastian et al, 2000 and 2004) have reported several variants of test prioritization. (Kim J. and A. Porter, 2002) propose a history based technique and discuss trade offs in the use of test selection using modification traversing tests and test prioritization. (Srivastava A. and J. Thiagarajan, 2002) have reported Echelon, which is an industrial strength tool used to prioritize test cases. (Srikanth H and Williams L, 2005) investigate economic application of test prioritization. (Do Hyunsook et al, 2004) performed a cost benefit analysis of prioritizing unit test cases. (Wong W. E et al, 1997) reported an experiment to investigate the fault detection effectiveness using all use criteria.

Many of the previous researchers prioritized the test cases based on faults detected and not version specific test case prioritization, hence in this chapter, the idea of version specific test case prioritization is being highlighted using a metaheuristic approach (i.e. cuckoo search) (Yang X S and Deb S, 2010). To efficiently search solution space, Cuckoo search algorithm is used, since it is more efficient and simple than other metaheuristic algorithms and moving towards an optimized solution by replacing a fraction of worse nests in each iteration till maximum number of iterations pre-defined by user. The idea of version specific test case prioritization being presented in this chapter is based on the various parameters such as time, cost and max_generations will be decided which will be used in Cuckoo algorithm. For example if time is the parameter on which the test cases are prioritized then in that stipulated time the maximum possible iterations i.e. max_generations of iteration will be decided and Cuckoo search there by presents the best solution in every generation relative to the previous one. In the next section how the Cuckoo search works is explained.

INTRODUCTION TO CONCEPT

Cuckoo search is an optimization metaheuristic algorithm which is more efficient relative to some other metaheuristic algorithms (Srivastava Praveen Ranjan et al, 2008).The main advantage of Cuckoo search algorithm is that it can easily solve global optimized problems. Based on the fitness value in every iteration a fraction of worse nests are abandoned which are not good solutions and in every generation moving towards an optimized solution by replacing the solutions with the good ones. Finally by the end of max_iterations (iterations until which loop continues), a fraction of solutions will be replaced and we will obtain the optimized solution (Yang X S Yang and Deb S, 2010).

Cuckoo Search Algorithm (Yang X S Yang and Deb S, 2009, 2010)

We can simply describe Cuckoo Search algorithm by using the following three idealized rules:

- Each cuckoo lays one egg at a time, and dumps it in a randomly chosen nest. The process of executing a program or system with the intent of finding errors or it involves any activity aimed at evaluating an attribute or capability of a program or system and determining that it meets its required results.
- The best nests with high quality of eggs (i.e. solutions) will carry over to the next generations.
- The number of available host nests is fixed, and a host can discover an alien egg with a probability of either 0 or 1. In this case, the host bird can either throw the egg away or abandon the nest so as to build a completely new nest in a new location. The pseudo code of Cuckoo search algorithm is shown in Appendix A.

The implementation of Cuckoo search algorithm in test case prioritization is explained in the next section phase 2.

THE PROPOSED STRATEGY

To generate prioritized test cases this approach consists of two phases. During phase 1(based upon the concept on Aggrawal K K et al, 2004 work as shown in Figure 1 (phase 1).This first phase concept is same as is reported in paper (Aggrawal K K et al, 2004). Some of the test cases from the initial test suite (T) will be removed and a new test suite T', which has less number of test cases will be generated so that by the end of phase 1 the test suite will be minimized. Step1 includes calculating NO_MATCHES for each test case and adding the maximum match's test case to T'. Step 2 repeatedly calculates step1 by removing the lines of code by the test case added to T' from the test cases and MOD_LINES and in every iteration a test case is added.In Step 3 considering the dependent test cases. There by considering the problem of test case prioritization with the test cases in T' during phase 2. In phase 2 Cuckoo Search is implemented on the permutations of test cases in T' and a prioritized test suite is generated.

Overview of the terms used:

Figure 1. Implementation of cuckoo search

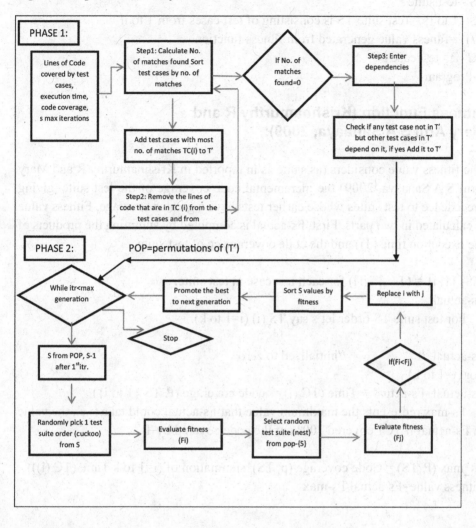

MOD_LINES=>the lines of code where the program has been modified.

S=>the population for each generation

N=> no of test cases in test suite

TL (i) => the lines of code covered by test case i;

NO_MATCHES=>the number of lines matched by TL (i) and MOD_LINES

TMATCH_LINES (i) =>the lines of code matched between TL (i) and MOD_LINES.

POP: All possible permutations of test cases in the test suite excluding the order preserved by dependent test cases.

TS =test suite

TS {1 to i} =Test suite TS is consisting of test cases from 1 to i.

F (i) =fitness value generated from fitness function

TC (i) =test case i

P-Program

Fitness Function (Krishnamurthy R and Mary Arul S A Sahaaya, 2009):

The fitness value considers (as same as in reported in Krishnamurthy R and Mary Arul S A Sahaaya, 2009) the incremental code coverage of the test suite, giving precedence to test suites whose earlier tests have a greater coverage. Fitness value is calculated in two parts. First, Fs-actual is computed by summing the products of the execution time (Ti) and the code coverage cc of test suite

TS_j {1, i} = (T1 …. Ti) for each test case in test suite.

Fs-actual

For test suite TS order let's say TS (i) (i=1 to k).

Fs-actual=0   //initialized to zero

For (i=1 to k)

Fs-actual=Fs-actual + Time (TC (i)) * code coverage (P, TS {1 to i})

Fs-max represents the maximum value that Fs-actual could take (i.e., the value of Fs-actual if TC1 covered 100% of the code covered by T

Fs_max (P, TS) = Code coverage (p, TS)*summation of (i=1 to k Time (TC (i)))

Fitness value=Fs-actual/Fs-max

FIRST PHASE (AGGRAWAL K K, SING Y AND KAUR A, 2004)

During Phase 1, only the lines of code where the program P has been modified will be considered. Here presenting the algorithm for the modified lines of code the same algorithm works well even with addition and deletion of lines in the Program P(as given in Aggrawal K.K. et al,2004). In step1 NO_MATCHES will be calculated for each test case and sorting the test case objects with the NO_MATCHES found. In Step 2 in each iteration a test case will be added to the test suite T' and repeating step1 again by removing lines of code that was covered by the test case added to the test suite T' from the test cases and modified lines to avoid a redundant coverage. Finally at the end of the phase 1 the program P can be executed with the minimum number of test cases where the program has been modified.

Step 1

As shown in Figure 1, initially a test suite T, let's say the test suite contains N test cases. The lines of code each test case (TL (i)) covers and the lines of code where the program has been modified (MOD_LINES) will be given for the program P. An object will be created for each test case and the lines covered by it will be stored in an array. The NO_MATCHES for each test case will be calculated with the new lines of code by using hash algorithm. Then sort the test case objects by NO_MATCHES found and then adding the test case to the new test suite T'.

Step 2

By calculating the intersection between MOD_LINES and TL (i), let's say i, the test case that was added before. The lines of code matched by test case i TMATCH_LINES(i) will be obtained.Then the lines of code TMATCH_LINES(i) will be removed from the remaining test cases TL(j),j=1 to N and in the MOD_LINES to avoid redundant coverage matching lines.. Then again the NO_MATCHES is calculated for the remaining test cases with the modified MOD_LINES.

By repeating Step 2 described above and removing the test cases that have NO_MATCHES is equal to zero in every iteration.A test case will be added to new test suite T' after each iteration.

Step 3

By the end of step 2 a new test suite which have less number of test cases than T, will be generated. Here then considering the dependent test cases since the test cases cannot be removed if there exists some other test cases which depends on the test cases that are removed, even though they're not covering new lines of code. To implement this, dependent test case will be taken in the form of a graph using the data structure adjacency matrix (Michael T Goodrich, 2006) where values 0 or 1 assigned as elements of matrix based on dependency of corresponding row to column of matrix. Then by using topological sort (Michael T Goodrich, 2006) on this graph dependent test case sets will be generated.

Suppose that a test case TC(i) is not in T' because it is not covering MOD_LINES while a test case let's say TC(j) which is in T' and depends on TC(i).Then TC(i) will be added to the test suite T'.

By the end of step 3, a new test suite T' will be generated which has a less number of test cases than T, initial test suite. This test suite T' will then be sent to phase 2 where the implementation of Cuckoo will take place on this test suite T'.

SECOND PHASE

In the second phase Cuckoo search will be implemented on a test suite T' as in Figure 1. Here the POP will be number of permutations that can be generated by N excluding the order of dependent test cases.

1. A population of size S will be chosen from the total population POP in each generation.
2. Get a random Cuckoo, one of the possible permutations from the set (POP-S), let's say i.
3. Calculate its Fitness Value let's say F (i).
4. Select a random nest from S, say j and calculate its fitness value say F (j).
5. Compare F(i) and F(j), if F(i)>F(j), replace j with i.
6. Sort S based on the fitness values and promotes the Cuckoo with highest fitness value to next generation.
7. In the next Generation take a new S-1 population from the set POP.
8. Go to step 2.
9. By repeating this process until with the user defined max_generation based on time or cost.

By the end of Phase 2 order of test cases will be obtained which then can be executed for the Program P during Regression testing.

ANALYSIS OF PROPOSED APPROACH

Cuckoo Search algorithm avoids the local optima problem of Genetic algorithm (GA) (Srivastava Praveen Ranjan, 2008). After every iteration, a new solution that is better than previous solution will be obtained. As the approach is based metaheuristic technique, the number of iterations taken to prioritize test-cases for a program may be in consistent. We can see that Cuckoo search is more efficient in finding the global optima with higher success rates. Each function evaluation is virtually instantaneous on a modern personal computer. For example, the computing time for 10,000 evaluations on a 3GHz desktop is about 5 seconds. In addition, for stochastic functions, genetic algorithms do not perform well, while on the basis of our experience particle swarm intelligence is better. However, CS is far more promising.

CASE STUDY

To determine the effectiveness of this approach the implementation of the algorithm is done on the sample program in Java which is described in Appendix B. The fitness values and the method are described below for various inputs. Here the input x value is changed (Emma code coverage eclipse plug-in, 2010).

Total 4 test cases are there TC1, TC2, TC3, and TC4 their coverage are showing below

TC1: x=6
Lines covered: 4, 5, 6, 7, 8, and 30
TC2: x=35
Lines covered: 4, 5, 6, 9, 10, 11, 12, 13, 14, 15, 30, 32, 33, 34, and 42
TC3: x=863
Lines covered: 4, 5, 6, 9, 16, 17, 18, 19, 20, 21, 22, 30, 32, 33, 34, 35, 36, 37, and 42 =19
TC4: x= 2341
Lines covered: 4, 5, 6, 9, 16, 23, 24, 25, 26, 27, 28, 29, 30, 32, 33, 34, 35, 39, 40, 41, and 42 =21

Suppose these lines are to be modified in a given code: 11, 12, 9, 22, 30, 32, 37, 42, and 41

Now we will try to execute step by step procedure for the proposed approach:

Phase 1:
Iteration 1:

	MATCHLIST	NO_MATCHES
TC1	{30}	1
TC2	{9, 11, 12, 30, 32, 42}	6
TC3	{9, 22, 30, 32, 37, 42}	6
TC4	{9, 30, 32, 41, 42}	5
MOD_LINES= {11, 12, 9, 22, 30, 32, 37, 42, 41}		

By the end of first iteration max NO_MATCHES is for TC2 and TC3. For illustration purpose here TC3 will be promoted to test suite T'. The lines of code that are common to TC3 and modified lines are removed from the remaining test cases. Calculation of MATCHLIST and NO_MATCHES will be calculated in next iteration.

Iteration 2:

	MATCHLIST	NO_MATCHES
TC1	{}	0
TC2	{11, 12}	2
TC4	{41}	1

By the end of second iteration TC2 will be promoted to T'. TC1 is removed from the list. Since it's NO_MATCHES is zero. Similarly in the next Iteration TC4 will be added to the new test suite T'. Hence by the end of phase 1 TC3, TC2, TC4 will be promoted to phase 2.

Now the POP, the total population will be {TC2, TC3, TC4}, {TC2, TC4, TC3}, {TC3, TC2, TC4}, {TC3, TC4, TC2}, {TC4, TC3, TC2}, {TC4, TC2, TC3}

Since here the total population is 6, for illustration purpose S=2 has been chosen. Here the max population in each generation S value depends on the POP size i.e. S=2;

For illustration purpose max_iterations =3 has been taken, the value of max_iterations directly depends on the time constraint and cost constraint.

Here showing the calculation of fitness value for the test suite order TC3, TC2, TC4. The above test suite order is taken in random.

Similarly other fitness values can be calculated. Here we have assumed the execution time of each test case as the lines covered by it.

Code Coverage for each test case is taken as = no of lines covered by the test case/total no of lines.

	Code coverage	Time
TC1	0.1623	6
TC2	0.4050	15
TC3	0.5233	19
TC4	0.5675	21

Fitness value for TC3, TC2, TC4

Fsactual=19*0.5233+15*(0.1633+0.5233) +21*(0.5233+0.1623+0.28) =42.064

Fs_max=1*(19+21+15)

Here in Fs-actual in the term 15*(0.1633+0.5233) under this expression 0.1633 represents additional code coverage by test case TC2 and it is calculated by considering the additional lines or new lines covered by the test case by total no of lines. Similarly 0.28 for TC4;

Fitness value =Fs-actual/Fs-max=0.7648;

Test suite order fitness value
1. TC3, TC2, TC4 0.7648
2. TC3, TC4, TC2 0.7766
3. TC2, TC3, TC4 0.7454
4. TC2, TC4, TC3 0.7568
5. TC4, TC3, TC2 0.7889
6. TC4, TC2, TC3 0.7849

Here for illustration purpose a (TC3, TC2, TC4), c (TC2, TC3, TC4) are chosen at random for S.

Iteration 1:

S= ({TC3, TC2, TC4}, {TC2, TC3, TC4})
Let j= {TC2, TC4, TC3} which is chosen randomly from POP-{S}
   i= {TC3, TC2, TC4} which is chosen at random from S.
F (i) =0.7648
F (j) =0.7568
F (i) > F (j)

So no replacement
Increasing order of fitness values in S
c (0.7454), a(0.7648) so 'a' will be promoted to next generation.

Iteration 2:

S= {a, e}   //e is chosen in random
j=b
i=a
F (i) < F (j)

So 'a' will be replaced by 'b'.
Increasing order of fitness values in S, based on the highest value the test suite will be promoted to next generation.
   b (0.7766),e(0.7889)
'e' will be promoted to next generation

Iteration 3:

S= {e, d}
i=d
j=f
F (j) > F (i)
Replace d with f
Increasing order of fitness values in S
f (0.7849), e(0.7889)

Termination condition occurred so 'e' i.e. {TC4, TC3, and TC2} is the prioritized order for appendix B and ensures 100% coverage.

The proposed algorithm was tested on real time software (some of in house development and few of open sources); the results we got are very encouraging. In general we compared (on the basis of redundant test case, complexity of a programme, dependent test cases etc) proposed algorithm over traditional approaches on test case prioritization which shown as in Figure 2. Since Cuckoo search is optimized algorithm, hence test case prioritization algorithm based on cuckoo search have always better result over any procedural method. In addition also under proposed strategy, we are getting minimal number of non-redundant test cases with maximum coverage, also run time are not so much complex, following Figure 2 represents superiority over traditional method.

Since this chapter used the concept of cuckoo search technique, this technique is very new in the area of software testing, so we can say this is state of art. Now solid comparison is possible between different metaheuristic techniques with newly developed cuckoo search technique in the area of software testing.

Figure 2. Comparison over various factors

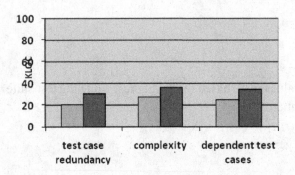

CONCLUSION AND FUTURE RESEARCH

This chapter presents a strategy for test case prioritization using cuckoo search and removing redundant test cases. The result of case study shows proposed approach is better, since the cuckoo search algorithm is more efficient than other algorithms. We are planning to enhance approach by calculating dependent test cases more efficiently.

REFERENCES

Aggrawal, K. K., Singh, Y., & Kaur, A. (2004). Code coverage based technique for prioritizing test cases for regression testing. *SIGSOFT Software Engineering Notes*, *29*(5), 1–4. doi:10.1145/1022494.1022511

Do, H., Rothermel, G., & Kineer, A. (2004). *Empirical studies of test case prioritization in a Junit testing environment. Proceeding in ISSRE* (pp. 113–124). IEEE Press.

Elbaum, S., Malishevsky, A., & Rothermel, G. G. (2000). *Prioritizing test cases for regression testing. Proceeding in ISSTA* (pp. 102–112). ACM Press.

Elbaum, S., Malishevsky, A., & Rothermel, G. G. (2004). Selecting a cost-effective test case prioritization technique. *Software Quality Control*, *12*(3), 185–210.

Emma Code. (2010). *Coverage eclipse plug-in*. Available at www.eclemma.org/

Goodrich, M. T. (2006). *Data structures and algorithms in C*. Wiley Publisher.

Horgan, J. R., & London, S. (1992). ATAC: A data flow coverage testing tool for C. In *Proceeding of Symposium on Assessment of Quality Software Development Tools*, May 1992, (pp. 2-10). IEEE Press.

Kim, J., & Porter, A. (2002). A history based test prioritization technique for regression is testing in resource constrained environments. *Proceeding of the 24th International Conference on Software Engineering* (ICSE), (pp. 119-129). ACM Press.

Krishnamoorthi, R., & Sahaaya, M. A. S. A. (2009). Regression test suite prioritization using genetic algorithms. *International Journal of Hybrid Information Technology*, *2*(3), 35-52. SERSC publication house Korea.

Mathur, A. P (2007). *Foundation of software testing*, 1st ed. India Pearson Education.

McMinn, P. (2004). Search-based software test data generation: A survey. *Software Testing, Verification and Reliability, 14*(3), 212-223.

Pressman, R. S. (2005). *Software engineering: A practitioner's approach* (6th ed.). India: TMH.

Ranjan, S. P. (2008). Test case prioritization. *Journal of Theoretical and Applied Information Technology, 4*(2), 178-181. Asian Research Publishing Network. ISSN 1992-8645

Ranjan, S. P., et al. (2008). Generation of test data using meta heuristic approach. *Proceeding of IEEE TENCON 2008.*

Ranjan, S. P., & Raghurama, G. (2009). Function and path coverage based techniques for prioritization test cases for regression testing. *International Journal of Software Engineering and Computing, 1*(2), 85–91.

Singh, Y., Kaur, A., & Bharti, S. (2010). Test case prioritization using ant colony optimization. *ACM SIGSOFT Software Engineering Notes, 35*(4), 1-7.

Srikanth, H., & Williams, L. (2005). On the economics of requirements based test case prioritization. *Proceeding in EDSER*, (pp. 1-3). ACM Press.

Srivastava, A., & Thiagarajan, J. (2002). *Effectively prioritizing test cases in development environment. Proceeding in ISSTA* (pp. 97–106). ACM Press.

Wong, W. E., Horgan, J. R., London, S., & Aggrawal, H. (1997). *A study of effective regression in practice. Proceeding in ISSRE* (p. 264). IEEE Press.

Yang, X.-S., & Deb, S. (2009). Cuckoo search via Lévy flights. *Proceeding in World Congress on Nature & Biologically Inspired Computing* (NaBIC), (pp. 210–214). IEEE Publications.

Yang, X.-S., & Deb, S. (2010). Engineering optimisation by cuckoo search. *International Journal of Mathematical Modelling and Numerical Optimisation, 1*(4), 330–343. doi:10.1504/IJMMNO.2010.035430

APPENDIX A

```
Objective function:
Generate an initial population of n host nests;
While (t<max_generation) or (stop criterion)
    Get a cuckoo randomly (say, i) and replace its solution by
performing Lévy flights;
    Evaluate its quality/fitness Fi
[For maximization];
    Choose a nest among n (say, j) randomly;
If (Fi > Fj),
          Replace j by the new solution;
End If
Fractions (pa) of the worst nests are abandoned and new ones
are built;
    Keep the best solutions/nests;
    Rank the solutions/nests and find the current best;
    Pass the current best to the next generation;
End while
Post-processing the results and visualization;
```

APPENDIX B

Following is the Java code used for case study.

```
1.    Import java.util.*;
2.    Public class hello {
3.    Public static void main(String[]  args) {
4.    Scanner s=new Scanner(System. in);
5.    int b, y=0,x= s.nextInt();
6.    if(x<10) {
7.    System.out.println ("x lies in block 1.");
8.    System.out.println ("y:"+ x);}
9.    else if(x>=10 && x<100) {
10.   b=2;
11.   y=x;
12.   System.out.println ("x lies in block 2.");
13.   While(y>9)
14.   y= Todigit(y, b);
```

```
15.    System.out.println("y:"+y);}
16.    Elseif(x>=100 && x<1000) {
17.    y=x;
18.    b=3;
19.    System.out.println("x lies in block 3.");
20.    While(y>9)
21.    y= Todigit(y, b);
22.    System.out.println("y:"+y);}
23.    else if (x>999 &&  x<10000){
24.    y=x;
25.    b=4;
26.    System.out.println("x lies in block 4.");
27.    while(y>9)
28.    y= Todigit(y, b);
29.    System.out.println("y:"+y);}
30.    }
31.    public static intTodigit(int x, int b){
32.    int y=0,i=0,j=0;
33.    if(x>=10 && x<100)
34.    y=((x/10)+(x%10));
35.    else if(x>99 && x<1000){
36.    j=x%100;
37.    y=((x/100)+(j/10)+(j%10));}
38.    else{
39.    i=x%1000;
40.    j=i%100;
41.    y=(x/1000+i/100+j/10+j%10);}
42.    return y;}}
```

Chapter 7
A Review of Software Quality Methodologies

Saqib Saeed
University of Siegen, Germany

Farrukh Masood Khawaja
Ericsson Telekommunikation GmbH, Germany

Zaigham Mahmood
University of Derby, UK

ABSTRACT

Pervasive systems and increased reliance on embedded systems require that the underlying software is properly tested and has in-built high quality. The approaches often adopted to realize software systems have inherent weaknesses that have resulted in less robust software applications. The requirement of reliable software suggests that quality needs to be instilled at all stages of a software development paradigms, especially at the testing stages of the development cycle ensuring that quality attributes and parameters are taken into account when designing and developing software. In this respect, numerous tools, techniques, and methodologies have also been proposed. In this chapter, the authors present and review different methodologies employed to improve the software quality during the software development lifecycle.

DOI: 10.4018/978-1-4666-0089-8.ch007

INTRODUCTION

The abstract nature of software products make them very different from conventional products that we can touch and see being built. As a result, the probability of human induced errors in software systems becomes high. Software systems have revolutionized every field of life. It is hard to believe that software systems are not being applied in any organizational setting. Extensive use of software applications and products in everyday life requires dependable and efficient software applications to run the day to day activities smoothly. This is equally true in case of business organization and commercial environments. As a result, similar to other products, the quality is emerging as an important attribute of such software systems. Crosby (1979) defines quality as "conformance to requirements" and Pressman (2010) extends this definition to include "adherence to standards". Pressman (2010) defines software quality as "conformance to explicitly stated functional and performance requirements, explicitly documented development standards, and implicit characteristics that are expected of all professionally developed software." This definition not only focuses on functional requirements but also includes performance requirements, adherence to development standards and presence of generic professional quality attributes to determine the quality level of software artifact. However, the definition of software quality is a contested concept in the software engineering literature (cf. Kitchenham & Pfleeger, 1996; Petrasch, 1999). The suggestion is that, in defining software quality, user requirements and elicitation of such requirements must form an important aspect of quality. An important reason behind this is that, in contrast to the conventional products, elicitation of software requirements is regarded as the responsibility of the development team instead of the customers. As a result, the requirements are categorized in different types e.g. user requirements, functional requirement, non functional requirements, usability requirements, performance requirements. The additional difficulty is that these requirements may well conflict with each other; they may even have different priority levels among stakeholders (developer, user, financer etc.) depending on stakeholders' perspectives or the application domain. It is also quite possible that it may be difficult to achieve some of these requirements.

IEEE (1990) defines software quality as "the degree to which a system, component, or process meets customer or user needs or expectations." This definition only focuses on the conventional marketing principle that customer is right and quality is only measured based on the satisfaction level of customer needs. On the other hand, other quality parameters which are invisible to users, but extremely important, get neglected. It is not easy to quantify quality. It is, therefore, often assessed in terms of its characteristics. Ghezzi et al., (2003) describe following eleven characteristics of software quality.

- Correctness
- Reliability
- Robustness
- Performance
- Usability
- Verifiability
- Maintainability
- Reusability
- Portability
- Understandability
- Interoperability

Furthermore quality is also determined by the process employed to design the product, product characteristics and the project attributes in terms of life cycle stages. Every application area also has its own specialized quality requirements which need to be considered while designing quality objectives of a software project. This highlights the fact that there is no strict definition of quality as each software development project and product has its own quality goals. In this chapter, we highlight how the quality can be improved in each software lifecycle phase and also suggest methodologies that can be put in place to improve the software development projects.

The remaining of this chapter is structured as follows. Section 2 discusses quality and its attributes which need to be considered in the entire software development lifecycle. Section 3 highlights the prevailing methodologies employed to enhance quality in software projects. Section 4 presents our conclusion.

QUALITY IN SOFTWARE DEVELOPMENT LIFECYCLE (SDLC)

The importance of enhanced quality suggests that quality is not something that is added to a product after it has been realized (such as garnishing a dish that has already been cooked). It requires a quality culture where the raw materials and the processes involved have built-in quality. In such a culture, enhancement of quality becomes everyone's responsibility. Thus, it becomes an ongoing activity performed throughout the software development lifecycle, through all the various software development phases; requirements engineering, system design, development and testing. As previously mentioned, software quality can also be correctly classified in terms of product quality, process quality and the project quality. Process quality refers to the effectiveness of the procedures employed in producing high quality software artifacts during the software development life cycle. Product quality refers to the quality attributes built into the final software product. Project quality refers to the overall processes of assessment, monitoring and management. Process quality is relatively more important as it makes the foundation for the success of current as well as future projects whereas the product quality only focuses on the current Project which is under consideration. Similarly, quality management activities are categorized into quality assurance and quality control. Quality assurance is proactive whereas quality control is a reactive strategy. The objective of the quality assurance activities is to perform SDLC activities in an optimal way to reduce the inherent problems and increase the product and process quality, whereas quality control activities attempt to find whether the product or process meets the required quality standard and, if not, then what the discrepancies are. In the following subsections, we discuss the activities which need to be focused to improve the quality of software products in a SDLC process. Here, the process is seen as composed of a number of software project phases consisting of: initiation, planning, requirements elicitation, design, development, testing and configuration.

Project Initiation

Project initiation is a preliminary stage of any software development project where project proposals and contracts are established and project feasibility is carried out. In order to avoid problems later in the project lifecycle, it is important to accurately estimate the project scope, the software size and project effort to identify project cost, project duration and service level agreements. This could be realized by applying multiple estimation techniques, instead of a single estimation approach, and also by learning from other past projects while working on feasibility assessment. This stage may also be known as the feasibility step. At the end of the phase, either the project is abandoned or the next stage – planning – is entered to conduct a proper planning strategy before implementing it (cf. Wiegers, 2007; Greer & Conradi, 2009).

Project Planning

This is the most important stage of any development project. If this stage is conducted correctly then the project execution becomes straight forward. Projects costing too much or their late delivery or they not conforming to user requirements is often due to inappropriate planning. An important project aspect, which most of the software projects lack, is timely delivery of artifacts. One reason for this is the choice of inappropriate software development lifecycle model. There are also numerous issues at this stage relating to: cash flow forecasting, work breakdown structures, cost, time and effort estimation, analysis of resources availability, resource allocation planning, staff responsibility and progress monitoring strategies (cf. Walston

& Felix, 1977; Albrecht & Gaffney, 1983; Mohapatra, 2010). All these need to be appropriately developed to control the project schedule and ensure that planning is correct. In addition, it is at this stage that overall project quality assurance and monitoring policies needs to be developed for later implementation in the project lifecycle. These refer to ensuring that: 1) work breakdown structures are complete by conducting reviews; 2) estimation of time and cost is worked out following industry accepted approaches; 3) the entire project is conducted following set approaches as devised by organizations such as PMI (Project Management Institute).

Requirements Engineering

Once the planning is over, the requirements elicitation stage can be entered. The objective of this software development lifecycle phase is to gather, classify and document software requirements (cf. Nuseibeh & Easterbrook, 2000; Lamsweerde, 2000; Wiegers, 2003; Wiegers, 2006). Majority of software project fail due to weak and incomplete requirement engineering phase. It is important to employ multiple requirement elicitation techniques to better understand the software requirement. It is important that enough appropriate time is spent to discuss system requirements with the customers. Furthermore, the requirements classification, prioritization and validation need to be carried out in a well planned manner to understand the relationships among requirements. At the end of this stage, a well documented software requirement specification should be available as a requirement baseline for the entire lifecycle project. Quality procedures at this stage refer to ensuring that: 1) each meeting achieves the aim set; 2) reviews for documents are conducted so that ambiguities and omission can be removed; 3) development team exhibit the professionalism and follow the code of conduct already set.

System Design

This stage is the first step in the execution of the project plan. During this stage, the system design and architecture is established. The typical quality attributes like performance, maintainability, understandability, ease of use (when the product is complete), and maintainability are taken into account during system design and architecture. In order to avoid later problems, it is important to measure the performance of proposed system design and architecture and benchmark it with required performance levels by conducting complexity analysis. This would give an early indication if our approach lacks required performance level. The design approach depends on the application domain; however, one way to instill quality is to follow the engineering approach, practicing principles such as abstraction, information hiding and modularity (cf. Song, & Osterweil, 1994)). As an example: modularity will help to reduce complexity and information hiding will aid the functional independence. As a result, the final product will be better constructed.

Coding

The coding phase is the realization of requirements in a programming environment. Here, the design is implemented to develop the software artifact. The selection of programming environment also affects the quality, so it is important to evaluate the benefits and limitations of programming environment and project quality goals. Furthermore, it is recommended to follow the best practices for coding, to improve the code readability and understandability and also ensure modularity (cf. Seacord. 2005). Coding standards walkthroughs and coding review procedures must be in place to ensure quality.

Testing

Software testing refers to verification and validation activities in software development lifecycle. These activities are as important part of software development lifecycle as the development phase. Here, the requirements are validated to ensure that the final product conforms to the requirements set at the beginning. A weak verification strategy (often mainly to save time as perhaps the project is already behind schedule) can allow the product to pass through, which does not meet quality criteria. It is pertinent that these verification activities should not only focus on software artifacts by conducting code testing, instead the artifacts produced throughout the lifecycle (such as software requirement specification, project plan, configuration management plan etc.) should also be subject to verification. In other words, testing of the product is as important as ensuring that the procedures followed are also of good quality. Here, quality needs to be instilled in all aspects of software testing including test planning, automation of testing, requiring ample execution time for this stage.

Configuration Management

Software configuration management is not always part of a SDLC. However, it is a process to control and track changes in software artifacts as well as other elements of software configuration throughout the SDLC. Software artifacts and other associated elements (including design and documentation) keep on changing due to different set of changes which could be corrective, adaptive, perfective or preventive (cf. Lientz & Swanson, 1980). The changes can affect each artifact in software development lifecycle so there should be an effective configuration management plan in place, to control these different variants of artifacts. In the absence of a configuration management plan, the final product may not be integrated based on the updated artifacts and as a result, it is quite possible that it may not meet the customer requirements or expectations. This activity is often neglected, mainly due to lack of time, however, it is important that appropriate time is devoted to this activity.

QUALITY METHODOLOGIES

In order to evaluate and improve the quality of products and processes, a number of different methodologies have been suggested. This section reviews the prevailing methodologies which are employed at different instances in software development lifecycle. Some of these have already been mentioned, the following sections will provide some more detail.

Software Quality Standards

Knowledge has become a strategic asset for every organization to improve the organizational processes (cf. Grant, 1996; Spender, 1996). Knowledge about best practices in software development life cycle activities can help to improve the quality of the software products as well as processes. As a result, notion of software quality standards have gained considerable importance. Since software development is a human centric activity, complete automation of software development activities is not possible but it has been observed that, when provided a set of guidelines, the activities in software development lifecycle work better as compared to a scenario where every team member is open to experiment. Numerous quality models have been suggested. Generally, these models are classified into two categories:

- Those commonly referred to as process improvement guidelines and
- Those often referred to as assessment frameworks

Some quality models work in a hybrid manner i.e. as a combination of the two approaches. Table 1 provides a list of a number of important software quality models, currently available. When selecting a quality model, one has to keep in mind the similarities and differences of the current project with the standardized approach. This will then help in instantiating the activities according to the project needs.

Software quality models provide a mechanism for channeling knowledge about development of complex software. However, recent literature has highlighted that many software companies having failures in adapting to defined software standards or simply not adhering to the standards. The typical reasons of this behaviour are

Table 1. Software quality models

ISO9000:2000	International organization for standardization (ISO) has approved different set of quality standards. The latest quality standard for computer software and related services is termed as ISO/IEC90003:2004. The standard documents provide guidelines to users on adopting this standard for software development organizations.
IEEE Software Engineering Standards	Institute of Electrical and Electronics engineering (IEEE) has established different set of standards for users to understand how different activities in software development lifecycle could be performed optimally. The examples of IEEE standard are IEEE Standard 730 (Standard for Quality Assurance Plan), IEEE Standard 828 (Software Configuration Management Plan), IEEE Standard 829 (Software Test Documentation), IEEE Standard 830 (Software Requirement Specification) etc.
CMM-I	Capability maturity model- Integrated (CMM-I) has converged from Capability Maturity Models (CMM). CMM-I could be followed in a staged or continuous manner depending upon the needs and resources of organizations (CMMI-Dev, 2006). The evaluation of CMMI is conducted through SCAMPI (Standard CMMI Appraisal Method for Process Improvement) appraisal approach. Since software development may not be carried out by each organization as a result CMMI is categorized into two classes which CMMI-ACQ and CMMI-Dev (cf. Frank et al., 2008).
ISO/IEC JTC1/ SC7	JTC1 is a joint technical committee of International organization of standardization and international electro technical commission. The SC7 charter advocates for cost minimization of software engineering activities by improving communication among suppliers and buyers and to improve the system quality (cf. Frank et al., 2008).
TL9000	TL 9000 quality management system focuses on meeting quality requirements of telecommunication industry. This model is developed by quality excellence for suppliers of telecommunication forum (cf. Frank et al., 2008).
ISO Spice	International organization for standardization has developed a software process assessment mechanism in software process improvement for capability determination project (cf. Frank et al., 2008).
Trillium	Bell Canada, Northern telecom and Bell northern research has developed a model for continuous improvement program. This model is based on CMM version 1.0 but its architecture is different from it (cf. Frank et al., 2008).
Bootstrap	Bootstrap is used for software process assessment, quantitative measurement and improvement. This project was completed in 1983 as European Strategic program for research in information technology (ESPRIT). This model enhanced the assessment mechanism of SEI and adapted according to European software industry (cf. Frank et al., 2008).
Tick-IT	Tick-IT is a quality management system supported by British and UK software industry. It is an assessment mechanism for the accreditation of ISO 9000 quality standard.

lack of resources on the part of software companies. In the context of knowledge society, since, smaller companies are not in the position to benefit from these standards, there is a need for light weight software quality models which are easy to implement with limited resources. This section reviews the available software quality models and discusses important issues which are worth investigating for the improvement of software quality models.

There are numerous quality models that present associated sets of recommended practices in a number of key process areas. These practices provide software organizations with guidance on how to gain control of their processes for developing and maintaining software and how to evolve towards a culture of management excellence. Setting sensible goals for different key process areas requires an understanding of the difference between mature and immature organizations. The Standards like CMMI, CMM, ISO 9001 etc. provide an evolutionary path for software organizations to transform their immature processes to mature processes. It is a common notion that software being produced from mature organizations would be mature, too. The success of software standards has not been so visible, especially as a lot of workload and resources are required to gain a certification with respect to standards and quality. This has resulted into a divide among the software development companies, as small companies are not in the position to invest much in a standardization activity. Since the outsourcing and global software development has encouraged the small and medium scale enterprises to conduct projects outside the geographical boundaries, this has resulted in a mushroom growth of small and medium scale enterprises. There is, thus, a need to focus this important group so they could also benefit from software standardization efforts. Secondly, as the notion of knowledge society emphasizes for equal opportunities for effective knowledge management strategies by all fractions of society, so there is a need for an effective software equality standard which is light weight so that smaller companies can also benefit. This could be realized by empirically evaluating the practices of successful small and medium enterprise companies not only in developed regions but also in regions like North America, South Asia and Eastern Europe.

Software Metrics

Software metrics are set of measures to quantify the value of various quality aspects. Fenton (1991) describes software metric as an approach to measure some property of software product or process. Generally, metrics can be classified into four categories which are product, process, project and resource metrics (cf. Frank et al., 2008). Metrics can also be designed based on the need and type of attributes using differnt frameworks such as plan-do-check-act cycle (Deming, 1986) or goal-question-metric (Basili & Rombach, 1984).

Product metrics highlight the properties of a particular software product e.g. number of defects in the product which highlights a product quality attribute. Another example of this could be the software size for which source line of codes and function points could be used as metrics. Process metrics highlight the quality and productivity aspect of overall software development process. This category of metrics provides the status of different aspects of software development process which helps in identifying the current improvement levels. The example of this type of metric is defect removal metric (Kan, 1995), which can be used to evaluate process effectiveness and reliability. Project attributes highlight the effectiveness of a project. The process and product metrics can be extended to project level as well. Resource metrics are used to determine the quantity of resources which are consumed for the realization of software projects. An example is the effort that has gone into the project, which can be a measure in person months or total development time.

Reviews and Inspections

Reviews and Inspections are another important set of procedures which are applied to work products in software projects (cf. Wiegers, 2002). The objective is similar to auditing i.e. to improve software processes and product qualities through reviews and inspections. IEEE standard for software reviews define reviews as "A process or meeting during which a software product is presented to project personnel, managers, users, customers, user representatives, or other interested parties for comment or approval."

Inspections are also defined in IEEE standards for software reviews as follows: "The purpose of an inspection is to detect and identify software product anomalies. This is a systematic peer examination that:

- Verifies that the software product satisfies its specifications
- Verifies that the software product satisfies specified quality attributes
- Verifies that the software product conforms to applicable regulations, standards, guidelines, plans, and procedures
- Identifies deviations from standards and specifications
- Collects software engineering data (for example, anomaly and effort data) (optional)
- Uses the collected software engineering data to improve the inspection process itself and its supporting documentation (for example, checklists) (optional)".

Reviews are used to uncover error and to verify that software meets its requirements, follows predefined standards and is developed uniformly. The review results contain decisions about the product and all the team members need to sign off (Frank et al., 2008). The products, here, refer to requirement documents, design diagrams, source listings, test plans as well as any other associated products of the SDLC activities. Proper views will help to develop products with appropriate quality.

SOFTWARE TESTING

Software testing is an important tool to analyze the quality of software systems and to test correctness and performance of the system. It has two aspects to it: verification and validation. Verification refers to conformation to user requirements and validation refers to it being 'correct' from users' perspective. The objective is to verify that the software system adheres to the software requirements and is free of bugs and the final product is one that the users originally asked for. There has been an extensive literature available discussing the software testing challenges, research issues and implications (cf. Borba et al., 2007; Bertolino, 2003; Bertolino, 2007; Lazic, 2005). A comprehensive test plan should be established for each software development project highlighting scope, approach, resources and schedule of testing activities. The selection of appropriate test strategy is important in test planning. We highlight different testing strategies which can be adopted depending upon the status and requirements of the software project.

Top Down Testing

Top level module is tested first, and then the module whose calling module has been already tested, has the turn (cf. Myers, 1979). A "stub" module is used when the module under testing needs to exchange data from its subordinate modules. This approach is quite helpful in identifying problems earlier if the errors are profoundly occurred in top level modules.

Bottom Up Testing

In contrast to top level testing approach if it is expected that majority of flaws will occur in internal modules then a bottom up testing strategy maybe more productive in identifying flaws quickly. In this approach the bottom level module is tested first and if it requires data exchange with its higher module then a "driver" module is realized to simulate the functionality of higher modules. Once the testing of bottom level module is completed, then its upper level module has the next turn.

Black Box Testing

The objective of black box testing approach is to verify that the output of the program is correct with respect to a given input data. In this approach knowledge of program logic and internal structure is not required; instead test cases are designed using the software requirement specification.

White Box Testing

In contrast to black box strategy, white box testing focuses on program internals and logic. The objective of this approach is to verify that the program code behaves correctly. This requires thorough code knowledge to carry out statement and branch testing to evaluate control flow and dataflow.

Grey Box Testing

Like black box testing, grey box testing involves testing the software by evaluating the output for a give input value, but the input values are selected in such a way that different internal program paths are evaluated. This requires extensive knowledge of software's internal components and their interaction behavior.

Time Box Testing

With the increasing popularity of agile software development approaches, similar testing methodologies have emerged. In time box testing we have a predefined hard deadline when the testing tasks need to be finished. The testing tasks are scheduled in a manner that this deadline is achieved.

Test Driven Design

Beck (2003) describes that in this testing approach, a test case is written before the software code describing some functionality. In the absence of software code this test case fails then the appropriate code is written to satisfy this test case. Later refactoring technique may be used to improve the quality of written code.

Good Enough Testing

Software testing is quite expensive as it requires considerable resources. Good enough testing approach tries to make a balance between software cost and quality. Its objective is to realize a software product that is good enough to meet customers' requirements and organization's expectations (cf. Bach, 1998; Elather, 2008).

Risk Based Testing

Risk based testing is another approach where preference is given to test cases which have high probability of occurrence. In this approach test cases are defined taking into account the most important risk factors and prioritizing the test cases of most critical areas first (cf. Redmill, 2004; Souza et al., 2010)

Simulation

The software systems (especially embedded system settings) where physical testing is difficult to conduct, simulation is an important tool to analyze the behavior of the system. Simulation provides replicated real life environment to understand the operation of the system and test its behavior before the software is actually deployed (cf. Henry, 2000; Bai et al., 2007).

Input / Output First Testing

It has been observed that the input and output from the software system are often error prone. In this testing approach every valid input is used as a test case to demonstrate every valid output (cf. Frank et al., 2008).

Certification

Testing tasks maybe outsourced to some independent third party entities or tied with some external well known standard. This could be the demand of the customer or maybe exploited by the company to better market their software product.

Random Input

Carrying out complete software testing is difficult due to required time, effort and cost. In random input testing strategy a sub set of randomly selected inputs is applied. The random selection of input maybe influenced by some heuristics, and/ or prior experiences. This technique is quite useful in cases where possibility of number of input events is relatively very high (cf. Mayer & Schneckenburger, 2006; Ciupa et al., 2007).

Usability Testing

The objective of usability testing is to evaluate how easy it is to understand the graphical user interface of the system (cf. Andreasen et al., 2007; Andrzejczak & Liu, 2010).

Qualification Testing

The objective of this testing strategy is to evaluate whether the software product is suitable for operational use (cf. Frank et al., 2008).

Operational Testing

The operational testing takes qualification testing to next level and to analyze whether the software system works properly in its operational environment (cf. Frank et al., 2008).

Acceptance Testing

The objective of acceptance testing is to verify the finished product from end-user/customer's perspective in order to see if it meets the specified functional requirements set earlier by the customer during the requirements engineering. Acceptance testing is generally performed by the customer by using his test cases/business scenarios and is conducted before the end product is delivered (cf. Hsia et al., 1997; Park & Maurer, 2008).

Alpha Testing

Alpha testing is conducted by end users to identify the potential bugs in software system. The testing is normally conducted at developer's site which simulates the end user environment. The objective of this testing methodology is to reduce the potential problems before the actual release of software product.

Beta Testing

Beta testing is carried out by conducting external acceptance testing at customer's site. The real world situation helps in identifying faulty behavior and bugs which were not visible during in house testing.

Performance Testing

The performance of software systems is vital for the acceptability by customers. Performance testing focuses on factors like effectiveness, reliability, speed, resource consumption and efficiency in operational conditions (cf. Hoskins et al., 2005; Shams et al., 2006; Goldin & Tennant, 2007).

Environmental Load

This testing approach is similar to performance and stress testing; its objective is to find the highest load level under which the software system can work properly.

Worst Case Testing

In the software testing literature it is described that mostly the errors are found on the boundary / extreme values of input classes used. In this approach extreme values are entered to see system behavior (cf. Bright, 2000).

These different software testing strategies can be applied at different levels of software testing which are highlighted in Table 2.

SOFTWARE AUDITS

Software audits are an important tool to identify the discrepancy much earlier in a software development lifecycle. A worthwhile objective of auditing is to examine the product components and processes and improve as necessary to improve the product and process quality. IEEE standard for software reviews define audit as "An independent examination of a software product, software process, or set of software processes to assess compliance with specifications, standards, contractual agreements, or other criteria." Frank et al., (2008) describe that auditing consists of four stages which are planning and preparation, performance, reporting, corrective action and follow-up. They further classify audits into 12 classes as described in Table 3. The output of software audit is a report which is sent to audit initiator and then to audited organization. It contains audit findings and type and timing of follow up activities (Frank et al., 2008).

CONCLUSION

Software quality is an important characteristic of all well designed products which needs to be an important aspect of all phases of software development. It is important that the development process is correctly followed and products are built in a 'quality-aware' environment. The difficulty is that quality is an abstract concept and cannot be easily quantified. However, it can be determined or its level established in terms of the quality attributes such as the product's correctness, reliability, performance, usability, portability etc. To get the quality right, it is also important that

Table 2. Software test levels

Functional Testing	In functional testing approach testing the overall functionality of software system is verified. The functional testing can be carried out by adopting different strategies such as black box, white box, grey box etc. The focus of this testing is to verify that functional requirements described in software requirement specification are fulfilled by the software (cf. Shen & Su, 1988; Omar & Mohammed, 1991)
Non Functional Testing	The non functional testing approach aims to verify the presence of non functional requirements in end products. The strategies like usability testing and performance testing could be applied to evaluate non functional requirements (cf. Metsa et al., 2007; Afzal et al., 2009)
Exploratory Testing	It is a kind of free-style testing which generally requires a good knowledge of the product under tests by the tester so that by utilizing his/her intuition and product knowledge he can devise new and better tests. The methodology like random input could be used to perform this kind of testing (cf. Whittaker, 2009).
Perfective Testing	Changes in software development lifecycle are must and as the end user's requirements are added, logic of features is changed, new set of functionality is added, and other general enhancements are conducted, this may introduce new set of errors. Perfective testing focuses on this aspect and verifies the quality of these changes (cf. Frank et al., 2008).
Unit Testing	In order to avoid problems at later stages it is recommended to perform testing alongside the software development. Unit testing is the most basic level of testing. The primary goal of unit testing is to test the smallest possible piece of source code in isolation from other components to verify their operation individually. The calling and called components of the unit under test are replaced by drivers, trusted super-components, stubs, simulators, or trusted components (cf. Ellims et al., 2006).
Component Testing	Similar to the unit testing the component testing focuses on a single component, this could be either a unit/ composition of different units. In contrast to unit testing components are tested using real time code instead of stubs or simulators (cf. Silva et al., 2009).
Integration Testing	Individually tested components may confront with errors once they are integrated as new data flow paths are introduced. Integration testing aims to identify these problems (cf. Bashir & Paul, 1999; Rehman et al., 2007).
Regression Testing	Regression testing advocates for re-run of test cases for integrated modules/components. The integration of two components may introduce problems in already tested parts of individual components. In integration testing test cases are designed only to verify that the combining modules work in proper way, whereas regression testing highlights that already tested components need to re-run those test cases as integration of two components may resulted into a problem within already tested component (cf. Rothermal et al., 2004; Mahdian et al., 2009).
System Testing	Integration testing is followed by this black box kind of testing methodology. In system testing, complete/larger component of the integrated system as a whole is verified to see if it complies with the specified system requirements (cf. Almeida et al., 2010; Sneed, 2010).

quality is looked at in terms of the process and project attributes. It is also imperative there is a quality culture and instilling quality is seen as everyone's responsibility.

This chapter has discussed the various aspects of quality as well as the quality approaches that should be taken into account in the development phases of an SDLC. The chapter has also provided a comprehensive review of different methodologies and standards approaches that currently exist. Due to enormous complexity of software artifacts and limited available time, a majority of these quality aspects have also

Table 3. Software audit types (adopted from Frank et al., 2008)

First Party Audit	This type of audit is performed within the organization. Its example could be an internal software quality audit.
Second Party Audit	This type of audit is carried out by customers on suppliers. Supplier survey by customer before contract signing to evaluate suppliers' procedure is an example of second party audit.
Third party Audit	This type of audit is conducted by an independent party which is deputed by client. A certification registration audit is an example of this type of audit. The registration organization doesn't have direct link with either company nor certification agency but it carries out audit on behalf of certification authority.
Internal Audit	Internal audit is performed within organization to identify the strengths and weaknesses of the organization.
External Audit	External audit is carried out by a company on an external entity. The company may depute its own employees or a third party to perform audit activities.
System Audit	System audit takes a holistic view of the organization and/or project, so they have wide scope and larger boundaries.
Process Audit	Process audit investigates an activity to verify that input, actions and output are compatible with defined requirements.
Product Audit	The objective of product audit is to assess the final product for its suitability for use.
Compliance Audit	Compliance audits highlight that defined activities have been properly carried out and adhere to criteria mentioned in contracts, agreements and standards.
Regulatory Audit	These audits are carried out to make sure that requirements put by regulatory bodies are adhered.
Management Audit	Management audit verifies that organizational rules and policies are effective and adhered.
Quality Audit	The objective of quality audit is to evaluate whether quality activities and their results are compatible with established procedures.

been automated. In this context, automation of testing is of particular importance as exhaustive testing is just not possible and developing test cases of all combination of data is physically impractical. This, often, incorporates executing predefined and pre-recorded test cases using specialized automation tools to minimize human efforts in testing process – and, thereby, reducing the possibility of further errors. This also results in increased effectiveness, efficiency and test coverage of the end product with minimal human intervention. Similarly, there are a variety of automated auditing and review tools to facilitate the software development process.

In this chapter, various approaches for conducting the review process have also been discussed. The emphasis has been on quality methodologies and, in particular, with respect to software testing. The aim is to provide some useful information to software engineers to enable them to build software that satisfies the user requirements and is also of high quality. Professionalism requires nothing less than this.

REFERENCES

Afzal, W., Torkar, R., & Feldt, R. (2009). A systematic review of search-based testing for non-functional system properties. *Information and Software Technology, 51*(6), 957–976. doi:10.1016/j.infsof.2008.12.005

Albrecht, A. J., & Gaffney, J. E. (1983). Software function, source lines of code, and development effort prediction: A software science validation. *IEEE Transactions on Software Engineering, 9*(6), 639–648. doi:10.1109/TSE.1983.235271

Almeida, E. C., Sunye, G., Traon, Y., & Valduriez, P. (2010). Testing peer-to-peer systems. *Empirical Software Engineering, 15*(4), 346–379. doi:10.1007/s10664-009-9124-x

Andreasen, M. S., Nielsen, H. V., Schroder, S. O., & Stage, J. (2007) *What happened to remote usability testing? An empirical study of three methods*. Paper presented at the SIGCHI Conference on Human factors in Computing Systems (CHI '07). New York, NY: ACM.

Andrzejczak, C., & Liu, D. (2010). The effect of testing location on usability testing performance, participant stress levels, and subjective testing experience. *Journal of Systems and Software, 83*(7). doi:10.1016/j.jss.2010.01.052

Bach, J. (1998). A framework for good enough testing. *Computer, 31*(10), 124–126. doi:10.1109/2.722304

Bai, X., Lee, S., & Chen, Y. (2007). *Mutation-based simulation test data generation for testing complex real-time software*. Paper presented at the 40th Annual Simulation Symposium (ANSS '07). Washington, DC: IEEE Computer Society.

Bashir, I., & Paul, R. A. (1999). Object-oriented integration testing. *Annals of Software Engineering, 8*(1-4), 187–202. doi:10.1023/A:1018975313718

Basili, V. R., & Rombach, H. D. (1984). The TAME project: Towards improvement oriented software environments. *IEEE Transactions on Software Engineering, 14*(6), 758–773. doi:10.1109/32.6156

Beck, K. (2003). *Test-driven development by example*. Addison Wesley.

Bertolino, A. (2003). *Software testing research and practice*. Paper presented at 10th International Conference on Advances in Theory and Practice (ASM'03). Berlin, Germany: Springer-Verlag.

Bertolino, A. (2007). *Software testing research: Achievements, challenges, dreams.* Paper presented at 2007 Future of Software Engineering (FOSE '07). Washington, DC: IEEE Computer Society.

Borba, P., Cavalcanti, A., Sampaio, A., & Woodcock, J. (Eds.). (2007). *Testing techniques in software engineering.* Berlin, Germany: Springer-Verlag.

Briand, L. C., Labiche, Y., & Shousha, M. (2005). Stress testing real-time systems with genetic algorithms. In H.-G. Beyer (Ed.), *2005 Conference on Genetic and Evolutionary Computation* (GECCO '05). New York, NY: ACM.

Bright, D. I. (2000). *A practical worst-case methodology for software testing.* Ph.D. Dissertation. Colorado Technical University.

Ciupa, I., Leitner, A., Oriol, M., & Meyer, B. (2007). *Experimental assessment of random testing for object-oriented software.* Paper presented at the 2007 International Symposium on Software Testing and Analysis (ISSTA '07). New York, NY: ACM.

CMMI-Dev. (2006). *CMMI for development, version 1.2: Improving processes for better products.* SEI CMU.

Crosby, P. B. (1979). *Quality is free.* New York, NY: Mentor Books.

Deming, W. E. (1986). *Out of the crisis.* Cambridge, MA: Massachusetts Institute of Technology.

Ellims, M., Bridges, J., & Ince, D. C. (2006). The economics of unit testing. *Empirical Software Engineering, 11*(1), 5–31. doi:10.1007/s10664-006-5964-9

Eltaher, A. (2008). *Towards good enough testing: A cognitive-oriented approach applied to infotainment systems.* Paper presented at the 23rd IEEE/ACM International Conference on Automated Software Engineering (ASE '08). Washington, DC: IEEE Computer Society.

Fenton, N. (1991). *Software metrics- A rigorous approach.* Chapman and Hall.

Frank, B., Marriott, P., & Warzusen, C. (2008). *CSQE primer.* Quality Council of Indiana.

Ghezzi, C., Jazayeri, M., & Mandrioli, D. (2003). *Fundamentals of software engineering* (2nd ed.). Prentice Hall.

Golding, P., & Tennant, V. (2007). Performance testing: Evaluating an RFID library inventory reader. *International Journal of Internet Protocols and Technology, 2*(3/4), 240–251. doi:10.1504/IJIPT.2007.016224

Grant, R. M. (1996). Toward a knowledge-based theory of the firm. *Strategic Management Journal, 17*, 109–122.

Greer, D., & Conradi, R. (2009). An empirical study of software project initiation and planning. *IET Software, 3*(5), 356–368. doi:10.1049/iet-sen.2008.0093

Henry, J. E. (2000). Test case selection for simulations in the maintenance of real-time systems. *Journal of Software Maintenance: Research and Practice, 12*(4), 229–248. doi:10.1002/1096-908X(200007/08)12:4<229::AID-SMR212>3.0.CO;2-S

Hoskins, D. S., Colbourn, C. J., & Montgomery, D. C. (2005). *Software performance testing using covering arrays: efficient screening designs with categorical factors.* Paper presented at the 5th International Workshop on Software and Performance (WOSP '05). New York, NY: ACM.

Hsia, P., Kung, D., & Sell, C. (1997). Software requirements and acceptance testing. *Annals of Software Engineering, 3*, 291–317. doi:10.1023/A:1018938021528

IEEE. (1990). *IEEE standard 610.12-1990: IEEE standard glossary of software engineering terminology.* New York, NY: IEEE Service Center.

Kan, S. (1995). *Metrics and models in software quality engineering.* Reading, MA: Addison-Wesley.

Kitchenham, B., & Pfleeger, S. L. (1996). Software quality: The elusive target. *IEEE Software, 13*(1), 12–21. doi:10.1109/52.476281

Lamsweerde, A. V. (2000). *Requirements engineering in the year 00: A research perspective.* Paper Presented at the 22nd International Conference on Software Engineering (ICSE '00). New York, NY: ACM.

Lazic, L. (2005). *The software testing challenges and methods.* Paper presented at the 9th WSEAS International Conference on Communications (ICCOM'05), Stevens Point, Wisconsin, USA.

Lientz, B., & Swanson, E. (1980). *Software maintenance management.* Reading, MA: Addison Wesley.

Mahdian, A., Andrews, A. A., & Pilskalns, O. J. (2009). Regression testing with UML software designs: A survey. *Journal of Software Maintenance and Evolution, 21*(4), 253–286. doi:10.1002/smr.403

Mayer, J., & Schneckenburger, C. (2006). *An empirical analysis and comparison of random testing techniques.* Paper presented at the 2006 ACM/IEEE International Symposium on Empirical Software Engineering (ISESE '06). New York, NY: ACM.

Metsa, J., Katara, M., & Mikkonen, T. (2007). Testing non-functional requirements with aspects: An industrial case study. Paper presented at the Seventh International Conference on Quality Software (QSIC '07). Washington, DC: IEEE Computer Society.

Mohapatra, S. (2010). Improvised process for quality through quantitative project management; an experience from software development projects. *International Journal of Information and Communication Technology, 2*(4), 355–373. doi:10.1504/IJICT.2010.034977

Myers, G. (1979). *The art of software testing.* New York, NY: John Wiley and Sons.

Nuseibeh, B., & Easterbrook, S. (2000). *Requirements engineering: A roadmap,* (pp. 35-46). Paper presented at the Conference on The Future of Software Engineering (ICSE '00). New York, NY: ACM.

Omar, A. A., & Mohammed, F. A. (1991). A survey of software functional testing methods. *SIGSOFT Software Engineering Notes, 16*(2), 75–82. doi:10.1145/122538.122551

Park, S. S., & Maurer, F. (2008). *The benefits and challenges of executable acceptance testing.* Paper presented at the 2008 International Workshop on Scrutinizing Agile Practices or Shoot-out at the Agile Corral (APOS '08). New York, NY: ACM.

Petrasch, R. (1999). *The definition of software quality: A practical approach.* Paper presented at the 10th International Symposium on Software Reliability Engineering.

Pressman, E. S. (2010). *Software engineering: A practitioner's approach* (7th ed.). McGraw Hill.

Pursak, L. (1997). *Knowledge in organizations.* Oxford, UK: Butlerworth-Heinemann.

Redmill, F. (2004). Exploring risk-based testing and its implications: Research articles. *Software Testing and Verifying Reliability, 14*(1), 3–15. doi:10.1002/stvr.288

Rehman, M. J., Jabeen, F., Bertolino, A., & Polini, A. (2007). Testing software components for integration: A survey of issues and techniques: Research Articles. *Software Testing and Verifying Reliability, 17*(2), 95–133. doi:10.1002/stvr.357

Rothermel, G., Elbaum, S., Malishevsky, A. G., Kallakuri, P., & Qiu, X. (2004). On test suite composition and cost-effective regression testing. *ACM Transactions on Software Engineering and Methodology, 13*(3), 277–331. doi:10.1145/1027092.1027093

Seacord, R. C. (2005). *Secure coding in C and C++ (SEI series in software engineering).* Addison-Wesley Professional.

Shams, M., Krishnamurthy, D., & Far, B. (2006). A model-based approach for testing the performance of web applications. *The 3rd International Workshop on Software Quality Assurance* (SOQUA '06), (pp. 54-61). New York, NY: ACM.

Shen, L., & Su, S. Y. H. (1988). A functional testing method for microprocessors. *IEEE Transactions on Computers, 37*(10), 1288–1293. doi:10.1109/12.5992

Silva, F. R. C., Almeida, E. S., & Meira, S. R. L. (2009). An approach for component testing and its empirical validation. In *Proceedings of the 2009 ACM Symposium on Applied Computing* (SAC '09), (pp. 574-581). New York, NY: ACM.

Sneed, H. M. (2010). Testing object-oriented software systems. In *Proceedings of the 1st Workshop on Testing Object-Oriented Systems* (ETOOS '10). New York, NY: ACM.

Song, X., & Osterweil, L. J. (1994). Experience with an approach to comparing software design methodologies. *IEEE Transactions on Software Engineering, 20*(5), 364–384. doi:10.1109/32.286419

Souza, E., Gusmão, C., & Venâncio, J. (2010). Risk-based testing: A case study. In *Proceedings of the 2010 Seventh International Conference on Information Technology: New Generations* (ITNG '10), (pp. 1032-1037). Washington, DC: IEEE Computer Society.

Spender, J. C. (1996). Making knowledge the basis of a dynamic theory of the firm. *Strategic Management Journal, 17*, 45–62.

Walston, C. E., & Felix, C. P. (1977). A method of programming measurement and estimation. *IBM Systems Journal, 16*(1), 54–73. doi:10.1147/sj.161.0054

Whittaker, J. A. (2009). *Exploratory software testing: Tips, tricks, tours, and techniques to guide test design* (1st ed.). Addison-Wesley.

Wiegers, K. A. (2002). *Peer reviews in software: A practical guide.* Addison-Wesley.

Wiegers, K. A. (2003). *Software requirements.* Microsoft Press.

Wiegers, K. A. (2006). *More about software requirements: Thorny issues and practical advice.* Microsoft Press.

Wiegers, K. A. (2007). *Practical project initiation - Best practices, a handbook with tools.* Microsoft Press.

Zhang, J., & Cheung, S. C. (2002). Automated test case generation for the stress testing of multimedia systems. *Software, Practice & Experience, 32*(15), 1411–1435. doi:10.1002/spe.487

Chapter 8
Model–Based Testing of Distributed Functions

Thomas Bauer
Fraunhofer IESE, Germany

Robert Eschbach
Fraunhofer IESE, Germany

ABSTRACT

The standard-compliant development of component-based embedded systems calls for systematic coverage of product requirements and for testing component interactions at the system integration stage. System functionality is represented by a set of complex distributed functions, i.e., functions that are spread across several system components. This chapter presents a novel automated model-based testing approach for distributed functions that uses informal system requirements and component behavior models. The test modeling notation makes it possible to model component interactions and composite functions with defined pre- and post-conditions. Test cases are automatically generated as scenarios of distributed functions represented by sequences of component interactions.

INTRODUCTION

In embedded systems, such as automotive or industrial automation, the majority of new innovations are realized via interactions of different system components. Examples are comfort functions in info- and entertainment systems or safety-critical driver assistance functions like park lane and brake assistants. In the past decade,

DOI: 10.4018/978-1-4666-0089-8.ch008

industrial development processes have been influenced by strict process and product standards, shorter development cycles, and higher quality needs. On the other hand, about 50% of all failures are caused by software faults, of which about 25% are caused by distributed software functions (Biagosch, Knupfer, Radtke, Näher & Zielke, 2005).

Complex embedded systems are often developed with third-party components provided by suppliers. The integration of third-party components requires particular efforts regarding systematic quality assurance on the part of the manufacturers, since neither the program code nor supplier-internal documentation is accessible. The manufacturer has to assure that the system assembled from externally developed components fulfills the system requirements and customer needs. A systematic integration test approach is needed to detect requirement violations and unspecified component interactions.

Integration and interoperability testing of distributed systems are essential quality assurance activities to check interactions within the system and functionalities that are spread across several system components. In integration testing, black-box testing techniques are usually applied, i.e., test cases are derived or selected based on the system specification. Integration testing is driven in practice by manual tests that highly depend on the experience of the test engineers and on their system knowledge. This approach leads to inefficient quality assurance in terms of effort, test coverage, and product quality.

By introducing model-based development approaches for software in embedded systems and standard-compliant component descriptions, different kinds of structural and behavioral models become available as valuable resources for early, systematic, and automated quality assurance on the component and subsystem levels.

Test automation usually deals with the use of automated methods supported by tools in software testing. In practice, available tools for test automation focus on the automated execution and evaluation of test cases, like x-unit frameworks for software unit testing, GUI tester and capture/ replay tools for testing via the graphical user interface, and hardware-specific solutions for hardware-in-the-loop (HiL) testing of electronic control units (ECUs).

In this article, a combined model-based approach for the systematic integration testing of distributed systems is presented; it uses functional system requirements and component models to avoid the generation of large system models. The approach bridges the gap between the informal requirements from the system view and the detailed event flow from the component view. The main contribution of our work is the systematic formalization of functional system requirements and component models for testing models that enable the automated generation of integration test cases.

Figure 1. Development process with manufacturer-supplier relationship

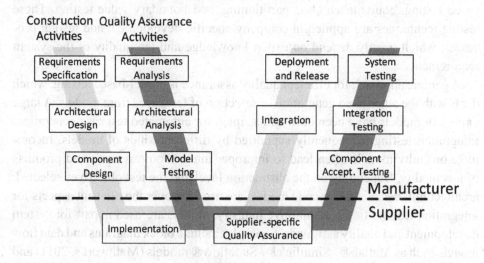

INTEGRATION TESTING IN PRACTICE

Industrial development processes are often driven by the involvement of suppliers and third-party components. The integration of third-party components requires particular efforts regarding systematic quality assurance on the part of the manufacturer, since neither the component implementation nor supplier-internal documentation is accessible. The manufacturer usually provides detailed component specifications, which may include textual requirements, executable component models, or acceptance test cases. The supplier develops the components and conducts supplier-specific unit testing. The manufacturer is the integrator of the externally developed components. He/she has to assure that the component fulfills the system requirements. A systematic integration test approach is needed to detect requirement violations and unspecified component interactions.

Figure 1 shows a simplified development process for embedded systems that takes into consideration the use of third-party components and the relationship between system manufacturers and suppliers. The process is divided into construction and quality assurance activities. Integration testing is usually performed together with the integration stage where system components are systematically assembled. In the example process, the components have been externally developed by the supplier and approved during the component acceptance testing stage.

International standards for the development of software-intensive critical systems, such as IEC 61508 (IEC 61508, 2010), call for systematic integration testing by different means depending on the criticality of functions and components. In industry, traditional function-oriented testing techniques are used, such as requirements-based testing, equivalence class partitioning, and boundary value testing. These testing techniques are applied in company-specific development and testing processes, which greatly depend on expert knowledge and the quality of the system requirements.

A generic approach for efficient quality assurance is model-based testing, which deals with the automated generation or selection of test cases from models. A large variety of models have been used and adapted for automated test case generation. Integration testing is frequently supported by different kinds of models. Incomplete or faulty models often lead to improper integration test cases and products of low quality. Depending on the abstraction level and the test objectives selected, architectural, behavioral, or code models are used to cover the relevant aspects for integration testing. In the automotive industry, models are used in part for system development and quality assurance. Examples include block diagrams and data flow models such as Matlab® / Simulink® / Stateflow® models (Mathworks, 2011) and UML models such as UML state charts.

COMPONENT-BASED SYSTEMS

Systems are complex entities composed of a set of components. They provide high-level functionality stated in the system requirements specification. *Distributed systems* are systems that consist of multiple autonomous computers or processes that communicate through a computer network or a communication middleware. The processes interact with each other in order to achieve a common goal (Attiya & Welch, 2004).

Components are system parts with defined interfaces and functionalities. In many areas, the manufacturers of complex embedded systems use third-party components from suppliers, such as software packages or complete ECUs. Their main task is to specify the desired component functionality and integrate it into their system. When third-party components are used, the manufacturer often provides the supplier with textual specifications, enriched with some models for interesting or critical aspects. The integration test of the assembled system becomes an important quality assurance activity.

Components may be triggered by the environment (stimuli) and may respond internally (to other system components) or externally (to the environment). The environment comprises all test-relevant entities and components that are outside the system boundary, i.e., they are not part of the system under test. The definition of the system boundary, i.e., the determination of the concrete set of components and the abstraction level of their interfaces, is an important activity of the test planning stage (Prowell & Poore, 2003). In complex embedded systems with many ECUs, sensors, and actuators, the definition of the system boundary for certain test stages is a non-trivial task that influences the determination of relevant stimuli, external responses, and internal component interactions.

The components may communicate via different communication mechanisms, such as exchange of messages, shared data, files, and shared resources. The communication middleware is the infrastructure used to connect components and perform component interactions. Most infrastructures have well-defined communication protocols with known quality properties, such as maximum bandwidth, response time, and reliability. The communication protocol of the middleware is often described by different kinds of behavior models, such as finite state machines. Some test approaches explicitly consider the communication middleware (Bochmann & Petrenko, 1994).

THE CASE STUDY

The test object is derived from the automotive example presented in (Robinson-Mallett, Hierons, Poore & Liggesmeyer, 2008), a simplified component-based automatic transmission control system. Automotive transmissions are complex software-intensive subsystems in road vehicles, which consists of several ECUs connected via communication busses (Naunheimer, Bertsche, Ryborz, & Novak, 2011).

Figure 2 shows the simplified system structure of the feasibility study, which is derived from the case study described in (Robinson-Mallett et al., 2008). For demonstration purposes, the system was reduced to six components that communicate via automotive-specific communication busses. The component *vehicle* describes the vehicle- and engine-specific aspects of the transmission, such as acceleration and deceleration, calculation of engine RPM, and velocity. Furthermore, the vehicle may affect the shift strategy when certain thresholds for engine RPM and velocity are reached. The *shift lever* is responsible for selecting the desired shift mode (neutral automatic, manual). The *shift control* evaluates the inputs from the vehicle and from the shift lever and controls the clutch and transmission components. The control depends on the transmission type such as single or dual clutch transmission (Naunheimer et al., 2011). The *clutch control* and *transmission control* components execute the commands from shift control. The *ignition* is connected to the shift lever to assure stationary safety-related functionalities (e.g., the ignition can only be turned off when the shift lever is in the parking position).

Figure 2. System structure of the test object

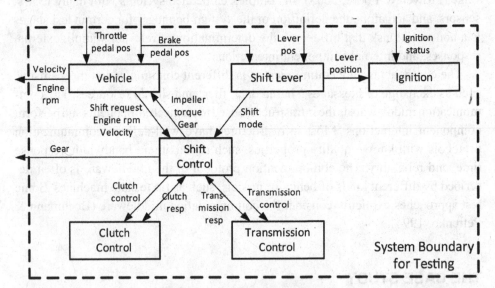

DISTRIBUTED AND COMPOSITE FUNCTIONS

The behavioral aspects of the system are described by a set of functions. Functions are subroutines and portions of program code that perform specific tasks and fulfill specific requirements. Functions are composite, i.e., they can contain or invoke other functions. Furthermore, functions can be used by several complex functions, e.g., an exception handling routine can be invoked by different system functions. Functions are enabled at specific system states, i.e., certain combinations of component states. These states describe the pre-condition for the function. During the execution of the function, the system state, i.e., the corresponding component states, may be changed. The result of the state change describes the post-condition of the function.

Functions are executed by stimulating the system via its interface. The system behavior is represented by system state changes, system responses to the environment, and internal component interactions. Distributed systems usually provide a set of functions that are implemented by the interplay of the system components, the so-called *distributed functions*. A function is distributed if at least two components are involved and at least one component interaction takes place between the components. An interaction is triggered by external stimulation of at least one component. The assumption is that the system works in a slow environment, i.e., the environment sends inputs only when the system is in stable mode (Lanet & Requet, 1998). The system is in stable mode when all components are in stable states, i.e., no outward transitions of the components are enabled.

Figure 3. Function graph

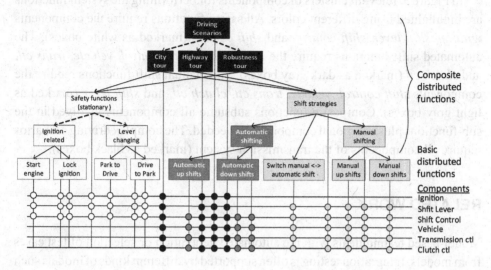

Figure 3 shows the different distributed functions of the case study and their relationships in an acyclic hierarchical function graph. The hierarchy describes the composition of functions. The *basic functions* at the bottom do not use any of the other functions specified. They represent the lowest level in the functional hierarchy. The highest functions in the hierarchy are complex scenarios. The composition may use different operators. A special case is the integration of semantically related functions into a function container (marked as dashed arrows in the graph). In later steps, the graph is the basis for the derivation of the functional model. The function graph is retrieved from the system requirements specification by mapping chapters, sections, paragraphs, and cross-references to graph nodes and transitions between them. The graph is acyclic to avoid design flaws. Functions may be referenced by multiple functions.

The application of the case study contains a set of complex driving scenarios covering typical long-term usages of the device and robustness cases covering untypical system usages. In addition, the requirements describe the different shift strategies and safety functions in the stationary mode, i.e., when the car is not moving. The safety functions cover ignition-specific and lever-specific sub-functions. The shift strategies comprise manual and automatic shift strategies. The safety functions and shift strategies are both sub-functions of the complex driving scenarios. For each function, the components involved are marked. By definition, a component is involved in a distributed function when its state is changed or a component response is used in the functional implementation.

In Figure 3, relevant clusters of components for performing the system functions are highlighted using different colors. All safety functions require the components *ignition, shift lever, shift control,* and *shift control* (marked as white boxes). The automated shift functions require the components *shift control, vehicle, trans ctl,* and *clutch ctl* (marked as dark gray boxes). The manual shift functions require the components *shift control, vehicle, trans ctl, clutch ctl*, and *shift lever* (marked as light gray boxes). Composite functions subsume all components involved in the sub-functions plus additional components if needed. The complex driving scenarios require all components of the transmission system (marked as black boxes).

RELATED WORK

Model-based testing deals with the automated generation or selection of test cases from models. Integration testing is often supported by different kinds of models such as structural, behavioral, or code models. A widely accepted taxonomy for model-based testing is presented in (Utting, Pretschner & Legeard. 2011). This taxonomy has been extended to cover the specific aspects for integration testing.

Figure 4 shows the taxonomy proposed for integration test approaches. Six dimensions have been defined: test objectives, model types, modeling paradigm, test selection criteria, test generation technology, and integration order.

Three common *test objectives* in terms of coverage have been identified, namely, code, component interactions, and use cases / scenarios. Code coverage in integration testing deals with the modeling and coverage of the inter-functional, inter-component, and inter-class control and data flow. The coverage of component interactions focuses on more abstract component interplay without accessing the concrete control and data flows in the program. The coverage of complex interactions, use cases, and scenarios represents the requirements-based system view. The systems and its subsystems have to fulfill the functional and non-functional requirements stated in the specification.

The *integration order* determines the approach for assembling the system components. The classification used here is re-used from (Borner, 2010). Most of the approaches derive the integration order based on the system structure, some on functional system aspects such as use case or thread-based integration order. Traditional hierarchical approaches comprise top-down or bottom-up ordering. Other approaches transform the system structure by using cycle splitting, cluster analysis, or genetic algorithms to identify communicating subsystems and minimize the number of stubs and the effort for creating them. Only few integration test approaches explicitly consider the integration order, for example (Robinson-Mallett et al., 2008).

Figure 4. Taxonomy dimensions of model-based integration testing

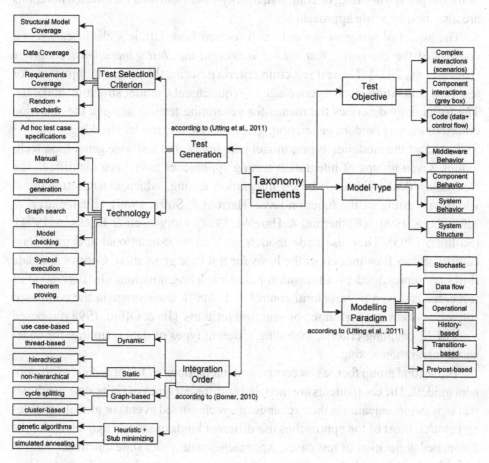

The *model type* represents the generic kinds of models used as a basis for test case generation. Component-based systems have a defined system structure and interfaces that can be exploited for the derivation of test cases. Behavior models define the dynamic properties of the test object from the system or component perspective. System behavior models describe interesting use cases and scenarios. Component behavior models represent the component-specific input-output trajectories stimulated and produced via the component interfaces. The communication of a distributed system relies on a middleware infrastructure, which can be specified by particular middleware behavior models.

The *model paradigms* are re-used from Utting's classification (Utting et al., 2011). The main paradigms are transition-based, pre-/post-based, operational, history-based, data flow-based, and stochastic. Most of the approaches use transition-based notations, but pre-/post-based, operational, history-based and data flow-based notations are also used by some approaches.

The aspect of *test generation* is also re-used from Utting's classification and consists of the categories *test selection criteria* and *test generation technology* (Utting et al., 2011). The test selection criteria describe the different objectives for test case generation, such as coverage of requirements, model structure, and data. The technology describes the means for generating tests to achieve the selection criterion, such as random generation, graph search, and model checking.

Based on the modeling types, model paradigms, and test case generation techniques, seven groups of integration testing approaches have been identified. The first group deals with code-based integration testing, which extends traditional white-box testing on the function level (Harrold & Soffa, 1989), (Linnenkugel & Müllerburg, 1990), (Rothermel & Harrold, 1994), (Jorgensen & Erickson, 1994), (Spillner, 1995). They use code models such as inter-functional and inter-class control or data flow models as the basis for test case generation. Control and data flows are represented by a transition-based modeling notation. The derivation of test cases is driven by structural control and data flow coverage in the composed software system and performed by search algorithms. (Jin & Offutt, 1998) proposed a set of 12 coupling criteria, including different types of data coupling, for code-based integration testing.

The second group focuses on component interactions and uses dedicated component models. The components are modeled as different types of finite state machines that may communicate via the exchange of synchronized events or global variables and clocks. Most of the approaches use different kinds of search algorithms for the automated generation of test cases. Approaches with finite state machines without variables, guards, and clocks focus on the coverage of synchronized events (Henninger, 1997), (Wu, Pan & Chen, 2001), (Koppol, Carver & Tai, 2002), (Seol, Kim, Kang & Ryu, 2003), Wang, Wu. & Yin, 2004), (Desmoulin & Viho, 2007), (Hashim, Ramakrishnan & Schmidt, 2007). The second sub-group uses extended finite state machines, i.e., state machines with variables, guards, and clocks, and re-uses the coverage of the non-extended finite state machines (Hartmann, Imoberdorf & Meisinger, 2000), (Pelliccione, Muccini, Bucchiarone & Facchini, 2005), (Robinson-Mallett et al., 2008). Other approaches use extended finite state machines and define specific criteria for additionally covering data coupling and data flow dependencies on subsystem level (Gallagher & Offutt, 2006), (Saglietti & Pinte, 2010).

(Robinson-Mallett et al., 2008) created partial models from component state machines. Model checking is used to derive a partial test model and test cases based on several communication coverage criteria. The approach also works for extended finite state machine (EFSMs) with variables and conditions. The partial testing model considers only single interactions. Distributed system functions that contain sequences of component interactions are not considered. Robinson-Mallett's approach proposes a bottom-up integration order for the extraction of partial test models and for stepwise test case generation.

The third group of approaches is based on the operational notation Petri nets, which is a suitable notation for specifying concurrency on the level of component interactions (Jin & Offutt, 2001), (Zhu & He, 2000), (Reza & Grant, 2007). Jin and Reza additionally use architectural models to describe components and connectors in the system. Petri net-specific coverage criteria (such as transition, state, and flow coverage) are combined with architectural coverage criteria (such as component and connector interface coverage). For analysis and test case generation, the reachability graph of the Petri net has to be created, which becomes very large in complex concurrent systems.

The fourth group deals with the generation of integration test cases from component test cases (Pretschner, Slotosch, Aiglstorfer & Kriebel, 2004), (Schätz & Pfaller, 2010). The component test cases are derived from component models or code models. The approaches avoid the construction of large integration test models by generating integration test cases directly from the component test cases. Symbolic execution and model checking are used as test case generation technologies.

The fifth group deals with scenario-based testing without component models. The approaches describe system functions, use cases, and usage scenarios via UML behavior diagrams such as sequence diagrams, collaboration diagrams, and interaction activity diagrams (Abdurazik & Offutt, 2000), (Basanieri & Bertolino, 2000), (Briand & Labiche, 2001), (Fraikin & Leonhardt, 2002), (Lee, Kim & Cha, 2002), (Pilskalns, Andrews, 2003), (Muccini, Bertolin & Inverardi, 2004), (Machado, de Figueiredo, Lima, Barbosa, Lima, 2007), (Fan, Shu, Liu & Liang, 2009). Structural model coverage criteria are applied for test case generation. Another approach uses the operational notation CSP (Communicating Sequential Processes) to represent functional aspects of concurrent systems (de Figueiredo, Andrade & Machado, 2006), (Nogueira, Sampaio, Mota, 2008), (Cabral & Sampaio, 2008). Test cases are generated by structural coverage and the coverage of test objectives specified as CSP as well.

The sixth group works with scenario-based testing supported by state-based component models, which are the most relevant approaches compared to this work. The approaches of this group use separate modeling notations to represent system and component behavior (Ali et al., 2007), (Benz, 2007), (Wieczorek et al., 2009). The use of separate models for the system view and for the component view has several advantages. It avoids the construction of the complete system state space from the component models by focusing on the system view, and it enables the generation of representative test cases from the system perspective. The use of component models assures the validity of test cases by considering interfaces and behavior from the component perspective. The component behavior is described as extended finite state machines such as UML state charts. The system behavior is modeled using different notations. Ali uses UML collaboration diagrams, Benz uses a tree-like feature interaction model, and Wieczorek uses extended finite state machines to represent the so-called global choreography model. Test case generation is performed in a top-down manner from the system models to the component models using structural coverage, searching, and model checking.

(Ali et al., 2007) proposed an approach that combines UML collaboration diagrams for the definition of relevant system functions and UML state charts for describing the component behavior. The collaboration depicts the sequence of interactions between different components in a notation similar to UML object diagrams. The author uses an intermediate state-based test model called SCOTEM (state collaboration test model) to summarize the relevant information. Test cases are generated based on the structural coverage of the SCOTEM model. The composition patterns for composite functions are restricted to sequences. Alternative execution paths can be annotated in single diagrams by introducing a hierarchical sequence number or can be modeled as additional diagrams. System functions are supposed to be executable in most of the system states.

(Benz, 2007) developed an approach focusing on interactions of system functions called features. Feature interaction occurs when one feature influences or modifies the behavior of another one. Benz uses a tree-like feature interaction model for the high-level description and UML state charts for the low-level component models. The connection of features to component models is provided by model annotations describing the pre- and post-conditions of features. The composition of features is restricted to sequences. State variables are not explicitly used. Features represent paths in the component models; more complex implementations of interactions are not supported. Test cases are generated on the basis of several feature interaction coverage criteria based on the feature model.

(Wieczorek et al., 2009) proposed an integration test approach for checking service protocols that are implemented as messages exchanged between pairs of components. The authors use different views: a high-level system perspective and a low-level component perspective. The high-level system model describes the sequences of component interactions allowed. The low-level component model describes the possible participation of the component in interactions. Additional channel models describe the behavior of the underlying communication middleware. The state-based models are transformed into B machines in order to enable more efficient test case generation by applying model coverage, model checking, and random walk. The viewpoints reduce the complexity of the state-based system models to a certain extent, but multiple complex scenarios lead to large system models. Furthermore, composite scenarios are not supported by the approach. The pre- and post-conditions of scenarios are implicitly defined by the component models involved in the scenario. State variables are not explicitly used in the component and system models.

The combined notations with system and component models provide advanced solutions for testing high-level scenarios and low-level component interactions. The approaches presented in the state-of-the-art section are missing a systematic description of distributed functions. The expression of functional pre- and post-conditions and the possibilities for composing functions by using different operators are limited. The reason is that the selected modeling notations offered by the start-of-the-art approaches do not allow efficiently describing functional composition and execution conditions. Since both aspects are necessary to describe distributed functions, a novel modeling notation is proposed.

MODELS AND NOTATIONS

The modeling notation of the approach consists of the three model types: pre/post, operational, and transition-based models. Each one is used for a disjoint modeling aspect. By combining the three models, the composite distributed functions with defined pre- and post-conditions and their implementation as component interactions can be described efficiently and completely.

Modeling Pre- and Post-Conditions of Basic Functions

The first modeling notation used for representing the execution context of a function, i.e., its pre- and post-conditions, is a *pre-/post-notation*. A function can be executed if the system fulfills its pre-condition. After the execution of a function in a defined pre-condition, the system fulfills a defined post-condition. Two functions may be concatenated if the post-condition of one function and the pre-conditions of the other function overlap. In the approach, the modeling notation *B machines* is used, a formal notation for state-based systems using an abstract machine notation (Abrial, 1996).

A B machine consists of a set of variables for describing system states, a set of invariants, and a set of operations for modifying the system state. Invariants are used to restrict the values of state variables. Each system specified as a B Machine has a unique initial state, which is defined in the initialization part of the B machine. The system operations have designated pre- and post-conditions and provoke the change of state variables. B supports the refinement and abstraction of operations and state space, but does not support composition. Each valid and reachable combination of state variable values is a valid system state. Concrete system states, i.e., concrete

Figure 5. Description of the functional pre- and post-conditions in B

```
...
VARIABLES
ignition_Status ⊂ {IGN_LOCKED, IGN_OFF, IGN_ON};
vehicle_status ⊂ {STOPPED, DRIVE_FORW, DRIVE_BACKW};
shift_detected ⊂ {NONE, UP, DOWN}
lever_pos ⊂ {N, D, M};
shift_mode ⊂ {MANUAL, AUTO};
gear_engaged ⊂ {-1, ... , 5};
...
OPERATIONS
auto_up =
PRE vehicle_status= DRIVE_FORW & shift_detected=NONE &
shift_mode=AUTO & lever_pos=D & 1≤gear_engaged≤4
THEN
      gear_engaged = gear_engaged+1
END;

man_up =
PRE vehicle_status= DRIVE_FORW & shift_mode=MAN &
      lever_pos=M & (1≤gear_engaged≤5)
THEN
      If ((1≤gear_engaged≤4) THEN
           gear_engaged = gear_engaged+1
END;
...
```

combinations of state variable values, are reachable if a sequence of operations exists that leads to these states. Test cases generated from the model are represented by traces, i.e., by a sequence of operations through the B machine state space, starting from the initial state. An example of the modeling of the pre-/post-conditions in B is given in Figure 5.

Modeling Operational Behavior of Composite Functions

The second modeling notation used for describing the composition of functions is an *operational notation*. In the approach, the modeling notation *CSP* is used, a formal notation for describing, analyzing, and verifying systems consisting of concurrent, communicating processes (Hoare, 1985). CSP works with compositional processes and different kinds of synchronization and communication between processes. The model elements of CSP are events and processes.

CSP processes represent the externally visible behavior of a component. A component consumes input events and produces output events. Processes may synchronize with other processes on certain events. CSP events represent system inputs, system outputs, and direct communication or interaction between the system processes. Processes may synchronize with other processes on certain events. Events are assumed to be indivisible and instantaneous. The concrete behavior

Figure 6. CSP operators used for function composition

Operator	Description	Example as Petri net	CSP Syntax
Sequential processing of events	Concatenation of basic functions	 e1 ▷→○→▷ e2	**e1->e2**
Sequential composition	Concatenation of composite functions	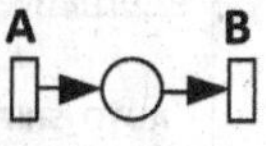 A ▷→○→▷ B	**A; B**
External choice	Alternative execution paths	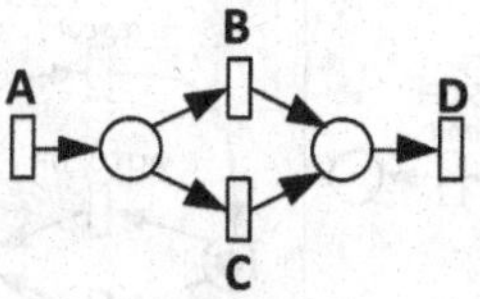 A ▷→○ ⇉ B / C ⇉ ○→▷ D	**A; (B [] C); D**
Parallel composition	Concurrent executions of functions	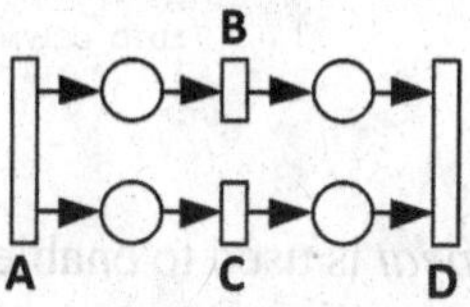 B / A ▷→○→▷→○ ... C ... D	**A; (B || C); D**

of the process is described by processing events and composing the behavior of other processes using algebraic composition operators. In this work, the following composition operators provided by CSP are used: *sequential composition* for concatenating functions, *external choice* for alternative paths, and *parallel composition* for concurrent executions.

Figure 6 shows the CSP operators used in the approach. Events can be processed and concatenated to sequences using the operator →. The sequential composition of processes is defined as their consecutive execution. In the example, A is executed first and then B. External choice represents alternative paths through the process; valid paths in the example are A-B-D and A-C-D. Parallel composition requires the execution of concurrent processes in an arbitrary order with the assumption that processes are not executed simultaneously. Valid paths in the example are A-B-C-D and A-C-B-D.

In the example in Figure 7, the three composite functions *lever changing (LE-VER_CHANGE), automatic shifting (AUTO_SHIFT),* and *driving scenarios (DRIVE_SCN)* are defined. *LEVER_CHANGE* is defined as alternating sequences of the functions *park to drive (PARK_DRIVE)* and *drive to park (DRIVE_PARK).* The term *LEVER_ CHANGE [ ] SKIP* represents the multiple execution of the function *LEVER_CHANGE.* The transition *SKIP* leads to the exit state of the func-

Figure 7. Examples of composition in CSP

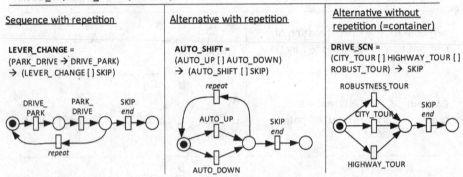

Definition of event channels

CHANNEL
PARK_DRIVE, DRIVE_PARK,
START_IGN, LOCK_IGN,
AUTO_UP, AUTO_DOWN, SWITCH, ...

Sequence with repetition	Alternative with repetition	Alternative without repetition (=container)

LEVER_CHANGE =
(PARK_DRIVE → DRIVE_PARK)
→ (LEVER_ CHANGE [ ] SKIP)

AUTO_SHIFT =
(AUTO_UP [ ] AUTO_DOWN)
→ (AUTO_SHIFT [ ] SKIP)

DRIVE_SCN =
(CITY_TOUR [ ] HIGHWAY_TOUR [ ]
ROBUST_TOUR) → SKIP

tion. The transition *repeat* is used to enable multiple executions of the functions by connecting the post-state of the composition with its start state. *AUTO_SHIFT* is defined as arbitrary sequences of the functions *automatic up shifts (AUTO_UP), automatic down shifts (AUTO_DOWN),* and *switch between manual and automatic shifts (SWITCH)*. The third example on the right-hand side of the figure describes the composite function *DRIVE_SCN*, which is implemented as an external choice of the three functions *CITY_TOUR, HIGHWAY_TOUR*, and *ROBUSTNESS_TOUR* without repetition. By executing all sub-functions once, the function is completely covered. This construct represents a kind of container for semantically related functions.

Modeling Composite Functions with Pre-/Post-Conditions

Both modeling notations, CSP and B, can be combined to guide and restrict the decision complexity for traversing the large B state space (Butler & Leuschel, 2005). The combination of CSP and B uses the B machines to specify abstract system states and operations and CSP models to coordinate the execution of operations. In the approach, B operations are mapped to CSP channels. The B machine is represented as an additional process in CSP. The combination of CSP and B leads to the parallel composition of both specifications. A certain operation can only be executed when it is enabled in both the CSP and the B specification. In the test approach, the combination of CSP and B models is used to design complex functions as a composition of other functions with defined pre- and post-conditions. Every composite function is represented by a new process in CSP.

Modeling the Transition-Based Behavior of Component Interactions

The third modeling notation used for describing the composition of functions is a *transition-based notation*. Transition-based notations describe the control logic of components with their major states and actions which lead to state transitions. For describing complex systems, additional modeling elements like data variables, clocks, hierarchical machines, parallelism, and synchronization have been introduced. In the approach, the modeling notation *timed automata* is used. Timed automata are finite state machines extended with variables and clocks (de Alfaro & Henzinger, 2001). A timed automaton consists of locations, an initial location, variables and clocks, actions (input and output events), edges between locations, and invariants assigned to locations. Clocks are special variables that progress synchronously. Locations represent the vertices of the automaton and may have invariants related to system variable values. Every automaton has a designated initial location. Locations are connected by edges. Edges may be annotated with an event (either sending or receiving), guards related to the variable values, and actions for setting variable values.

A system is modeled as a parallel composition of timed automata. Timed automata support the synchronous and asynchronous component interactions through synchronized events and shared variables. An example of communicating finite state machines modeled as timed automata is shown in Figure 8.

The timed automata are derived from the case study described in (Robinson-Mallett et al., 2008). Synchronous communication between two automata is provided when edges labeled with complementary events synchronize over a common channel (e.g., *MODE_D!* for sending and *MODE_D?* for receiving). Asynchronous communication between timed automata is modeled by means of shared global variables, i.e., different automata can read and write variables and react depending on their values.

APPROACH OVERVIEW

The models described above are systematically constructed from the *systems requirements specification* and the *component models*. The system requirements specify the distributed system functions. A system function is defined by pre- and post-conditions, its implementation as a composite function, and the concrete component interactions that realize the function. Figure 9 shows the main steps of the approach.

Figure 8. Example of modeling component interactions[1]

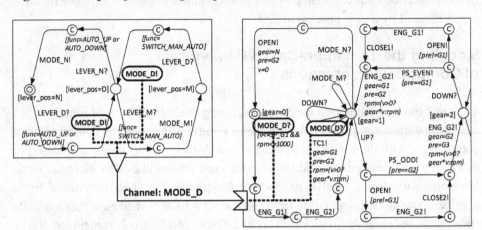

In the first step, the distributed system functions and their relations are extracted from the requirements specification and transformed into the *function graph* (1a). Based on the function graph and the requirements, the *functional model* (1b) is derived, which describes the global view of the system. The functional model is a combined CSP and B model that represents, on the one hand, the compositional aspect of functions and, on the other hand, the pre- and post-conditions for the execution of functions. Component models may be incomplete or outdated. In this case, the models can be updated based on the requirements specifications and the design decisions made during functional modeling (1c). Furthermore, the elements of the component models, i.e., states, transitions, inputs, and outputs, are annotated with function tags. The tags allow extracting those elements that are involved in the implementation of a certain distributed function.

Functional and component models are analyzed statically to retrieve model faults and inconsistencies (2). The model shall not contain any deadlocks and all relevant system states shall be reachable. Furthermore, it has to be assured that each function referred to in the high-level functional models is represented in the low-level component models, i.e., with start states, end states, and defined paths.

Based on the functional model, the *integration strategy* is defined. The integration strategy determines the system assembly order (3a) and the aspects to be covered at each integration step (3b). In this work, a function-driven approach is proposed. The system components are composed according to their relevance for the distributed functions. For each integration step, a reduced version of the functional models (3c) and component models (3d) is generated from the original test models by using the

Figure 9. Steps and elements of the testing approach

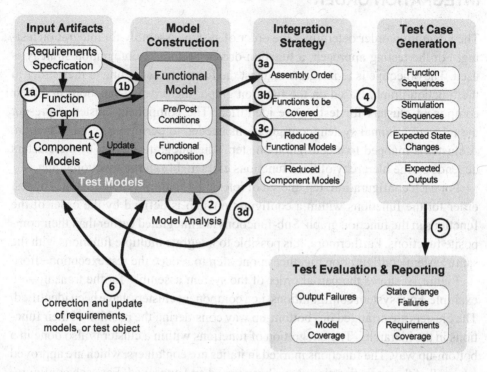

functions tags. The reduced models contain the information for deriving test cases that is specific for each integration step.

Test cases are automatically generated from the reduced models for each integration step. Different coverage criteria are proposed for the test case generation. The generation starts with the reduced functional models. Test scenarios, i.e., traces of distributed functions, are derived for each integration step. From the reduced component models, valid input-output trajectories of the assembled system are extracted. The trajectories represent abstract test cases on the component interface level. To enable the automated execution and evaluation of test cases, a test adapter has to be provided, e.g. by annotating executable test scripts. In the next step, the test results are evaluated in terms of failures and coverage of models and requirements (5). Based on the evaluation results, the modeling of artifacts and requirements may be corrected (6).

INTEGRATION ORDER

The integration order determines the order of system assembly for integration testing. For the testing approach, a function-driven bottom-up integration strategy is used. The objective is to integrate and test the functions according to their order in the function graph. Based on the function graph, the order of functions and their component clusters for testing are identified. The component clusters represent the relevant minimal system configurations needed to perform a certain function. A cluster is mapped to a configuration step. The integration order of the clusters depends on the hierarchy of their functions extracted from the function graph.

For each configuration step, the set of relevant functions is determined. The test order for the functions within a configuration step is defined by the order of the functions in the function graph. Sub-functions are integrated earlier than their composite functions. Furthermore, it is possible to integrate multiple functions with the same system configuration together in one step to reduce the test execution effort.

Figure 10 shows the partial order of the system assembly for the transmission example. Four system configurations, i.e., component clusters, have been identified. The clusters are arranged in a bottom-up way considering the position of their functions in the hierarchy. The integration of functions within a cluster is also done in a bottom-up way. The functions marked in italics are containers, which are approved when all of their sub-functions have been tested and approved. For each configuration step, the sets of involved components (marked as white boxes), required stubs (marked as gray boxes), and irrelevant components (marked as black boxes) are annotated. The annotations are related to the system structure shown in Figure 2.

In the example, cluster configuration 1 with the components *shift control, ignition,* and *shift lever* is tested first. It contains the set of safety-related system functions. The functions *Start engine* and *Lock ignition* are tested together, followed by the composite function *Ignition related*. In the next step, the functions *Park to drive* and *Drive to park* are covered. Finally, the composite function *Lever changing* is tested. After this step, all safety-related functions are tested and the container *Safety functions* is approved.

In the next step, configuration 2 (with the components *shift control, vehicle, transmission ctl,* and *clutch ctl*) is assembled and its functions are tested, which is followed by configuration 3. After testing and approving the last function *robustness tour*, the container *driving scenarios* is also approved. Thus, all system functions have been approved and the product is released to the next stage.

For each configuration step, reduced versions of the test models are created, i.e., a reduced CSP model showing the relevant functional compositions, a reduced B

Figure 10. Integration strategy for the transmission case study

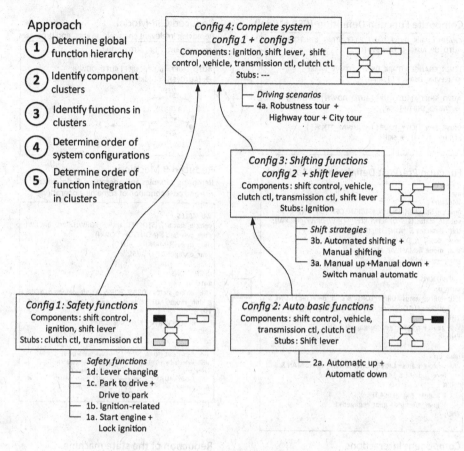

Approach

1 Determine global function hierarchy

2 Identify component clusters

3 Identify functions in clusters

4 Determine order of system configurations

5 Determine order of function integration in clusters

Config 4: Complete system
config 1 + config 3
Components : ignition, shift lever, shift control, vehicle, transmission ctl, clutch ctL
Stubs : ---

— *Driving scenarios*
— 4a. Robustness tour +
   Highway tour + City tour

Config 3: Shifting functions
config 2 + shift lever
Components : shift control, vehicle, clutch ctl, transmission ctl, shift lever
Stubs: Ignition

— *Shift strategies*
— 3b. Automated shifting +
   Manual shifting
— 3a. Manual up +Manual down +
   Switch manual automatic

Config 1: Safety functions
Components : shift control, ignition, shift lever
Stubs : clutch ctl, transmission ctl

— *Safety functions*
— 1d. Lever changing
— 1c. Park to drive +
   Drive to park
— 1b. Ignition-related
— 1a. Start engine +
   Lock ignition

Config 2: Auto basic functions
Components : shift control, vehicle, transmission ctl, clutch ctl
Stubs: Shift lever

— 2a. Automatic up +
   Automatic down

model showing the relevant functions with their pre-/post-conditions, and a reduced set of component models for showing relevant system interactions on the component level. These step-specific models are created by removing irrelevant information from the original test models.

Figure 11 shows an example of the generation of step-specific test models from the original component models for the function *automatic shifting* in integration step 2a. The CSP model is reduced by removing irrelevant channels, events, and processes. The B machine is reduced by removing state variables and operations and simplifying the pre- and post-conditions of the remaining operations. Finally, the component models are reduced by removing irrelevant events, states, and transitions.

Figure 11. Example of reduced step-specific test models[2]

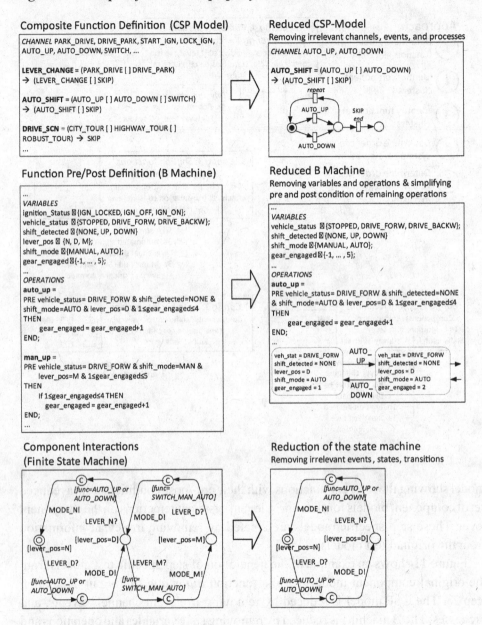

TEST CASE GENERATION

For the test case generation, an approach based on stepwise coverage and considering all three model types is proposed. Test cases are generated for each configuration

Figure 12. Test case generation and coverage criteria

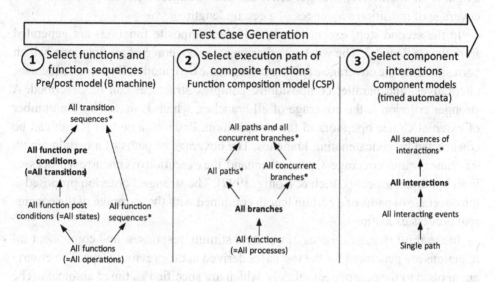

step from its reduced test models. For scalability reasons, different criteria are proposed for each model type. Depending on the type of function (basic or composite) appropriate coverage criteria are selected. Test cases for basic functions focus on the coverage of the B states space and the component interactions related to the function. Test cases for composite functions aim at covering the functional composition in CSP and the B state space affected by the functional pre- and post-conditions.

Figure 12 shows the test case generation approach for the heterogeneous test models together with the coverage criteria for each modeling notation. The graphs describe the subsumption relation of the coverage criteria, which is represented by the order in the graph. An upper criterion subsumes the lower criterion by assuring a higher coverage of the model. The criteria are globally applied at each integration step, i.e., the set of all test cases of a certain step covers function sequences, execution paths in composite functions, and component interactions. The symbol * means that the test case generation is bounded by a sequence length, path length, or the number of loop and cycle executions. The criteria that are marked in bold are proposed as minimum coverage criteria for the approach.

In the first step, sequences of functions are generated from the B model. The weakest criterion is the coverage of all functions, which is related to the coverage of all reachable operations. A stronger criterion is the coverage of all reachable transitions of the B model, which corresponds to the coverage of all functions calls and functional pre-conditions. The coverage of function sequences of a certain length is an alternative, stronger criterion. The strongest criterion proposed is the coverage of transition sequences of a certain length.

In the second step, execution paths of the composite functions are generated from the CSP model. The weakest criterion is the coverage of all functions, which corresponds to the coverage of all processes in the CSP model. By using sequences, alternatives, and parallel compositions, complex structures can be described. A stronger criterion is the coverage of all branches, which is driven by the number of external choice operators in the composition. Paths of a certain length can be constructed by concatenating branches. The coverage of paths of a certain length subsumes branch coverage. On the other hand, the execution of concurrent processes is an important aspect (Ulrich & König, 1997). The strongest criterion proposed is the coverage of paths of a certain length combined with the coverage of the concurrent process executions.

In the third step, sequences of concrete stimuli, responses, and component interactions are generated for the test cases derived in the previous steps. The criteria are applied to the component models, which are specified as timed automata. The weakest criterion generates one path through the component models for each function call derived from the CSP and B-models. Stronger criteria are the coverage of all interacting events for a certain function and the coverage of all reachable and valid component interactions provoked by the exchange of interacting events. Interactions can be concatenated to sequences of a certain length, which represents the strongest coverage criterion.

Figure 13 presents an example of a test case for the basic function *automatic upshift*. The test case generation for basic functions focuses on the coverage of functional pre and post conditions in the B state space and component interactions described in the component models. On the left hand side a trace through the B state space with the state variable changes is shown. The diagram on the right hand side shows the sequence diagram of the test case with system inputs from the environment (driver), component interactions, and expected state changes.

The test case starts in the initial system state which is defined in the original B model. In order to execute the function *automatic upshift*, the system state has to be changed. Therefore, the auxiliary function *initialize* is specified to provoke the required state change by setting the system mode to D (driving mode) and engaging the first gear. The upshift is performed when the car accelerates and a defined engine rpm threshold is achieved. The shift control interacts with the clutch control and the transmission control to execute the upshift in the transmission. Finally, an acknowledge signal is sent back to the vehicle component.

Figure 13. Example of a test case for the basic function automatic upshift

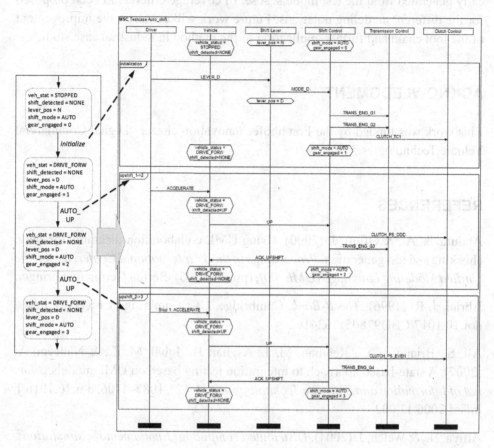

CONCLUSION AND OUTLOOK

In this chapter, a novel model-based approach for the systematic testing of distributed functions in component-based systems has been presented. The focus of the work was on the systematic construction of models for covering the system requirements and enabling the automated generation of test cases. The test problem was solved by a heterogeneous modeling approach consisting of three models for describing the function composition, the pre- and post-conditions of functions, and the component behavior. For each model type, an appropriate notation was proposed. The modeling notations can be changed according to the system properties and the test designers' expertise with the notations. An approach for the systematic construction of the models from the system requirements was presented. The stepwise system assembly is supported by a function-driven integration order. Test cases are automatically generated from the test models. A set of coverage criteria has been proposed for the different modeling notations. Future work will comprise the improvement of the tool chain and further application of the method in industrial case studies.

ACKNOWLEDGMENT

This work was funded by the Fraunhofer innovation cluster "Digital Commercial Vehicle Technologies."

REFERENCES

Abdurazik, A., & Offutt, J. (2000). Using UML collaboration diagrams for static checking and test generation. *Proceedings of the 3rd International Conference on the Unified Modeling Language (UML '00)*, (pp. 383-395). Berlin, Germany: Springer.

Abrial, J.-R. (1996). *The B-Book*. Cambridge, UK: Cambridge University Press. doi:10.1017/CBO9780511624162

Ali, S., Briand, L. C., Rehman, M. J., Asghar, H., Iqbal, M. Z., & Nadeem, A. (2007). A state-based approach to integration testing based on UML models. *Journal of Information and Software Technology*, *49*(11-12), 1087–1106. doi:10.1016/j.infsof.2006.11.002

Attiya, H., & Welch, J. (2004). *Distributed computing: Fundamentals, simulations, and advanced topics*. Wiley-Interscience.

Basanieri, F., & Bertolino, A. (2000). A practical approach to UML-based derivation of integration tests. *Proceedings of the Software Quality Week (QWE2000)*.

Benz, S. (2007). Combining test case generation for component and integration testing. *Proceedings of 3rd International Workshop on Advances in Model-Based Testing*, (pp. 23-33). London, UK: ACM Press.

Biagosch, A., Knupfer, S., Radtke, P., Näher, U., & Zielke, A. (2005). *Automotive electronics - Managing innovations on the road*. McKinsey Brochure.

Bochmann, G., & Petrenko, A. (1994). Protocol testing: Review of methods and relevance for software testing. *Proceedings of the ACM International Symposium on Software Testing and Analysis (ISSTA '94)*, (pp. 109-124). ACM-Press.

Borner, L. (2010). *Integrationstest: Testprozess, Testfokus und Integrationsreihenfolge*. PhD thesis, Heidelberg (Germany).

Briand, L. C., & Labiche, Y. (2001). A UML-based approach to system testing. *Proceedings of the 4th International Conference on The Unified Modeling Language, Modeling Languages, Concepts, and Tools*, (pp. 194-208). Berlin, Germany: Springer.

Butler, M. J., & Leuschel, M. (2005). Combining CSP and B for specification and property verification. *Proceeding of the International Symposium of Formal Methods Europe, Lecture Notes in Computer Science vol. 3582*, (pp. 221–236). Berlin, Germany: Springer.

Cabral, G., & Sampaio, A. (2008). Formal specification generation from requirement documents. [ENTCS]. *Journal of Electronic Notes in Theoretical Computer Science, 195*, 171–188. doi:10.1016/j.entcs.2007.08.032

de Alfaro, L., & Henzinger, T. A. (2001). Interface automata, *Proceedings of the 9th Annual Symposium on Foundations of Software Engineering (FSE)*, (pp. 109-120). ACM-Press.

de Figueiredo, J. C. A., Andrade, W. L., & Machado, P. D. L. (2006). Generating interaction test cases for mobile phone systems from use case specifications. *SIGSOFT Software Engineering Notes, 31*(6), 1–10. doi:10.1145/1218776.1218788

Desmoulin, A., & Viho, C. (2007). A new method for interoperability test generation. *Proceedings of the TestCom/FATES 2007*, (pp. 58-73). Berlin, Germany: Springer.

Fan, X., Shu, J., Liu, L., & Liang, Q. (2009). Test case generation from UML sub-activity and activity diagram. *Proceedings of the 2nd International Symposium on Electronic Commerce and Security (ISECS '09)*, (pp. 244-248). Washington, DC: IEEE Computer Society.

Fraikin, F., & Leonhardt, T. (2002). SeDiTeC - Testing based on sequence diagrams. *Proceedings of the 17th IEEE International Conference on Automated Software Engineering*, IEEE Computer Society, (pp. 261-266).

Gallagher, L., & Offutt, J. (2006). Automatically testing interacting software components. *Proceedings of the International workshop on Automation of software test (AST '06)*, (pp. 57-63). New York, NY: ACM Press.

Harrold, M. J., & Soffa, M. L. (1989). Interprocedual data flow testing. *Proceedings of the ACM SIGSOFT '89 Third Symposium on Software Testing, Analysis, and Verification*, (pp. 158-167). New York, NY: ACM.

Hartmann, J., Imoberdorf, C., & Meisinger, M. (2000). UML-based integration testing. *Proceedings of the ACM SIGSOFT International Symposium on Software Testing and Analysis (ISSTA '00)*, (pp. 60-70). New York, NY: ACM Press.

Hashim, N. L., Ramakrishnan, S., & Schmidt, H. W. (2007). Architectural test coverage for component-based integration testing. *Proceedings of the International Conference on Quality Software (QSIC 2007)*, IEEE Computer Society, (pp. 262-267).

Henninger, O. (1997). On test case generation from asynchronously communicating state machines. *Proceeding of the 10th International Workshop on Testing of Communicating Systems*. Chapman & Hall.

Hoare, C. A. R. (1985). *Communicating sequential processes*. Prentice Hall.

IEC 61508. (2010). *IEC 61508: 2010 - Functional safety of electrical/electronic/programmable electronic safety related systems.*

Jin, Z., & Offutt, J. (1998). Coupling-based criteria for integration testing. *Journal of Software Testing, Verification, and Reliability*, 8(3), 133–154. doi:10.1002/(SICI)1099-1689(1998090)8:3<133::AID-STVR162>3.0.CO;2-M

Jin, Z., & Offutt, J. (2001). Deriving tests from software architectures. *Proceedings of the 12th International Symposium on Software Reliability Engineering (ISSRE '01)*, (pp. 308-313). Washington, DC: IEEE Computer Society.

Jorgensen, P. C., & Erickson, C. (1994). Object-oriented integration testing. [New York, NY: ACM Press.]. *Communications of the ACM, 37*(9), 30–38. doi:10.1145/182987.182989

Koppol, P. V., Carver, R. H., & Tai, K. C. (2002). Incremental integration testing of concurrent programs. *IEEE Transactions on Software Engineering, 28*(6), 607–623. doi:10.1109/TSE.2002.1010062

Lanet, J. L., & Requet, A. (1998). Formal proof of smart card applets correctness. *Proceeding of the Third Smart Card Research and Advanced Application Conference (CARDIS '98)*, (pp. 85-97). Berlin, Germany: Springer.

Lee, N. H., Kim, T. H., & Cha, S. D. (2002). Construction of global finite state machine for testing task interactions written in message sequence charts. *Proceedings of the 14th International Conference on Software Engineering and Knowledge Engineering (SEKE 2002)*, (pp. 369-376). ACM Press.

Linnenkugel, U., & Müllerburg, M. (1990). Test data selection criteria for (software) integration testing. *Proceedings of the 1st International Conference on Systems Integration*, (pp. 709-717). Piscataway, NJ: IEEE Press.

Machado, P. D. L., Figueiredo, J. C. A., Lima, E. F. A., Barbosa, A. E. V., & Lima, H. S. (2007). Component-based integration testing from UML interaction diagrams. *IEEE International Conference on Systems, Man and Cybernetics (SMC 2007)*, (pp. 2679-2686). Washington, DC: IEEE Computer Society.

Mathworks. (2011, May 15). *Mathworks™ website: Simulink - Simulation and model-based design*. Retrieved from http://www.mathworks.com/products/simulink/

Muccini, H., Bertolino, A., & Inverardi, P. (2004). Using software architecture for code testing. *IEEE Transactions on Software Engineering, 30*(3), 160–171. doi:10.1109/TSE.2004.1271170

Naunheimer, H., Bertsche, B., Ryborz, J., & Novak, W. (2011). *Automotive transmissions: Fundamentals, selection, design and application* (2nd ed.). Berlin, Germany: Springer.

Nogueira, S., Sampaio, A., & Mota, A. (2008). Guided test generation from CSP models. *Proceedings of the 5th International Colloquium on Theoretical Aspects of Computing*, (pp. 258-273). Berlin, Germany: Springer.

Pelliccione, P., Muccini, H., Bucchiarone, A., & Facchini, F. (2005). TeStor: Deriving test sequences from model-based specifications. *Proceedings of the 8th International SIGSOFT Symposium on Component-Based Software Engineering*, (pp. 267-282). Berlin, Germany: Springer.

Pilskalns, O., Andrews, A., Ghosh, S., & France, R. (2003). Rigorous testing by merging structural and behavioral UML representations. *Proceedings of the 6th International Conference on the Unified Modeling Language*, (pp. 234-248). Berlin, Germany: Springer.

Pretschner, A., Slotosch, O., Aiglstorfer, E., & Kriebel, S. (2004). Model based testing for real--The in house card case study. [STTT]. *International Journal on Software Tools for Technology Transfer, 5*(2), 140–157. doi:10.1007/s10009-003-0128-3

Prowell, S. J., & Poore, J. H. (2003). Foundations of sequence-based software specification. *IEEE Transactions on Software Engineering, 29*(5), 417–429. doi:10.1109/TSE.2003.1199071

Reza, H., & Grant, E. S. (2007). A method to test concurrent systems using architectural specification. *The Journal of Supercomputing, 39*(3), 347–357. doi:10.1007/s11227-006-0017-0

Robinson-Mallett, C., Hierons, R., Poore, J., & Liggesmeyer, P. (2008). Using communication coverage criteria and partial model generation to assist software integration testing. *Software Quality Journal, 16*(2), 185–211. doi:10.1007/s11219-007-9036-1

Rothermel, G., & Harrold, M. J. (1994). Selecting tests and identifying test coverage requirements for modified software. *International Symposium on Software Testing and Analysis (ISSTA 94),* (pp. 169-184). New York, NY: ACM Press.

Saglietti, F., & Pinte, F. (2010). Automated unit and integration testing for component-based software systems. *Proceedings of the International Workshop on Security and Dependability for Resource Constrained Embedded Systems* (S&D4RCES '10). New York, NY: ACM Press.

Schätz, B., & Pfaller, C. (2010). Integrating component tests to system tests. [ENTCS]. *Electronic Notes in Theoretical Computer Science, 260,* 225–241. doi:10.1016/j.entcs.2009.12.040

Seol, S., Kim, M., Kang, S., & Ryu, J. (2003). Fully automated interoperability test suite derivation for communication protocols. *Computer Networks: The International Journal of Computer and Telecommunications Networking, 43*(6), 735–759.

Spillner, A. (1995). Test criteria and coverage measures for software integration testing. *Software Quality Journal, 4*(4), 275–286. doi:10.1007/BF00402648

Ulrich, A., & König, H. (1997). Specification-based testing of concurrent systems. *Proceedings of the Joint International Conference Formal Description Techniques and Protocol Specification, Testing and Verification (FORTE/PSTV97),* (pp. 7–22). Chapman & Hall.

Utting, M., Pretschner, A., & Legeard, B. (2011). A taxonomy of model-based testing. *Journal of Software Testing. Verification and Reliability, 21*(2), 72–90.

Wang, Z., Wu, J., & Yin, X. (2004). Generating interoperability test sequence for distributed test architecture: A generic formal framework. *Proceedings of the International Conference on Information Networking (ICOIN 2004),* (pp. 1135-1144). Berlin, Germany: Springer.

Wieczorek, S., Kozyura, V., Roth, A., Leuschel, M., Bendisposto, J., Plagge, D., & Schieferdecker, S. (2009). Applying model checking to generate model-based integration tests from choreography models. *Proceedings of the 21st International Conference on Testing of Software and Communication Systems and 9th International FATES Workshop (TESTCOM '09/FATES '09),* (pp. 179-194). Berlin, Germany: Springer.

Wu, Y., Pan, D., & Chen, M.-H. (2001). Techniques for testing component-based software. *Proceeding of the 7th International Conference on Engineering of Complex Computer Systems (ICECCS 2001)*, (pp. 222-232). IEEE Computer Society.

Zhu, H., & He, X. (2000). A methodology of testing high-level Petri nets. *Journal of Information and Software Technology*, *44*(8), 473–489. doi:10.1016/S0950-5849(02)00048-4

ENDNOTES

[1] derived from example in (Robinson-Mallett et al., 2008, fig.21)
[2] component models are derived from example in (Robinson-Mallett et al., 2008, fig.21)

Chapter 9
Testing E-Learning Websites

Kamaljeet Sandhu
University of New England, Australia

ABSTRACT

Testing e-learning websites may provide an insight to characteristics that are useful and others that are not so useful to the users. From a technical or systems development perspective, such understanding may not be known till it is finally tested and used by the users. Therefore this research aims to explore the effectiveness of e-learning websites in relation to user's perceptions (either positive or negative) that are developed when interacting with e-learning system and the features that they have to use.

INTRODUCTION

User's engaged in web-based learning activities tend to focus on prior information experience and perception, especially from the offline environment. The effect of information on user experience in web-based learning on first time user's compared to the frequent user's will vary, a user with no experience can form high (or low) perception, especially via word of mouth communications. Such perceptions may behave differently from those developed via experience. The concept of flow is important because it has a clear set of antecedent conditions and consequences that have implications for web-based learning. User's information experience on a website, its impact, retention of that web-based learning experience can be related to the flow concept.

DOI: 10.4018/978-1-4666-0089-8.ch009

For the flow state to be experienced the user must perceive skills and challenges to be in balance and above a critical threshold and the user must be paying attention. That is a user must be in state of learning. Hoffman and Novak (1996) suggest that the consequences of flow in web-based environments relates to increased learning, increased exploratory and participatory behaviours, and more positive subjective experiences, that a critical objective of a commercial website is to facilitate the flow experience. Karahanna et al. (1999) suggest that user's acquire personal experience and their own source of evaluative information in using the information system. Such an experience can have a strong affect on the user in remembering their learning experience on a particular website.

User information experience in web-based systems learning is an important area that is gradually growing with introduction and adoption of web-based technology (i.e. WebCT, Firstclass, and Blackboard). The information available in web-based systems learning may be one of the determinants which direct the user in achieving the desired objectives that form the purpose of using the system. The user information requirements may be based from prior experience in similar or related traditional learning environment. Information search form the initial need in the activity to achieve the desired objectives, and hence the acquisition of information experience process. Information if not available to users in e-learning or traditional learning environments may direct the user in adopting the search process based on experience.

Web-based user services are generally perceived as being successful, but there has been little evaluation of how well the web meets its user's' primary information requirements (D'Ambra and Rice 2001). The freedom and flexibility offered by the Internet allow users to connect to other websites of their interest and at the same time build upon their e-learning experience on the web. A number of researchers suggested that flow is a useful construct for describing interactions with websites (Csikszentmihalyi 1975; Johnson and Mathews 1997; Zeithaml et al. 1993; Zeithaml et al. 2000; and Chea and Lou 2008). Flow has been described as "the process of optimal experience" (Csikszentmihalyi and LeFevre 1990) achieved when sufficiently motivated user perceives a balance between their skills and challenges of the interaction, together with focused attention (Hoffman and Novak 1996).

This study assumes that user's experience with information already exists in the traditional environment (i.e., offline). Understanding the traditional learning complexities of user experience with information and transforming it to the web-based environment is a challenge for both practitioners and researchers. The dimension and scale of such complexity in terms of technology and its alliance with information may provide an integration point where technology requirements may meet with the user's learning experience. Defining user learning experience with information is not an easy and straightforward process. Rather developing an approach to studying the learning experience process on the basis of web-based learning and user interaction is suggested. This paper specifically investigates issues related to user learning experiences in web-based learning adoption and the process involving continued use of web-based learning services. With technology constantly changing it will subsequently have an effect on the user's learning experience and perception.

Davidow and Uttal (1989) suggest user's expectation is formed by many uncontrollable factors, from the experience of user's…to a user's psychological state. It is argued that a user web-based learning experience is formed and based on wider range of prior experiences that may be recalled or narrowed in a similar situation. The flow of information over the Internet is faster and communication between user's leads in enhanced learning. Understanding user's web-based learning experience and perception solely on the basis of online or offline experience would tend to limit the research dimension; rather a combination approach is adopted.

RESEARCH METHODOLOGY

The aim of the study is to investigate the adoption of web-based learning on websites amongst users. This led to the development of converging lines of inquiry, a process of triangulation (Yin 1994). In the first instance discussions were held together with three senior staff members involved in implementing the web-based learning project. They included the executive director, IT Manager, and an outside Consultant. In the second round separate individual interviews are conducted with these participants. The third round of interviews was conducted with the admissions manager and separate individual interviews with two other staff members. Altogether six separate interviews with participants were held. Though the participant's gender is not a major factor for introspection, it coincided to balance, three males and three females. In the first round interviews the data collected were compared with the second round and third round interview data, for consistency, clarity and accuracy of the information.

Interview data were also compared to test for the factors having effect on users with high and low performance in learning how to use the web-based system. This provided the advantage of not duplicating the data with just one set of evidence. The discussions and interviews were open-ended (Yin 1994), the researcher in the beginning provided the topic, and the respondents are probed of their opinion about the events. The questions are directed towards user's learning experience with the web-based system. This led the users in reflecting their recent learning experiences with the system and demonstrating its effectiveness in the web-based task. It provides the opportunity of capturing rich information that is fresh and part of the user-learning interface within the web-based system. It not only provides information about the user's learning experience, but also demonstrates the boundaries of the web-based learning system, in other words the scope of the system in providing enhanced learning is clearly reflected from the data the user's provided to what the system was capable of doing within the parameters. This approach took into consideration the users and the system context in understanding the web-based learning process. It provides important information from the user's perspective in the terms of the learning process available in the web-based system.

THE CASE STUDY

The case study examines the testing of web-based framework of the University of Australia (not the real name). International students have the option to lodge an admission application through either of: web-based e-service on the Internet, phone, fax, or in person. On receiving the application a decision is made by the staff on the admission status. Within this process the department is implementing an electronic delivery of its services on the website.

Web-based e-service has been in use for the last two and half years. The complete process involves students making the application and the staff processing applications on the website. The staff is currently using the web-based e-service and the paper-based system in conducting the tasks. Transition from paper-based to web-based e-service is believed by the department to be a significant step in the direction of moving the complete student admission process over the website and gradually removing the paper-based system. The users learning experience in adopting the web-based system is focus of attention in the study.

TESTING USER'S INFORMATION EXPERIENCE ON WEBSITES

The staff and Management acceptance of the e-Services system and its continued usage in processing international student's admission applications is considered a major organisational requirement to meet Departmental targets in the university's Strategic Plans. However, the Executive Director noted:

"One of our problems is that we have a lot of trouble with our staff coping with the new e-Services system. To get them to work with the two systems is troublesome for them. But actually we have 'realised' that the e-Services system is part of everyday work. And it probably deserves more attention instead of paper-based print applications in many ways. Our e-Services practices had to change."

Electronic services system were perceived by Management to provide benefits including less paperwork, quick delivery of information, easy editing and updating of information. Rogers (1995) argue that attributes of the innovation should be compatible to the organisation. At the same time Management realised that new systems challenge staff on implementation. Rogers (1995) suggests that complexity of systems implementation, trialability of the system, and ease of observability are the perceived characteristics of innovation. Through prior analysis of the situation, the Management's perception of introducing the new technology was based on the belief that such technology would have a positive impact on staff work when the advantages were reflected in their work.

The user perception of web electronic service is a burden and acted as a barrier to their work. The users learnt that it increased the workload, slowed the work process, and brought in complexity to the task. The department did not implement electronic services or introduce technology into jobs at the same time. The effect on user learning experience in using the e-service is not estimated when the system was being developed. Understanding the task sequence from start to finish, and integrating those functions into web-based learning process is missing. It lacks coherence. Individual users did not have consistent skills in learning how to use the system because of differing levels of expertise (i.e., user category). Specific expertise needed for conducting the task was lacking.

The users were asked to enter all information directly to the web. To expect a user to start using an electronic service without prior learning the user's experience is not perceive to be appropriate. Despite providing regular training the user resistance to use the electronic system increased. The following quote support this notion:

"There are quite a few fields where we can't use the web-based e-services."

Martin (1991) suggest that user learning experience evolves, or ranges, from naïve (no system knowledge) through inexperienced to competent and finally to expert. On such basis user's can be divided into following categories: novice, intermediate, and experienced. It is important to remember that different categories of user's learning experience vary at different stages in performing the task. It is anticipated the user's are in a learning process and shift from one mode to another, with experience sliding up or down on the learning swing and the user experience varies, till they reach a point (see Figure 1, point A) where the learning experience flow is at the optimum level in doing the task.

Different task requires different skills when done on paper, doing it electronically requires different experience with information and knowing what was happening beyond the user's computer screen. In the paper-based system, it was known to the user how different process of a task and where information was stored and

Figure 1. Learning-experience swing

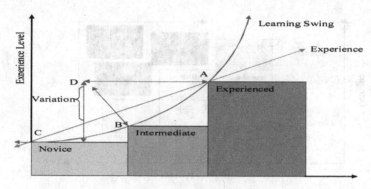

A- Optimum point; B- Improving point; C- Learning starting point;
D- Experience variation point

retained when needed, such as the filing, organizing, storing of documentation was systematically interconnected, in case of electronic service little was known by way what constituted as web-based e-service task process beyond the computer screen. Proper documentation providing information to the user's for referencing were either missing or unknown. The users didn't have learning experience in how to operate the system. One participant mentioned:

"User's had no confidence in the system and decision making." Sandhu and Corbitt (2002)

The assimilation and dissimulation of learning experience in conducting the web-based e-service task may provide the user an option in retaining that experience which can be remembered easily. A participant claimed:

"Need to **rely on paper documents** *and another database to complete the task... have to use all..."*

The information disclosed by the participant point to the fact that the web-based system was short from offering the user a learning process which if available would have gradually build on user's prior information experience, rather the user's were juggling with multiple sources to collect the information that was needed in completing the web-based task.

The experience attained in online or offline environment is likely to direct the user in retaining the most recent learning experience because this would be much easier to recall, provided that the information is relevant to the current context.

Figure 2. User experience grid (Adapted from Zemke and Connellan (2001))

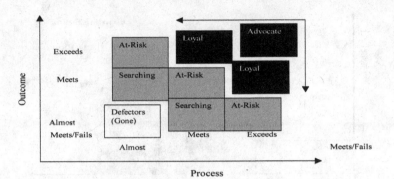

Zemke and Connellan (2001) posit that each learning experience, regardless of whether it's online or offline, sets the stage of expectations for future interactions. The user tends to focus on ease of use (more than the usefulness), familiarity, skills needed, website-to-website learning comparison, and on the task complexity. The task complexities can be defined in terms of navigation on the website, information search, transaction processing, and online support (i.e., help). A participant related this in terms of the web-based system as:

*"System **is not intelligent** to check simple errors like spell checks, grammar checks..."*

The statement referred to the user's learning expectation of the systems capabilities in terms of their prior experience. The user's had used this functionality in another system and expected to match with their prior information experience in the web-based system. The user's perceived experience about the current system being below its standard and not helpful in doing the task. It did not meet the user's information requirement for the task.

Zemke and Connellan (2001) developed a model (Customer Experience Grid, see Figure 2) to capture the sum total of a user learning experiences. The vertical axis of the user experience grid is the outcome the user receives, and offered on a website. On the horizontal axis the user's goes through the learning process to obtain the outcome, such as navigating the website, printing out information, looking for pricing, ordering a product etc. User compares similar outcomes on other website or in an offline environment in user transaction process. Zemke and Connellan (2001) claim that the process – the way they are served – is what makes it into learning experience, positively or negatively for users.

If the user's needs are not met on the process and outcome axes, they tend to go elsewhere, and hence called defectors. Similarly if the user's needs are met on one dimension and unmet on another, they are actively searching for an alternative on another website or in offline environment. This is supported in our study; the participants reported switching to the paper-based system, as the learning process and its outcome was easier to understand and follow. Zemke and Connellan (2001) suggest that to succeed on the website, it is important to consistently manage the total user learning experience (i.e. information experience) in the categories in upper three (black) boxes (see Figure 2). They claim to have successfully used the model at Dell Computers in understanding the total user's interaction. However, there is no quantitative data and analysis of the model that suggest how well the model works across web-based e-learning.

The user's interaction in computer mediated environment is an intense flow being a continuous variable ranging from none to intense (Berthon and Davies 1999; Foulkes 1994; Hasher and Zacks 1984; Chea and Lou 2008; and Chellappan 2008). The user's purpose of visit to the website may be perceived as more encouraging of exploratory behaviors than others (Trevino and Webster 1992). If the website meets the primary information need of the user, it may positively affect the user in further progressing with the activity leading to a state of intense flow. It is likely that user's developing a high flow will visit those websites more regularly and for longer duration (Berthon et al. 1996; and Berthon and Davies 1999). The state of intense learning flow was either missing or faced obstacles. The users weren't able to proceed with the task in the electronic environment. User may tend to reflect on the past experience for future interaction. A participant reflected this in a statement:

*"The system is **not 100% ready**... " "Adds on to the task...increases our task load."*

It was believed that the users were losing learning interest in the web-based system due to continuously being put down. To retain interest in a site, there should be enjoyment on the part of the user during the interaction of the site. A participant statement highlights this concern:

*"If the system can be fixed it can be fixed, otherwise we will **continue using it as it is**."*

It was known to the users that if the web-based system didn't work they could depend on an alternative system (i.e., paper-bases system) in doing the task. The shifting of learning experience between the paper-based and web-based emerged as a continuum on which the user viewed the web-based system effectiveness before proceeding with the task, which was based on an understanding from past experience. If the user felt the task could be (not only) performed and also completed they went ahead with the web-based system; otherwise they opted for the paper-based system. Any adverse feelings were filtered towards learning the web-based system at that time affecting the decision making to use the web-based system. Those claims were supported by participant statements:

*"**Verifying information** on the Internet is not possible; we still have to check student's education credential in paper form"*

*"Site needs to **be improved with better features and functionality** that will make it **easier for us to use**."*

In the flow state, the user's focus or attention is narrowed to a limited stimulus field, and irrelevant thoughts are filtered out. Csikszentmihalyi (1975) suggest that in a flow state the person becomes absorbed in the activity, while increasing his awareness of his own mental processes in the interaction with the web, the computer screen can serve as the limited stimulus field, focusing the individual's attention (Trevino and Webster 1992). The user faced hurdles during the flow state affecting their learning in doing the task. A participant expressed this:

*"Due to time out period that disconnect, the user has to reenter all the information once again...this **creates duplicity of information** for us...as the same user is reapplying again and it is hard to differentiate between the same application."*

As users become more frequent users they place more reliance on learning from internal sources (memory) than external sources (advertisements, word of mouth, etc) (Johnson and Mathews 1997). Many researchers have noted the ways in which memory is biased (Foulkes 1994). Frequent events are easier to recall than infrequent ones (Hasher and Zacks 1984). Therefore remembering an event is biased by the availability of information within memory (Johnson and Mathews 1997). The mechanical process of conducting the task with the available tools on the website forms a basis of interactivity for the user and is similar to recalling frequent and infrequent events. Prior research suggests the application of tools to vary across different users from novice to advance (see Martin 1991).

The development of intelligent agents guiding the user in conducting the task from start to completion tends to improve the user learning interface and reduce uncertainty in learning and problematic experience. This has led to smart software taking over the task, reducing and limiting user's interactivity with the task, and completion of task within a few ticks and clicks of a mouse. The whole process tends to be reduced, removing the intricacies the user can encounter, and at the same time standardizing the users web-based learning across all domain and user developing a positive experience.

The intelligent agent capability in storing and remembering user's transaction details, and displaying on revisits has also reduced the user's need to keep paper record of transaction, making it easier for the user in conducting the task with the availability of past, current and future information records available online. This has an effect on the user learning experience in using the traditional service where the information available is not swift and quick. A reliance on internal search means that the user's memory will have considerable influence on the formation of "learning expectancies" (Foulkes 1994). Hasher and Zacks (1984) argue that the accuracy with which people encode information increases with the frequency of encoding. Although their research focuses on consumers' exposure to advertising, a parallel can be drawn with consumers' exposure to web-based e-learning.

Similarly, Zeithaml et al. (1993;2000) in their study pointed to information gap on the basis of users learning experience with website that leads to providing incomplete or in accurate information to the users. It is anticipated that the application of intelligent agents in user interactivity will further enhance and integrate into the user learning experience with information, and become part of the user guidance in conducting web-based task. A participant directed the claim:

"If any information is missed, there is no way to check, there are no **compulsory fields** *to inform of missing information."*

Meuter et al. (2000) report that 80% of the customer complaints are made in person to the company, either by phone or by visiting a service facility. This suggests that the when the user is effected with a problematic experience on websites, and to resolve the issue, the user adopts the traditional approach of face-to-face interaction, rather than online approach. The participant in the study evaluated the web-based task, and weighted its effectiveness by comparing it to the paper-based service.

"We can't offer admission letters to higher degree research students on the web-based system, as letter templates not there; we have to offer it on paper."

The degree of tolerance for web-based system may be intense due to the competitor's service being a click away (Zeithaml et al 2000). The users are quick in changing over to paper-based service, which is believed competing with the web-based system. Thus user's tolerance level for web-based system, their immediate reactions to the service failure and their consecutive behavior, are interrelated and forms part of the user learning experience. A participant expressed:

"If the system can be fixed it can be fixed, otherwise we will **continue using as it is.**"

When the web-based system fails it has fallen outside the user's zone of tolerance (Zeithaml et al. 1993). So far nothing is known about user's tolerance levels of web-based systems, or the user's propensity to complain about online service failures (Riel et al. 2001), and user's reaction to it. Zeithaml et al. (2000) claim that customers have no expectations, customers have been found to compare web-based service to competitor's services and to brick and mortar stores (Meuter et al. 2000 and Szymanski and Hise 2000). The degree of user's tolerance is not known. Another participant states;

"They are frightened for asking help if needed…rather they ask for help than provide wrong information."

It seemed there are considerable obstacles the user's developed in their learning experience to use web-based system.

CONCLUSION

The case study data shows that the both staff and the Management were excited about the web-based e-services system in terms of user-work management. Those inspirations were short-lived when the web e-services system did not meet with the staff expectations. The perceived usefulness of the web-based e-services system in this case was not considered an important factor as the users perceptions were based on that system, one that was not capable of delivering.

The level of interaction from traditional services such as paper-based to web-based services and simultaneous use of both has laid a new set of implications for the universities, organizations, government, consumers, practitioners, and researchers. In understanding the new set of implications, initial research revealed that though uptake and use of this new innovation has been positive, its acceptance and continued use has been limited. The available research though identifies some main issues it lacks in understanding the impact of the critical success factors. Further research will attempt to explore a more structured understanding to web-based systems user learning within a referenced theoretical construct.

In line with the preceding discussion it is suggested that web-based systems adoption takes into account the user learning experience that develops with user interaction with the system. Though prior studies even adopted the general technology user models like the TAM model (Davis 1989; Davis et al. 1989; and Davis 1993), which is of significance, they do not take into account the user context issues on a commercial situation basis. To study web-based system from a user learning perspective centered context and combining it with adoption and acceptance models may enhance that understanding. To explore the context further, issues related to situation specific personalization of individual user learning needs in online and offline environment may be used to produce evaluation guidelines that would facilitate the adoption and continuation process.

Earlier studies investigated the adoption of web-based system in different contexts, but not provide insight into acceptance and continued use by users. Though a consumer may use a web-based system for the first time, its continued use relates to the success. The user's web-based learning experience may form an impression of the system in terms of how easy or how difficult it is to operate the system.

From the preceding discussion it has been clear that web-based system adoption is not a simple and straightforward process. Rapid development in technology delivery is gradually shaping the consumer learning in uptake and usage of this new innovation.

REFERENCES

Berthon, P., Pitt, L., & Watson, R. T. (1996). The World Wide Web as an advertising medium: toward an understanding of conversion efficiency. *Journal of Advertising Research, 36*(1), 43–45.

Berthon, P., & Davies, T. (1999). Going with the flow: Websites and customer involvement. *Internet Research: Electronic Networking Applications and Policy, 9*(2), 109–116. doi:10.1108/10662249910264873

Csikszentmihalyi, M. (1975). *Beyond boredom and anxiety*. San Francisco, CA: Jossey-Bass.

Csikszentmihalyi, M., & LeFevre, J. (1990). Optimal experience in work and leisure. *Journal of Personality and Social Psychology, 56*(5), 815–822. doi:10.1037/0022-3514.56.5.815

D'Ambra, J., & Rice, R. E. (2001). Emerging factors in user evaluation of the World Wide Web. *Information & Management, 38*, 373–384. doi:10.1016/S0378-7206(00)00077-X

Davidow, W. H., & Uttal, B. (1989). Service companies: Focus or falter. *Harvard Business Review*, (July/August): 17–34.

Davis, F. D. (1989). Perceived usefulness, perceived ease of use, and user acceptance of Information Technology. *Management Information Systems Quarterly, 13*(2), 319–340. doi:10.2307/249008

Davis, F. D., Bagozzi, R. P., & Warshaw, P. R. (1989). User acceptance of computer technology: A comparison of two theoretical models. *Management Science, 34*(8), 982–1002. doi:10.1287/mnsc.35.8.982

Davis, F. D. (1993). User acceptance of Information Technology: Systems characteristics, user perceptions and behavioral impacts. *International Journal of Man-Machine Studies, 38*(3), 475–487. doi:10.1006/imms.1993.1022

Foulkes, V. S. (1994). How consumers predict service quality: what do they expect? In Rust, R. T., & Oliver, R. L. (Eds.), *Service quality, new directions in theory and practice*. Beverly Hills, CA: Sage.

Hasher, L., & Zacks, R. T. (1984). Automatic processing of fundamental information: The case of frequency of occurrence. *The American Psychologist, 39*, 1372–1388. doi:10.1037/0003-066X.39.12.1372

Hoffman, D. L., & Novak, T. P. (1996). Marketing in hypermedia computer-mediated environments: Conceptual foundations. *JMR, Journal of Marketing Research, 60*(7), 50–68.

Johnson, C., & Mathews, B. P. (1997). The influence of experience on service expectations. *International Journal of Service Industry Management, 8*(4), 290–305. doi:10.1108/09564239710174381

Karahanna, E., & Straub, D, W., & Chervany, N. L. (1999). Information tecHnology adoption across time: A cross sectional comparison of pre-adoption and post-adoption beliefs. *Management Information Systems Quarterly, 23*(2), 183–213. doi:10.2307/249751

Martin, M. P. (1991). *Analysis and design of business information systems*. New York: Macmillan Publishing Company.

Meuter, M. L., Ostrom, A. L., Roundtree, R. I., & Bitner, M. J. (2000). Self-service technologies: Understanding customer satisfaction with technology-based service encounters. *Journal of Marketing, 64*, 50–64. doi:10.1509/jmkg.64.3.50.18024

Riel, A. C. R., Liljander, V., & Jurriens, P. (2001). Exploring consumer evaluations of e-services: A portal site. *International Journal of Service Industry Management, 12*(4), 359–377. doi:10.1108/09564230110405280

Rogers, E. M. (1995). *Diffusion of innovations*. New York, NY: The Free Press.

Sandhu, K., & Corbitt, B. (2002). *WG8.6: Exploring an understanding of electronic service end-user adoption*. Sydney, Australia: The International Federation for Information Processing.

Szymanski, D. M., & Hise, R. T. (2000). E-satisfaction: An initial examination. *Journal of Retailing, 76*(3), 309–322. doi:10.1016/S0022-4359(00)00035-X

Trevino, L. K., & Webster, J. (1992). Flow in computer-mediated communication: electronic mail and voice evaluation. *Communication Research, 19*(2), 539–573. doi:10.1177/009365092019005001

Yin, R. K. (1994). *Case study research: Design and methods* (2nd ed.). Sage Publications.

Zemke, R., & Connellan, T. (2001). *E-service: 24 ways to keep your customers when the competition is just a click away*. American Management Association.

Zeithaml, V. A., Berry, L., & Parasuraman, A. (1993). The nature and determinants of customer expectations of service. *Journal of the Academy of Marketing Science, 21*(1), 1–12. doi:10.1177/0092070393211001

Zeithaml, V. A., Parasuraman, A., & Malhotra, A. (2000). *A conceptual framework for understanding e-service quality: Implications for future research and managerial practice*. Marketing Science Institute, Working paper, Report no: 00-115.

Chapter 10
Testing E–Services

Kamaljeet Sandhu
University of New England, Australia

ABSTRACT

This research is about testing the effectiveness of Web-based e-services system. The problem facing the department is the staff resistance to accept and use e-services in their work. There are technical issues that impact negatively on staff users of the e-services system. Case analysis reveals that there are wider issues stemming from the interaction with the system which has a low impact on e-services acceptance. E-services drivers such as user training and experience, motivation, perceived usefulness and ease of use, acceptance, and usage were not clearly understood by the technical development team, hence not integrated when implementing the e-services system.

1. INTRODUCTION

E-Services system are being rapidly introduced on websites with the expectation that the users are going to utilise them (Khalifa and Liu 2003). The application of e- Services system on websites is widely expected to be a more effective, efficient and productive communication for businesses and users alike (Rust and Lemon 2001). However, whether or not it leads to continued use of e-services is not known. One of the purposes of using e-services is that it provides instant delivery of service (placing an order, payment etc) and accompanying information to the user. Whatever the purpose, e-services systems have one thing in common — they provide an

DOI: 10.4018/978-1-4666-0089-8.ch010

information service on the website. The primary requirement for e-services is the conducting of actions of personal benefit to the customer in a timely fashion and with instant feedback on its state of execution and level of performance.

With the development of information technology allowing user participation in service delivery on websites, customers' roles in the e-services process have become more important. Therefore, it can be argued that researchers need to pay more attention to customers' and users' evaluations of technology-based services (Parasuraman and Grewal 2000; Chea and Lou 2008; and Chellappan 2008). In general, existing research suggests that e-services system translate into fast delivery of services on websites and portals without the users investing much time or effort. The flexibility in service delivery offered by e-services system provides users with quick selection of the best services available, choice from a wider range of service providers, the availability of interaction in their own time and space, easier access to several related services, access to unlimited content, and excellent retrieval facilities (van Riel et al. 2001).

The implications of using e-services are significant for business (Xue et al. 2004). Customer participation in and acceptance of e-services provides them with a broader choice of services that meet their requirements. In some organisations this has led to the overhaul of the service delivery system (Xue et al. 2004). It is therefore important to understand the user roles in e-services system development. User - e-services interaction behaviour on websites is unique in the sense that the interface takes place in cyberspace within a short time. It is therefore important for business to understand what influences the use of an e-services system with in that short time frame (Grönroos et al. 2000).

Organisations engaged in e-business are providing e-services such as banking, airline ticket booking, car rental, management consulting, and the selling of music and software. Educational institutions are increasingly opting for interactive, e-services system delivery to meet user demand (Forrest and Mizerski, 1996). E-services system offer advantages such as instant and 24 X 7 access, immediate feedback and receipting, effective and immediate ordering etc, to business and government organisations delivering online services. For example, Hewlett Packard is rapidly transforming their after-sales service to e-services system business units (McCarthy 1999; Ruyter et al. 2001). Organisations have realised it would be easier for both businesses and their customers to put information up on the web than to answer repeated requests from users (Berners-Lee 1999:65).

Organisations and governments worldwide have established e-services system on websites, including services as diverse as bill paying, taxation, online delivery of education, medical information, legal consultancy, business consultancy, cultural awareness, real estate buying and selling, and transport information on timetables and registration (for example www.firstgov.com in the USA; www.europa.eu.int in Europe; www.ukonline.gov.uk in the UK; www.fed.gov.au in Australia; www.gov.sg in Singapore; and www.gov.hk in Hong Kong).

2. PERSPECTIVES TO THE RESEARCH PROBLEM

The Management believed that the e-services system, when fully developed, would be more useful for staff in their work. Management considered that the e-services system was a channel for delivering better, more useful and efficient services to students and at the same time would provide effective work administration for staff. The Management believed that, in the long term, such advantages would be reflected in better work management practices and increased work productivity. The most important factor from the Management perspective for staff acceptance, use, and continued use of the e-services system was the perceived usefulness of the e-services system.

The problem facing the international admission department is that the staff is not accepting the web electronic service system in processing the student admission application; instead continue to use the old system that is traditional paper based service. Printing documents, storing in folders, processing, and correspondence with students are through traditional mail and central to the workflow system. Reliance on paper-based service tends to duplicate and increase task load leading to errors and confusion. As a result of this, the department lacks behind in providing good service to its clients (students), resulting in considerable backlog. This is shown in Figure 1.

The case study examines the Web Electronic Service framework of the University of Australia (not the real name). The department is in the process of developing and implementing Web-based e-service system. International students have the option to lodge the admission application through either of any: web-based e-service system on the World Wide Web, phone, fax, or in person. On receiving the application a decision is made by the staff on the admission status. The department is implementing the electronic delivery of its services on the website. The web electronic service is believed to be in use for approximately last two and half years. The e-service process involves students making the application and the staff processing application on the website.

The department introduced the web electronic service to catch up with the increasing backlog and to improve the service. The staff indicated their resistance to accept web-based e-service system on the basis of factual information such as: it added additional load to their current task, lack of confidence, fear of providing wrong information on the web, and not seeking help when required.

Figure 1. Past-present situation and future goals

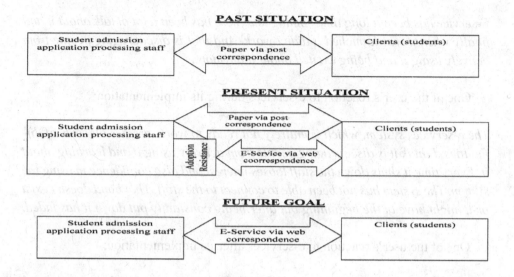

The Department has always used a paper-based administrative processing system to file information enquiries, process applications and support potential and existing overseas students at the university. With the volume of enquiries and numbers of applications increasing at 30% per year for the past 3 years, there has been a need to increase efficiency. The IT Manager said:

It is a pretty big area. When starting the enquiries we are looking at ...there are probably about 30,000 individual records and many come down to applications... but you are probably dealing with a number a lot less than that.

As a result the Manager of the Department initiated the development of an e-services system to undertake all of the tasks previously done manually. The system has now been in place for 2 years. The Management envisaged that this new e-services system would create new business opportunities by providing international students with an electronic platform for sending and receiving information. The system would also enable the Department to achieve its aim to provide quality customer service to these students and deliver all services electronically. The primary aim of the Department's Managers for the e-services system was to reduce paper processes and provide quicker and more efficient service to its clients (i.e. international students). Management expected the staff to use the e-services system in their regular work so that they could use it to manage and make day-to-day work more efficient and more significant in managing workflow.

One of the user's reaction to e-services prior to its implementation:

E-service has been a long time coming and there has been a lot of talk about it and finally when it was launched it didn't work. And that is discouraging people from actively using it and being excited about it anymore.

One of the user's reaction to e-services during its implementation:

The e-services system, which is entirely not ready to work, creates all sorts of difficulties. I think it is discouraging people from actively using it and learning about it. Every time it shuts down the staff looses interest and also confidence in using the system. The system has not been able to connect to the staff. That bond doesn't exist or it might have at the beginning but after being constantly put down it has faded.

One of the user's reaction to e-services after its implementation:

I think obviously there is resistance to using the e-services system because the staff feel that they were never consulted on the system's development so they are quite insulted. I mean it is a very obvious thing that the system should be able to do basic functions. Staff need to be consulted about this.

The senior staff outlined the department goals as – (1) processing all application by web electronic service on the Internet; (2) respond to student correspondence by web electronic service within 24 hours (and in peak time within 48 hours); and (4) diverting more students towards adopting the web electronic service application.

The theme of the case study is to investigate the uptake of web electronic services system amongst end-users especially based on user requirements. The benefits that the readers are expected to receive from reading this article is to understand the development process of e-services system from the user side (i.e. albeit reducing the technical focus), the use of qualitative data in solving the problem that can have an impact on e-services project, and the transition gap from paper-based to web-based e-services system.

The staff is using the web electronic service system along with another database system (which will be referred as- DA system- in this study). DA system is accessible only to the internal staff processing student applications, and offers all the functions in complementing the paper-based system in conducting the task. In simple terms it is known as the paper-based service system. It is believed to be in use approximately for last eight years. The DA system does not interact and neither offers its functionality directly with web electronic system. The staff at the time was using both systems to do the task. The transition from paper-based to web-based e-service system is anticipated by the department to be a significant step in the direction of moving the service process over the website and gradually removing the paper based system.

2.1. Case Analysis of the Problem

One of the staff reported that the attributes of the interface with the system, such as navigation and task button functionalities, were unclear despite being given some training. DeLone and McLean (1992) claim that the systems quality is one of the important characteristics for measuring Information Systems success. For example that staff member noted:

We have very little experience in the working of the e-services system. We don't know how it is supposed to function and what we can expect out of it. From our past experience in using e-services we know that it cannot be used in all areas of our work and it is still being developed and is incomplete. It is not 100% complete yet and there is a risk involved with its use.

Staff were asked to enter all information directly into the e-services system. Even with some training, staff resistance to using the e-services system appeared to increase over the case study period and in follow ups with staff over the next 12 months. This emerged as an issue because of different levels of confusion caused by the lack of complete functionality of the new systems and poor integration with the other systems in use at the Department. One staff member said:

There are quite a few fields where we can't use the e-services system. It just doesn't work. We have to use the paper-based system to complete the work, and that adds on to our workload to use both systems at same time. It takes a lot of time especially when we want to get a simple task done. The two systems are not compatible to each other and we have to depend on both and sometimes it is confusing to know which one works better than the other.

There was a consistent view amongst staff that the e-services system was inadequate and it was obvious in all of the interviews and in discussions with staff that no staff member believed that the training given was adequate. Land (1999) suggested that the skills in using the system can be acquired, providing an incremental learning experience exists. In its absence in this case study, staff were juggling with multiple paper-based sources to gather information needed to complete the e-services system task. One staff member added:

We need to rely on paper documents and another database to complete the tasks... we have to use both systems (i.e. paper-based and e-services based)... and sometimes we are busy; it is too much. We need to gather more expertise about using the system rather than the system helping us in our work. There are paper-based records, which have no connection with the e-services system. We keep using them as well. Plus we use another database, which is not connected to the e-services system, but the IT Manager told us that it should soon start working with the e-services system. It's been quite long and that hasn't happened yet.

In the discussions and interviews with the staff, they focused on issues of systems familiarity, work comparison with both systems, and on the task complexity when doing their work.

Electronic services system were perceived by Management to provide benefits including less paperwork, quick delivery of information, easy editing and updating of information. Parthasarathy and Parthasarathy and Bhattacherjee (1998) suggest that the utilization levels of e-services is through the user's ability to realise expected benefits via appropriate utilisation of their superior technological skills and ability to mobilise effort and resources to learn the innovation. Student evaluation of e-services acceptance is based on time they spent in doing work on the e-services system; money (dollars) spent in using the e-services, and proposed benefits in student's work to use e-services. Performing different tasks simultaneously on e-services system such as information searches, downloading information and emailing, may provide the user with a positive perception of the benefits. There was significant emphasis on the introduction of e-services system technology to improve efficiency and effectiveness of the staff and their operations within the Department.

The Management envisaged that this new e-services system would create new business opportunities by providing international students with an electronic platform for sending and receiving information. The system would also enable the Department to achieve its aim to provide quality customer service to these students and deliver all services electronically. The primary aim of the Department's Managers for the e-services system was to reduce paper processes and provide quicker and more efficient service to its clients (i.e. international students). Management expected the staff to use the e-services system in their regular work so that they could use it to manage and make day-to- day work more efficient and more significant in managing workflow.

The staff and Management acceptance of the e-services system and its use in processing international student's admission applications is considered a major organisational requirement to meet Departmental targets in the university's Strategic Plans. However, the Executive Director noted:

"One of our problems is that we have a lot of trouble with our staff coping with the new e-services system. To get them to work with the two systems is troublesome for them. But actually we have 'realised' that the e-services system is part of everyday work. And it probably deserves more attention instead of paper-based print applications in many ways. Our e-services practices had to change."

Electronic services system were perceived by Management to provide benefits including less paperwork, quick delivery of information, easy editing and updating of information. Rogers (1995) argue that attributes of the innovation should be compatible to the organisation. At the same time Management realised that new systems challenge staff on implementation.

Rogers (1995) suggests that complexity of systems implementation, trialability of the system, and ease of observability are the perceived characteristics of innovation. Through prior analysis of the situation, the Management's perception of introducing the new technology was based on the belief that such technology would have a positive impact on staff work when the advantages were reflected in their work.

3. RESEARCH METHODOLOGY

Multiple sources are used in data collection (Yin, 1994) - documentation, archival records, open-ended interviews, direct observation, participant-observation, and physical artifacts. This is a major strength of case study data collection to use many different sources of evidence (Yin, 1994) providing real life information on the existing problem. Information on the current system provided insight on the obstacles in the user acceptance in systems development and implementation process. This led to the development of converging lines of inquiry, a process of triangulation (Yin, 1994) in processing information from number of sources.

In the first instance discussions are held with three senior staff members involved in implementing the web-based e-service system. They included the executive director, IT Manager, and an outside Consultant. In the second round separate individual interview are conducted with these participants. The third round of interviews is conducted with the admissions manager and separate individual interviews with two other staff members. Altogether six separate interviews with participants are undertaken. In the study they are referred to as Participant 1, Participant 2, and so forth, due to participant confidentiality and their identity not disclosed in the study. Though the participant gender is not a major factor for introspection, it coincided to be balanced, three males and three females.

In the first round interview the data collected and compared with the second round and third round interview data, for consistency, clarity and accuracy of the

Figure 2. Triangulation – convergence of multiple sources of evidence (Adapted from Yin (1994))

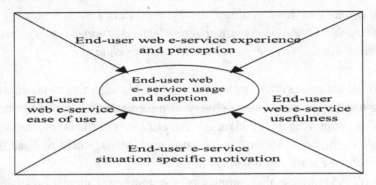

information. Participant 5 and 6 interview data were contrasted to test for the factors having effect on users with high and low performance in using the system. This provided the advantage of not duplicating the data with just one set of evidence.

The discussions and interviews were open-ended (Yin, 1994), the researcher in the beginning provided the topic, and the respondents were probed of their opinion about the events. A reasonable approach was taken to verify the responses with information from other sources (Yin, 1994). The respondents were encouraged to provide their own insight into the problem and this was later converged with responses from other respondents and sources pointing to the fact. The researcher avoided following sequence of certain set of questions only, as it would have limited the scope of study and may not have provided important and rich information. This is shown in Figure 2.

4. ANALYSIS OF THE QUALITATIVE EVIDENCE

The objective of this research is to examine the user acceptance and use of an e-services system. User's acceptance to use e-services relates to the initial use when users trial the use of e- Services system and evaluate its effectiveness in meeting their objectives for visiting the e- Services system. This is shown in Figure 3. For example, a student may use e-services system on a university website for emailing but its effective use can only be determined if such activities meet with the student's objectives. If the objectives are not met, the student is unlikely to accept e-services.

This case study follows the theoretical propositions that led to the case study (Yin, 1994). The original objectives and design of the case study were based on propositions, which reflected on research questions, review of literature, and the

Figure 3. End-users web electronic usage and acceptance

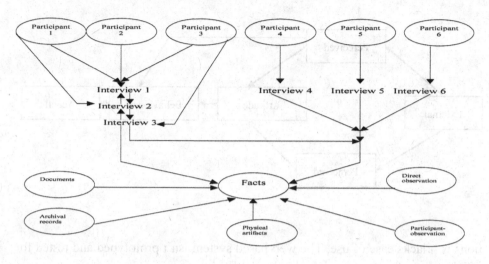

conceptual model. The central problem in the case study coincided with the research problem under investigation. This helped the researcher to focus attention on certain data and ignore other data (Yin, 1994), due to the scope of the study, limited time and resources.

TAM has been applied in a variety of end-user studies on the world-wide-web (Heijden, 2000; Gefen and Straub, 2000; Venkatesh 2000; Wright and Granger, 2001). These studies investigated the application of TAM in conjunction with one or more factors (i.e., experience, motivation, and usage frequency). Currently research on web-based e-services focus on understanding those factors that influence how successfully and rapidly users adopt web-based e-service. The Technology Acceptance Model (TAM) of Davis (1989, and 1993) represents an important theoretical contribution toward understanding IS usage and IS acceptance behaviour (Davis et al. 1989, and 1992; Figure 4).

Löfstedt (2007) suggests that Swedish research on e-services focuses on citizens, communication, the development of e-services, the design of e-services, the maintenance of e-services, e-participation, the quality of services, evaluation, organisational changes, interactions between different e-services, usability, cooperation, inter-organisational co-operation, accessibility, e-Health, the development of methods, and process orientation.

The staff experience of the web-based system to have high controls, lesser flexibility, and it is not intelligent to detect simple task errors. This remarkably reflects on prior experience and perception in doing the task with ease with the paper-based system. Though the web-based e-services system offers usefulness but users percep-

Figure 4. The technology acceptance model (Davis. 1989)

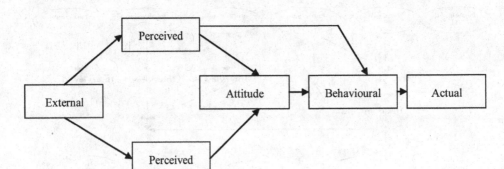

tions is it lacks ease of use. The web-based system isn't prototyped and tested for efficiency, performance and the bugs need fixing.

The user resistance in accepting web-based system also implicates some degree of perceived ease of use and perceived usefulness (Davis, 1989; Chea 2008; and Chellappan 2008) among staff in using the e-services. It is unveiled that the paper-based system is popular among staff, due to its ease of use and usefulness in conducting the task. It offers users with better control, self-service, and support, than the web-based system.

5. TESTING THE GAP BETWEEN THE PAPER BASED SYSTEM AND E-SERVICES SYSTEM

The gap between paper-based and web-based e-service system are identified emerging due to information gap, design gap, communication, and fulfillment gap. Zeithaml et al (2000) in their study pointed to each of these gaps on the basis of users experience with the website. Information gap leads to providing incomplete or in accurate information to the users. The initial design of a website not meeting the user's requirement may result in design gap. The presence of an information gap would exacerbate the design gap because incomplete or incorrect understanding of users might adversely affect the design of the website, therefore compounding user's frustration (Zeithaml et al., 2000).

Similarly communication gap reflects on a lack of accurate understanding about the websites features, capabilities, and limitations. Sometimes users are made promises that cannot be met, that contribute to the fulfillment gap. In the systems gap situation when the users expectations are not met their reactions is that of frustration.

Figure 5. Web-based e-service systems gap

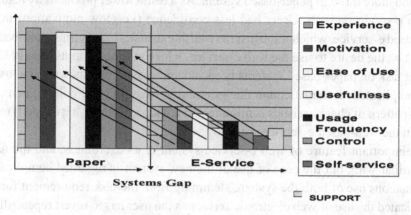

Although emotions such as anger and frustration are expressed when users report on problems arising from web electronic service quality, these appear to be less tense than those associated with traditional service quality experience (Zeithaml et al., 2000). It can be suggested that the contrast in being "less tense" may be due to the users perception of conveying their problem on web e-services system is relatively new and any expression will need further user experience.

Figure 5 points to the factors effecting users in paper based and web-based systems. User experience in paper-based service is considered as one of the factors having significant effect. Such experience is formed of different characteristics. One such contemporary characteristic is the email correspondence. Paper-based service has long been in existence before the web-based system, the user expertise is more concentrated and central to using the paper-based service. The web-based e-service is viewed as an alternative, which will replace the paper-based service but is far from matching user's expectation of the system when compared to the paper-based service system. This is believed to increase the gap. The two systems offer different functionality based on their system characteristics and functionality, at the same time meeting user's expectation of the system is critical to successful acceptance and continued use.

The emerging systems gap at the time is anticipated to be growing. Introducing new changes in web electronic workflow entirely without transferring the user-friendly characteristics (e.g., ease of use) of paper-based system is started effecting users motivation and usage frequency in using web-based e-service. There is underlying resistance in acceptance of the web-based e-service system and increasing negativity towards it features and usage. Low user perception and experience of the electronic system reflects in lower motivation to work with the new system and hence lower usage that results in doing less work within the web electronic framework and more through paper-based system. As a result lower productivity resulted in web e-service system. Users had less confidence (i.e., low motivation) in the web-based e-service, which is intrinsic as well as extrinsic. Low intrinsic motivation reflects on the desire to use the web e-service, which at times is at its lowest. Conducting task on paper-based systems is considered easy to do, known to the users, less complicated, systematic, and the users know what they are doing. Such consistent pattern of characteristics is missing and not known (though it existed) to the users in the web-based e-service workflow.

An important feature of web e-service system is its usefulness, and the users are familiar with, but the ease of use of the new system is regarded complicated. Simultaneous use of both the system, stemming from the task requirement further complicated the use of web electronic service as the user has to revert repeatedly to the paper based system to complete the web-based e-service task. The web-based system is believed not to be self-sufficient and being developed and updated from time to time, and in those times the users has to rely on the paper-based service system for information.

The scope of web-based system functionality isn't defined and the user didn't have a good experience from the beginning. Establishing the web electronic workflow frame within the system, after the system was developed, resulted in adjusting the other features of the system, and hence adjusting the user experience, which was not an easy and straightforward process. Though the user may have taken the new features into their experience but it formed an initial perception of the system as "being inadequate to perform the web electronic service task." Such early perception may have a down side effect on acceptance and further usage of the web electronic service.

User's guidelines in transferring work from paper-based system to web-based system may have greatly enhanced user's experience. Although such user experience already existed and transferring to the web-based system may have been easy. Users are aware of the guidelines that were verbally conveyed, written guidelines are either missing or unknown to the users. Important information that is not conveyed to the users is "how the new web-based e-service system makes their work easier to perform and save time and effort". Though this is not considered important at the time, it may have a positive effect on the user if known. A list outlining the benefits of the web-based e-service system may demonstrate to the users of their performance improvement when using the system.

Developing a system without involving the users is not based on a good system development life cycle (SDLC) principle. User participation in the development of the new system (i.e., web-based system) is very crucial before and after the system development. Such interaction allows the system to be custom made meeting the users expectations of what the system can do and not the other way around. Add-

Figure 6. The mirror effect for the two systems

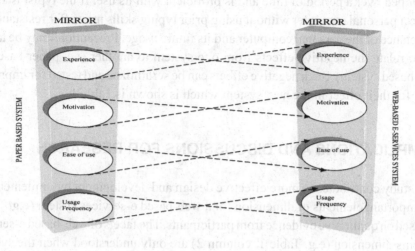

ing new features and upgrades to the existing system also requires close interaction with the user group, for testing and demonstrating its effectiveness, before finally integrating to the existing system.

6. THE MIRROR EFFECT

The web-based system is not tested with the users for its effectiveness before final deployment. It is important to know "what is expected from the web-based system", or which characteristics that can be migrated from the old system to the new one, even the ones that didn't work in the old system may be improved and tested and offered to the user with a better experience in the new system (Figure 6). This would have greatly enhanced the web electronic workflow system. Understanding and relating the users motivation and usage frequency characteristics from the old system (i.e. paper based) into the new (i.e. web electronic) may have offered the user with the same look and feel within the new system.

A different approach may not been appropriate in developing users experience based on the system (and not the user) requirement, this discouraged the users from parting their prior (old) experience. Rather the users examined the new experience (on the basis of system requirements) as rigid and not effective in the current electronic task. Keeping aside ones prior experience that has been developed over a period of time and used in everyday task is difficult to forget or separate.

A good system will complement and integrate user's prior experience within the new framework. For example a typist using a typewriter has prior experience developed over a period of time and is proficient with its use. If the typist is asked to use a personal computer without using prior typing skills may offer resistance in acceptance of the personal computer and its future usage. Precautions may be taken not to relate the negative effects from one system to another (i.e. paper-based to web-based system). Such negative effects can be scrutinized and tested for improvement for their effect in the new system which is shown is Table 1.

7. IMPLICATIONS AND DISCUSSIONS FOR RESEARCH

This study contributes to more effective design and development by implementing the important elements of dimension for a web-based e-services system (e.g. Table 1) based on qualitative evidence from participants. The facets of web-based e-service systems dimension (e.g. Table 1, column 2) are only understood when the system has been developed and running, thus capturing users understanding of the systems deficiency. This research differs from the previous literature by suggesting that the important aspects of the e-services dimension need to be 'early on designed and tested' and built into the system development cycle. This would reduce the negative impact on the users' attitude towards e-services system performance. E-services system are user driven, features that enhances the systems design will have an effect on the user adoption of e-services. This research also identifies the need to integrate qualitative data into the design for e-services system development projects.

The experiences learnt from the e-services system development are:

1. The users need to be involved in the systems development from a very early stage.
2. The use of qualitative data from users in e-services systems implementation need not be underestimated. No user group (e.g. administration staff, academic staff, and senior management staff) should be ignored.
3. Detail conceptualization of the e-services systems needs to be developed and mapped and shown to the user group and ask for their input. Any changes to that process needs to be implemented at that stage.

The key learning points for this article is to know the users effective role in using the e-services system based on user requirements, implement those requirements within the e-services system by reducing technical complexities and increasing task simplicity on the computer screen. Further, understanding the systems gap and the impact it can have on the e-services project, by tapping into the users knowledge about the features of the previous system (i.e. paper-based) and building those features into the new e-services system that would make the transition easy for the user.

210

Table 1. Perceived dimensions, attributes, and concrete cues for e-service quality and selected illustrative quotes

Dimension of Web-based System	Facets of Web-based E-Service Systems Dimension	Evidence from Selected Quotes
Reliability	Site is up and running Helps in doing the task	"The system is **not 100% ready**…" "Adds on to the task…increases task load." "the system is **not connected** to the financial system"
	Error checks	"If the system can be fixed it can be fixed, otherwise we will **continue using it as it is**." "System **is not intelligent** to check simple errors like spell checks, grammar checks."
	Does the site meet all the task needs	"If any information is missed, there is no way to check, there are no **compulsory fields** to inform of missing information". "Need to **rely on paper documents** and another database to complete the task… have to use all."
Responsiveness	Help available if there was a problem Support	"It is available…but if the system cannot do certain things, we have to **do it manually**."
	Manuals, guidelines, online help	"Mine has been chucked out…**haven't seen one**."
	When the system doesn't work	"Sometimes **have frustration** with the system when it doesn't work, of what we **expect of it**… it brings the motivation down, and when it works, it **bounces the motivation up**…tell everyone how well it works"
	Information search	"At home I am **more motivated** in using the system, as I am **relaxing**; at work I am **hurrying** as I have to do this quick…do that." "The site doesn't have a **search engine**…if there was one; information search would have been easier." "Students with high level of literacy good English language skills will be **confident to use** the site a lot".

continued on following page

Table 1. Continued

Dimension of Web-based System	Facets of Web-based E-Service Systems Dimension	Evidence from Selected Quotes
Access	To the site Login to the site	"**Too many log in screens**…"
	Site update	"Speed needs to be improved, **needs to be faster**." "Due to time out period that disconnect, the user has to reenter all the information once again…this **creates duplicity of information** for us…as the same user is reapplying again and it is hard to differentiate between the same application."
Flexibility	Choice of ways to do the task Available	"**Verifying information** on the Internet is not possible, we still have to check students education credential in paper form" "**We need more control**…we can get report, but that's only in numbers, whereas the other databases has more information providing us with more **control over information**…this makes the **work easier.**" "When students are filling the forms online…it is not compulsory for them to write email address…we **can't proceed** or get in contact if email address is not provided."
Ease of navigation	Easy to find what I need Easy to get anywhere on the website Contains a site map with links to everything on the site Has a search engine	"When I am in between different tasks it logs off…have to **login number of times**…due to time out period, loose work when login back…**its irritating**"
Efficiency	Simple to use Site that contains just the basics Doesn't require me to input a lot of information Structured properly Gives information in reasonable hunks Gives information on command rather than all at once No scrolling from side to side No fine print that is difficult to read and hard to find	"Site needs to **be improved with better features and functionality** that will make it **easier for us to use**."

continued on following page

Table 1. Continued

Dimension of Web-based System	Facets of Web-based E-Service Systems Dimension	Evidence from Selected Quotes
Site Aesthetics	Good pictures of items Color of items same as what it is on the screen	"Lot of pictures…in some countries computer is slower; it would take a long time to download images."
	Eye Catching Color is intriguing Brightness rather than dark background Simple Free of distraction Uncluttered Clean, not too busy No flashing things going across the screen	"Screen is fine, fonts are too small, and trying to fit everything in one page… **people whose first language is not English would like the fonts to be bigger in size.**"
Customization and Personalization	Site that help me find exactly what I want Easy to customize	"Can't **change or edit** letter templates, can't do anything, everything is fixed… whereas with the other system lets you do"

Adapted from Zeithaml et al. (2000)

The approach that was adapted for this development was just the opposite. Very few users were involved in the e-services systems development. The use of qualitative data was ignored. No detail conceptualization of the e-services system was solicited from the user group.

User's effective role in determining the contents of service and its outcome may require moderate levels of input in the form of information from users to deliver the service. Though such participation in developing the service in paper-based system was present its applicability in web-based e-service system is either missing or very low. Defining user jobs and managing the diverse user groups requires an initiative at the system development stage, which at its very central may be integrated with the workflow process.

The level of user's participation that may be increased or decreased depending on the user's experience thus shifting the complicated and repetitive task on technology, other task requiring minimum input can be done by the user, making the process easier for the user to complete. Such an understanding if applied may greatly enhanced user task. The senior staff had the view of "we don't want them to create things" which was getting to be difficult when user wanted to customize features such as letter templates, screen fonts size, other changes, that were not allowed within the web-based systems parameters. This may have brought in a sense of disconnected feeling among the users, as one participant put it "they (i.e. users) see themselves as backroom people and not front room they need to be in the front room".

It is not known whether the user are proficient in using the web-based database system, rather it is assumed on the basis of their past experience and interface with the paper based system. Working with a database system requires certain level of expertise, for which the users are not tested. It may not be possible for the user to understand the essential requirements of the task and what was expected from it. There weren't any rewards set for the expected performance because nothing is stated as "expected performance". The user isn't encouraged by the rewards rather they processed output on the basis of input.

From the service context it is encouraged to have user's participation in service evolving process as much as possible, which adds on users experience, motivation, and decision-making. The user's comment about the web-based e-service system is "we are not consulted and no one ever speaks to us about the online web processing system, it just suddenly appeared and we have to use it". One participant even went a step further and said, "they (the users) don't feel they have any ownership from the beginning" and "we are slowly trying to introduce that sense of ownership among users". Such experience may have been frequently shared among colleagues who were using the web-based system, and the overall general perception of the system is perceived to be low not as a result of its characteristics (not this time) but due to the intense downside collective feeling against accepting the system, due to lack of contribution in its development, participation, and consultation process.

A participant disclosed this as "when marketing managers are told to handle an inquiry, the reaction is, it isn't their job". This clearly demonstrated that either the users are shifting their task to their sub-ordinates or they didn't understand their contribution and responsibilities in the web-based system. No minimum standard is set for each task; rather the complete service output is taken as a final delivery of service. This has reduced the sense of user ownership, and the minimum standard expected in doing the task.

General models of employee behavior suggest that behavior is determined by role of clarity, ability to perform, and motivation to perform (Zeithaml and Bitner 2000; Sandhu and Corbitt 2008; and Sandhu 2009). Similarly, user behavior in a service production and delivery situation is facilitated when (1) users understand their roles and know how they are expected to perform, such as clearly defining their task; (2) users are able to perform as expected, that is the minimum standard expected to do the task; and (3) there are valued rewards for performing as expected (Schneider and Bowen, 1990), that is users will be motivated individually and collectively for their achievements. While working with both systems users had forgotten their actual roles within the systems.

8. CONCLUSION

The evidence in this study reveals that users' beliefs are created on the basis of impressions formed about e-services. These impressions play an important role in determining user thoughts about e-services acceptance and their evaluation is guided by their assessment of how well e-services meet their work requirements. Users did not recognize the benefits and rewards of effective participation unless they are specifically informed about its benefits, ease of use, and usefulness. The users are not informed about the accrued benefits not only to them, but also to their colleagues, the department, and the whole organization. All users are not motivated with the same types of rewards, efforts to include individualized rewards may be considered. Some may value the increased access and timesaving they can gain by performing their service roles effectively. Others may value recognition, monetary benefits, or still other may be looking for a promotion, autonomy, or greater personal control over the service outcome. If users are not satisfied and their motivation is lacking, it will result in negative outcomes such as, not understanding the service process, slowing down the change process, resistance to change affecting each other (i.e. their colleagues) as well as the customer.

The users may have been clearly informed about their contribution in developing the web-based e-service. Different user's contribution in forming the end-service requires a clear understanding of each user participation and contribution to the process. Interconnected task of different users may demonstrate the start and completion of each user task and responsibilities. Whatever the case, the expected level of user participation required to be communicated verbally or in writing in order to perform their roles.

Users need to be educated of their roles and their inputs so that they can perform the task effectively. To understand what is expected of them and the expertise to accomplish the task needs evaluation and feedback of their abilities necessary to perform within a specified context. Users education program can take the form of formal orientation programs, training, written literature provided to users (or manual, that were either missing or unknown), directional cues and signage in the service environment, learning from colleagues and customers, and personal experience. User's performing a specific task requires understanding of the task process (for example: What is needed? How to progress? What is user supposed to do?).

Observing other users doing the same task (brings confidence), exchanging information with other users, enhances users experience. Rewarding the users performing their roles effectively motivates the users and influences others in doing their task well, provides confidence, increases motivation, and job satisfaction. Rewards are likely to come in the form of increased control over the web-based e-service delivery process, timesaving, monetary savings, and psychological or physical benefits.

REFERENCES

Chea, S., & Lou, M. (2008). Post-adoption behaviors of e-service customers: The interplay of cognition and emotion. *International Journal of Electronic Commerce*, *12*(3), 29–56. doi:10.2753/JEC1086-4415120303

Chellappan, C. (2008). *E-services: The need for higher levels of trust by populace*. Chennai, India: Anna University.

Davis, F. D. (1989). Perceived usefulness, perceived ease of use, and user acceptance of Information Technology. *Management Information Systems Quarterly*, *13*(2), 319–340. doi:10.2307/249008

Davis, F. D. (1993). User acceptance of Information Technology: System characteristics, user perceptions and behavioural impacts. *International Journal of Man-Machine Studies*, *38*(3), 475–487. doi:10.1006/imms.1993.1022

Davis, F. D., Bagozzi, R. P., & Warshaw, P. R. (1989). User acceptance of computer technology: A comparison of two theoretical models. *Management Science*, *34*(8), 982–1002. doi:10.1287/mnsc.35.8.982

Davis, F. D., Bagozzi, R. P., & Warshaw, P. R. (1992). Extrinsic and intrinsic motivation to use computers in the workplace. *Journal of Applied Social Psychology*, *22*(14), 1111–1132. doi:10.1111/j.1559-1816.1992.tb00945.x

DeLone, W. H., & McLean, E. R. (1992). Information Systems success: The quest for the dependant variable. *The Institute of Management Sciences*, *3*(1), 60–95.

Forrest, E., & Mizerski, R. (1996). *Interactive marketing, the future present*. Chicago, IL: American Marketing Association.

Gefen, D., & Straub, D. (2000). The relative importance of perceived ease of use in IS adoption: A study of e-commerce adoption. *Journal of the Association for Information Systems*, *1*(8), 1–20.

Grönroos, C., Heinonen, F., Isoniemi, K., & Lindholm, M. (2000). The Netoffer model: A case example from the virtual marketplace. *Management Decision*, *38*(4), 243–252. doi:10.1108/00251740010326252

Heijden, H. (2000). *Using the technology acceptance model to predict website usage: Extensions and empirical test. Research Memorandum 2000-25*. Amsterdam: Vrije Universiteit.

Khalifa, M., & Liu, V. (2003). Determinants of satisfaction at different adoption stages of Internet-based services. *Journal of the Association for Information Systems, 4*(5), 206–232.

Land, F. (1999). *The management of change: Guidelines for the successful implementation of Information Systems.* Department of Information Systems, London School of Economics and Political Science.

Löfstedt, U. (2007). Public e-services research-A critical analysis of current research in Sweden. *International Journal of Public Information Systems, 2007,* 2.

McCarthy, V. (1999). *HP splits in two to focus on enterprise, e-services.* Retrieved from http://www.hpworld.org/hpworldnews/hpw903/news/01.html

Parasuraman, A., & Grewal, D. (2000). The impact of technology on the quality-value-loyalty chain: A research agenda. *Journal of the Academy of Marketing Science, 28*(1), 168–174. doi:10.1177/0092070300281015

Parthasarathy, M., & Bhattacherjee, A. (1998). Understanding post-adoption behaviour in the context of online services. *Information Systems Research, 9*(4), 362–379. doi:10.1287/isre.9.4.362

Rogers, E. M. (1995). *Diffusion of innovations.* New York, NY: The Free Press.

Rust, R. T., & Lemon, K. N. (2001). E-service and the consumer. *International Journal of Electronic Commerce, 5*(3), 85–101.

Ruyter, K. D., Wetzels, M., & Kleijnen, M. (2001). Customer adoption of e- services: An experimental study. *International Journal of Service Industry Management, 12*(2), 184–207. doi:10.1108/09564230110387542

Sandhu, K. (2009). Measuring the performance of electronic services acceptance model (E-SAM). *International Journal of Business Information Systems, 5*(4).

Sandhu, K., & Corbitt, B. (2008). A framework for electronic services system. *International Journal of Electronic Customer Relationship Management, 2*(1). doi:10.1504/IJECRM.2008.019568

van Riel, A. C. R., Liljander, V., & Jurriëns, P. (2001). Exploring consumer evaluations of e-services: a portal site. *International Journal of Service Industry Management, 12*(40), 359–377. doi:10.1108/09564230110405280

Venkatesh, V. (2000). Determinants of perceived ease of use: Integrating control, intrinsic motivation, and emotion into the technology acceptance model. *Information Systems Research, 11*(4), 342–365. doi:10.1287/isre.11.4.342.11872

Wright, K. M., & Granger, M. J. (2001). Using the Web as a strategic resource: an applied classroom exercise. *Proceedings of the 16th Annual Conference of the International Academy for Information Management*, New Orleans, Louisiana.

Xue, M., Harker, P. T., & Heim, G. R. (2004). *Incorporating the dual customer roles in e-service design. The working paper series*. The Wharton Financial Institutions Center.

Yin, R. K. (1994). *Case study research: Design and methods*. Sage Publications.

Zeithaml, V. A., & Bitner, M. J. (2000). *Services marketing: Integrating customer focus across the firm*. Irwin McGraw-Hill.

Zeithaml, V. A., Parasuraman, A., & Malhotra, A. (2000). *A conceptual framework for understanding e-service quality: Implications for future research and managerial practice*. Marketing Science Institute, Working paper, Report no: 00-115.

Compilation of References

Abdurazik, A., & Offutt, J. (2000). Using UML collaboration diagrams for static checking and test generation. *Proceedings of the 3rd International Conference on the Unified Modeling Language (UML '00)*, (pp. 383-395). Berlin, Germany: Springer.

Abrial, J.-R. (1996). *The B-Book*. Cambridge, UK: Cambridge University Press. doi:10.1017/CBO9780511624162

Afzal, W., Torkar, R., & Feldt, R. (2009). A systematic review of search-based testing for non-functional system properties. *Information and Software Technology*, *51*(6), 957–976. doi:10.1016/j.infsof.2008.12.005

Aggrawal, K. K., Singh, Y., & Kaur, A. (2004). Code coverage based technique for prioritizing test cases for regression testing. *SIGSOFT Software Engineering Notes*, *29*(5), 1–4. doi:10.1145/1022494.1022511

Alagar, V. S., & Periyasamy, K. (1998). *Specification of software systems*. New York, NY: Springer-Verlag, Inc.

Albrecht, A. J., & Gaffney, J. E. (1983). Software function, source lines of code, and development effort prediction: A software science validation. *IEEE Transactions on Software Engineering*, *9*(6), 639–648. doi:10.1109/TSE.1983.235271

Ali, S., Briand, L. C., Rehman, M. J., Asghar, H., Iqbal, M. Z., & Nadeem, A. (2007). A state-based approach to integration testing based on UML models. *Journal of Information and Software Technology*, *49*(11-12), 1087–1106. doi:10.1016/j.infsof.2006.11.002

Almeida, E. C., Sunye, G., Traon, Y., & Valduriez, P. (2010). Testing peer-to-peer systems. *Empirical Software Engineering*, *15*(4), 346–379. doi:10.1007/s10664-009-9124-x

Alsmadi, I. (2008). The utilization of user sessions in testing. In *Proceedings of the Seventh IEEE/ACIS International Conference on Computer and Information Science (ICIS 2008)*.

Alsmadi, I., & Al-Kabi, M. (2011). GUI structural metrics. *The International Arab Journal of Information Technology (IAJIT)*, *8*(2).

Alsmadi, I., & Magel, K. (2007). GUI path oriented test generation algorithms. *Proceedings of the Second IASTED International Conference on Human Computer Interaction, March 14-16, 2007, Chamonix, France.*

Alsmadi, I., & Magel, K. (2007b). *An object oriented framework for user interface test automation*. MICS07.

Ames, A., & Jie, H. (2004). *Critical paths for GUI regression testing*. University of California, Santa Cruz. Retrieved from http://www.cse.ucsc.edu/~sasha/ proj/ gui_testing.pdf

Amland, S. (2000). Risk based testing and metrics: Risk analysis fundamentals and metrics for software testing including a financial application case study. *Journal of Systems and Software, 53*, 287–295. doi:10.1016/S0164-1212(00)00019-4

Andreasen, M. S., Nielsen, H. V., Schroder, S. O., & Stage, J. (2007) *What happened to remote usability testing? An empirical study of three methods*. Paper presented at the SIGCHI Conference on Human factors in Computing Systems (CHI '07). New York, NY: ACM.

Andrzejczak, C., & Liu, D. (2010). The effect of testing location on usability testing performance, participant stress levels, and subjective testing experience. *Journal of Systems and Software, 83*(7). doi:10.1016/j.jss.2010.01.052

Attiya, H., & Welch, J. (2004). *Distributed computing: Fundamentals, simulations, and advanced topics*. Wiley-Interscience.

Bach, J. (1998). Good enough quality: Beyond the buzzword. *IEEE Computer, August*, (pp. 96-98).

Bach, J. (1998). A framework for good enough testing. *Computer, 31*(10), 124–126. doi:10.1109/2.722304

Bai, X., Lee, S., & Chen, Y. (2007). *Mutation-based simulation test data generation for testing complex real-time software*. Paper presented at the 40th Annual Simulation Symposium (ANSS '07). Washington, DC: IEEE Computer Society.

Basanieri, F., & Bertolino, A. (2000). A practical approach to UML-based derivation of integration tests. *Proceedings of the Software Quality Week (QWE2000)*.

Bashir, I., & Paul, R. A. (1999). Object-oriented integration testing. *Annals of Software Engineering, 8*(1-4), 187–202. doi:10.1023/A:1018975313718

Basili, V. R., & Rombach, H. D. (1984). The TAME project: Towards improvement oriented software environments. *IEEE Transactions on Software Engineering, 14*(6), 758–773. doi:10.1109/32.6156

Beck, K., et al. (2001). *Manifesto for agile software development*. Retrieved from http://agilemanifesto.org/

Beck, K. (2000). *Extreme programming explained: Embrace change*. Addison Wesley.

Beck, K. (2003). *Test-driven development by example*. Addison Wesley.

Bell, D. (2005). *Software engineering for students: A programming approach* (4th ed.). Prentice Hall International.

Benz, S. (2007). Combining test case generation for component and integration testing. *Proceedings of 3rd International Workshop on Advances in Model-Based Testing*, (pp. 23-33). London, UK: ACM Press.

Berard, B., Bidoit, M., Finkel, A., Laroussinie, F., Petit, A., & Petrucci, L. (2001). *Systems and software verification: Model-checking techniques and tools*. New York, NY: Springer.

Berthon, P., & Davies, T. (1999). Going with the flow: Websites and customer involvement. *Internet Research: Electronic Networking Applications and Policy, 9*(2), 109–116. doi:10.1108/10662249910264873

Compilation of References

Berthon, P., Pitt, L., & Watson, R. T. (1996). The World Wide Web as an advertising medium: toward an understanding of conversion efficiency. *Journal of Advertising Research, 36*(1), 43–45.

Bertolino, A. (2003). *Software testing research and practice.* Paper presented at 10th International Conference on Advances in Theory and Practice (ASM'03). Berlin, Germany: Springer-Verlag.

Bertolino, A. (2007). *Software testing research: Achievements, challenges, dreams.* Paper presented at 2007 Future of Software Engineering (FOSE '07). Washington, DC: IEEE Computer Society.

Biagosch, A., Knupfer, S., Radtke, P., Näher, U., & Zielke, A. (2005). *Automotive electronics - Managing innovations on the road.* McKinsey Brochure.

Bochmann, G., & Petrenko, A. (1994). Protocol testing: Review of methods and relevance for software testing. *Proceedings of the ACM International Symposium on Software Testing and Analysis (ISSTA'94),* (pp. 109-124). ACM-Press.

Borba, P., Cavalcanti, A., Sampaio, A., & Woodcock, J. (Eds.). (2007). *Testing techniques in software engineering.* Berlin, Germany: Springer-Verlag.

Borner, L. (2010). *Integrationstest: Testprozess, Testfokus und Integrationsreihenfolge.* PhD thesis, Heidelberg (Germany).

Bougé, L. (1987). Repeated snapshots in distributed systems with synchronous communications and their implementation in CSP. *Theoretical Computer Science, 49,* 145–169. doi:10.1016/0304-3975(87)90005-3

Briand, L. C., & Labiche, Y. (2001). A UML-based approach to system testing. *Proceedings of the 4th International Conference on The Unified Modeling Language, Modeling Languages, Concepts, and Tools,* (pp. 194-208). Berlin, Germany: Springer.

Briand, L. C., Labiche, Y., & Shousha, M. (2005). Stress testing real-time systems with genetic algorithms. In H.-G. Beyer (Ed.), *2005 Conference on Genetic and Evolutionary Computation* (GECCO '05). New York, NY: ACM.

Bright, D. I. (2000). *A practical worst-case methodology for software testing.* Ph.D. Dissertation. Colorado Technical University.

Butler, M. J., & Leuschel, M. (2005). Combining CSP and B for specification and property verification. *Proceeding of the International Symposium of Formal Methods Europe, Lecture Notes in Computer Science vol. 3582,* (pp. 221–236). Berlin, Germany: Springer.

Cabral, G., & Sampaio, A. (2008). Formal specification generation from requirement documents. *Journal of Electronic Notes in Theoretical Computer Science, 195,* 171–188. doi:10.1016/j.entcs.2007.08.032

Chandy, K. M., & Lamport, L. (1985). Distributed snapshots: Determining global states of distributed systems. *ACM Transactions on Computer Systems, 3*(1), 63–75. doi:10.1145/214451.214456

Charron-Bost, B., Delporte-Gallet, C., & Fauconnier, H. (1995). Local and temporal predicates in distributed systems. *ACM Transactions Programming Language Systems, 17*(1), 157–179. doi:10.1145/200994.201005

Chase, C. M., & Garg, V. K. (1995). Efficient detection of restricted classes of global predicates. In *WDAG '95: Proceedings of the 9th International Workshop on Distributed Algorithms* (pp. 303–317). Springer-Verlag.

Chase, C. M., & Garg, V. K. (1998). Detection of global predicates: Techniques and their limitations. *Distributed Computing, 11*(4), 191–201. doi:10.1007/s004460050049

Chea, S., & Lou, M. (2008). Post-adoption behaviors of e-service customers: The interplay of cognition and emotion. *International Journal of Electronic Commerce, 12*(3), 29–56. doi:10.2753/JEC1086-4415120303

Chellappan, C. (2008). *E-services: The need for higher levels of trust by populace*. Chennai, India: Anna University.

Chen, Y., & Probert, R. (2003). *A risk-based regression test selection strategy*. Fast Abstract ISSRE 2003.

Chess, B., & West, J. (2008). *Secure programming with static analysis*. Boston, MA: Addison-Wesley.

Ciupa, I., Leitner, A., Oriol, M., & Meyer, B. (2007). *Experimental assessment of random testing for object-oriented software*. Paper presented at the 2007 International Symposium on Software Testing and Analysis (ISSTA '07). New York, NY: ACM.

CMMI-Dev. (2006). *CMMI for development, version 1.2: Improving processes for better products*. SEI CMU.

Coenen, F., & Bench-Capon, T. (1993). *Maintenance of knowledge-based systems: Theory, techniques and tools*. Cornwall, UK: Hartnolls Ltd, Bodmin.

Collabnet. (2000). *SVN: An open source software revision control*.

Cooper, R., & Marzullo, K. (1991). Consistent detection of global predicates. *SIGPLAN Notices, 26*(12), 167–174. doi:10.1145/127695.122774

Crosby, P. B. (1979). *Quality is free*. New York, NY: Mentor Books.

Csikszentmihalyi, M. (1975). *Beyond boredom and anxiety*. San Francisco, CA: Jossey-Bass.

Csikszentmihalyi, M., & LeFevre, J. (1990). Optimal experience in work and leisure. *Journal of Personality and Social Psychology, 56*(5), 815–822. doi:10.1037/0022-3514.56.5.815

D'Ambra, J., & Rice, R. E. (2001). Emerging factors in user evaluation of the World Wide Web. *Information & Management, 38*, 373–384. doi:10.1016/S0378-7206(00)00077-X

Davidow, W. H., & Uttal, B. (1989). Service companies: Focus or falter. *Harvard Business Review*, (July/August): 17–34.

Davis, F. D. (1989). Perceived usefulness, perceived ease of use, and user acceptance of Information Technology. *Management Information Systems Quarterly, 13*(2), 319–340. doi:10.2307/249008

Davis, F. D. (1993). User acceptance of Information Technology: Systems characteristics, user perceptions and behavioral impacts. *International Journal of Man-Machine Studies, 38*(3), 475–487. doi:10.1006/imms.1993.1022

Davis, F. D., Bagozzi, R. P., & Warshaw, P. R. (1989). User acceptance of computer technology: A comparison of two theoretical models. *Management Science, 34*(8), 982–1002. doi:10.1287/mnsc.35.8.982

Compilation of References

Davis, F. D., Bagozzi, R. P., & Warshaw, P. R. (1992). Extrinsic and intrinsic motivation to use computers in the workplace. *Journal of Applied Social Psychology, 22*(14), 1111–1132. doi:10.1111/j.1559-1816.1992.tb00945.x

de Alfaro, L., & Henzinger, T. A. (2001). Interface automata, *Proceedings of the 9th Annual Symposium on Foundations of Software Engineering (FSE)*, (pp. 109-120). ACM-Press.

de Figueiredo, J. C. A., Andrade, W. L., & Machado, P. D. L. (2006). Generating interaction test cases for mobile phone systems from use case specifications. *SIGSOFT Software Engineering Notes, 31*(6), 1–10. doi:10.1145/1218776.1218788

DeLone, W. H., & McLean, E. R. (1992). Information Systems success: The quest for the dependant variable. *The Institute of Management Sciences, 3*(1), 60–95.

Deming, W. E. (1986). *Out of the crisis.* Cambridge, MA: Massachusetts Institute of Technology.

Desmoulin, A., & Viho, C. (2007). A new method for interoperability test generation. *Proceedings of the TestCom/FATES 2007*, (pp. 58-73). Berlin, Germany: Springer.

Do, H., Rothermel, G., & Kineer, A. (2004). *Empirical studies of test case prioritization in a Junit testing environment. Proceeding in ISSRE* (pp. 113–124). IEEE Press.

Duggal, G., & Suri, B. (2008). *Understanding regression testing techniques.* COIT 2008, India.

Elbaum, S., Malishevsky, A., & Rothermel, G. G. (2000). *Prioritizing test cases for regression testing. Proceeding in ISSTA* (pp. 102–112). ACM Press.

Elbaum, S., Malishevsky, A., & Rothermel, G. G. (2004). Selecting a cost-effective test case prioritization technique. *Software Quality Control, 12*(3), 185–210.

Ellims, M., Bridges, J., & Ince, D. C. (2006). The economics of unit testing. *Empirical Software Engineering, 11*(1), 5–31. doi:10.1007/s10664-006-5964-9

Eltaher, A. (2008). *Towards good enough testing: A cognitive-oriented approach applied to infotainment systems.* Paper presented at the 23rd IEEE/ACM International Conference on Automated Software Engineering (ASE '08). Washington, DC: IEEE Computer Society.

Emerson, E. A. (1990). *Temporal and modal logic.* Cambridge, MA: MIT Press.

Emma Code. (2010). *Coverage eclipse plugin.* Available at www.eclemma.org/

Fan, X., Shu, J., Liu, L., & Liang, Q. (2009). Test case generation from UML subactivity and activity diagram. *Proceedings of the 2nd International Symposium on Electronic Commerce and Security (ISECS '09)*, (pp. 244-248). Washington, DC: IEEE Computer Society.

Fenton, N. (1991). *Software metrics- A rigorous approach.* Chapman and Hall.

Forrest, E., & Mizerski, R. (1996). *Interactive marketing, the future present.* Chicago, IL: American Marketing Association.

Foulkes, V. S. (1994). How consumers predict service quality: what do they expect? In Rust, R. T., & Oliver, R. L. (Eds.), *Service quality, new directions in theory and practice*. Beverly Hills, CA: Sage.

Fraikin, F., & Leonhardt, T. (2002). SeDiTeC - Testing based on sequence diagrams. *Proceedings of the 17th IEEE International Conference on Automated Software Engineering*, IEEE Computer Society, (pp. 261-266).

Frank, B., Marriott, P., & Warzusen, C. (2008). *CSQE primer*. Quality Council of Indiana.

Free Software Foundation. (2007). *GNU lesser general public license*. Retrieved from http://www.gnu.org/copyleft/lesser.html

Gallagher, L., & Offutt, J. (2006). Automatically testing interacting software components. *Proceedings of the International workshop on Automation of software test (AST '06)*, (pp. 57-63). New York, NY: ACM Press.

Garg, V. K., & Mittal, N. (2001). On slicing a distributed computation. In *ICDCS '01: Proceedings of the the 21st International Conference on Distributed Computing Systems* (p. 322).

Garg, V. K., & Waldecker, B. (1992). Detection of unstable predicates in distributed programs. In *Proceedings of the 12th Conference on Foundations of Software Technology and Theoretical Computer Science* (pp. 253–264). London, UK: Springer-Verlag.

Garg, V. K. (2002). *Elements of distributed computing*. New York, NY: John Wiley & Sons, Inc.

Garg, V. K., & Waldecker, B. (1996). Detection of strong unstable predicates in distributed programs. *IEEE Transactions on Parallel and Distributed Systems*, 7(12), 1323–1333. doi:10.1109/71.553309

Gefen, D., & Straub, D. (2000). The relative importance of perceived ease of use in IS adoption: A study of e-commerce adoption. *Journal of the Association for Information Systems*, 1(8), 1–20.

Ghezzi, C., Jazayeri, M., & Mandrioli, D. (2003). *Fundamentals of software engineering* (2nd ed.). Prentice Hall.

Godase, S. (2005). *An introduction to software automation*. Retrieved from http://www.qthreads.com/articles/testing-/an_introduction_to_software_test_automation.html

Goga, N. (2003). *A probabilistic coverage for on-the-y test generation algorithms*. Retrieved from.

Golding, P., & Tennant, V. (2007). Performance testing: Evaluating an RFID library inventory reader. *International Journal of Internet Protocols and Technology*, 2(3/4), 240–251. doi:10.1504/IJIPT.2007.016224

Goodrich, M. T. (2006). *Data structures and algorithms in C*. Wiley Publisher.

Graff, M. G., & Van Wyk, K. R. (2003). *Secure coding: Principles and practices*. Sebastopol, CA: O'Reilly Media.

Grant, R. M. (1996). Toward a knowledge-based theory of the firm. *Strategic Management Journal*, 17, 109–122.

Greer, D., & Conradi, R. (2009). An empirical study of software project initiation and planning. *IET Software*, 3(5), 356–368. doi:10.1049/iet-sen.2008.0093

Grönroos, C., Heinonen, F., Isoniemi, K., & Lindholm, M. (2000). The Netoffer model: A case example from the virtual marketplace. *Management Decision*, *38*(4), 243–252. doi:10.1108/00251740010326252

Haban, D., & Weigel, W. (1988). Global events and global breakpoints in distributed systems. In *Proceedings of the Twenty-First Annual Hawaii International Conference on Software Track* (pp. 166–175). Los Alamitos, CA.

Hanna, S., & Abu Ali, A. (2011). Platform effect on Web services robustness testing. *Journal of Applied Sciences*, *11*(2), 360–366. doi:10.3923/jas.2011.360.366

Harrington, N., & Schardl, T. B. (December 10, 2008). *Speech recognition in hardware: For use as a novel* input device.

Harrold, M. J., & Soffa, M. L. (1989). Interprocedual data flow testing. *Proceedings of the ACM SIGSOFT '89 Third Symposium on Software Testing, Analysis, and Verification,* (pp. 158-167). New York, NY: ACM.

Hartmann, J., Imoberdorf, C., & Meisinger, M. (2000). UML-based integration testing. *Proceedings of the ACM SIGSOFT International Symposium on Software Testing and Analysis (ISSTA '00)*, (pp. 60-70). New York, NY: ACM Press.

Hasher, L., & Zacks, R. T. (1984). Automatic processing of fundamental information: The case of frequency of occurrence. *The American Psychologist*, *39*, 1372–1388. doi:10.1037/0003-066X.39.12.1372

Hashim, N. L., Ramakrishnan, S., & Schmidt, H. W. (2007). Architectural test coverage for component-based integration testing. *Proceedings of the International Conference on Quality Software (QSIC 2007)*, IEEE Computer Society, (pp. 262-267).

Heijden, H. (2000). *Using the technology acceptance model to predict website usage: Extensions and empirical test. Research Memorandum 2000-25*. Amsterdam: Vrije Universiteit.

Heimdahl, M. P. E., & Whalen, M. W. (1997). Reduction and slicing of hierarchical state machines. In *ESEC '97/FSE-5: Proceedings of the 6th European Conference held jointly with the 5th ACM SIGSOFT International Symposium on Foundations of Software Engineering* (pp. 450–467). New York, NY: Springer-Verlag, Inc.

Henninger, O. (1997). On test case generation from asynchronously communicating state machines. *Proceeding of the 10th International Workshop on Testing of Communicating Systems*. Chapman & Hall.

Henry, J. E. (2000). Test case selection for simulations in the maintenance of real-time systems. *Journal of Software Maintenance: Research and Practice*, *12*(4), 229–248. doi:10.1002/1096-908X(200007/08)12:4<229::AID-SMR212>3.0.CO;2-S

Hoare, C. A. R. (1985). *Communicating sequential processes*. Prentice Hall.

Hoffman, D. L., & Novak, T. P. (1996). Marketing in hypermedia computer-mediated environments: Conceptual foundations. *JMR, Journal of Marketing Research*, *60*(7), 50–68.

Horgan, J. R., & London, S. (1992). ATAC: A data flow coverage testing tool for C. In *Proceeding of Symposium on Assessment of Quality Software Development Tools*, May 1992, (pp. 2-10). IEEE Press.

Hoskins, D. S., Colbourn, C. J., & Montgomery, D. C. (2005). *Software performance testing using covering arrays: efficient screening designs with categorical factors.* Paper presented at the 5th International Workshop on Software and Performance (WOSP '05). New York, NY: ACM.

Howard, M., Leblanc, D., & Viega, J. (2009). *24 deadly sins of software security: Programming flaws and how to fix them.* New York City, NY: McGraw-Hill.

Howard, M., & Lipner, S. (2006). *The security development lifecycle: SDL: A process for developing demonstrably more secure software.* Sebastopol, CA: O'Reilly Media.

Hsia, P., Kung, D., & Sell, C. (1997). Software requirements and acceptance testing. *Annals of Software Engineering, 3,* 291–317. doi:10.1023/A:1018938021528

http://www.fmt.cs.utwente.nl/publications/Files/ 398_covprob.ps.gz

Hughes, G., & Cresswell, M. (1996). *A new introduction to modal logic.* London, UK: Routledge. doi:10.4324/9780203290644

Hurfin, M., Plouzeau, N., & Raynal, M. (1993). Detecting atomic sequences of predicates in distributed computations. In *Workshop on Parallel and Distributed Debugging* (pp. 32-42).

IEC 61508. (2010). *IEC 61508: 2010 - Functional safety of electrical/electronic/programmable electronic safety related systems.*

IEEE. (1990). *IEEE standard 610.12-1990: IEEE standard glossary of software engineering terminology.* New York, NY: IEEE Service Center.

Jain, N. (2005). *Agile maintenance.* Retrieved from www.thoughtworks.com

Jegou, R., Medina, R., & Nourine, L. (1995). Linear space algorithm for on-line detection of global predicates. In Desel, J. (Ed.), *Structures in Concurrency Theory, Proceedings of the International Workshop on Structures in Concurrency Theory (STRICT),* Berlin, 11–13 May 1995 (pp. 175–189).

Jin, Z., & Offutt, J. (2001). Deriving tests from software architectures. *Proceedings of the 12th International Symposium on Software Reliability Engineering (ISSRE'01),* (pp. 308-313). Washington, DC: IEEE Computer Society.

Jin, Z., & Offutt, J. (1998). Coupling-based criteria for integration testing. *Journal of Software Testing, Verification, and Reliability, 8*(3), 133–154. doi:10.1002/(SICI)1099-1689(1998090)8:3<133::AID-STVR162>3.0.CO;2-M

Johnson, C., & Mathews, B. P. (1997). The influence of experience on service expectations. *International Journal of Service Industry Management, 8*(4), 290–305. doi:10.1108/09564239710174381

Jorgensen, P. C., & Erickson, C. (1994). Object-oriented integration testing. *Communications of the ACM, 37*(9), 30–38. doi:10.1145/182987.182989

Kan, S. (1995). *Metrics and models in software quality engineering.* Reading, MA: Addison-Wesley.

Karahanna, E., & Straub, D, W., & Chervany, N. L. (1999). Information tecHnology adoption across time: A cross sectional comparison of pre-adoption and post-adoption beliefs. *Management Information Systems Quarterly, 23*(2), 183–213. doi:10.2307/249751

Khalifa, M., & Liu, V. (2003). Determinants of satisfaction at different adoption stages of Internet-based services. *Journal of the Association for Information Systems, 4*(5), 206–232.

Kim, J., & Porter, A. (2002). A history based test prioritization technique for regression is testing in resource constrained environments. *Proceeding of the 24th International Conference on Software Engineering* (ICSE), (pp. 119-129). ACM Press.

Kitchenham, B., & Pfleeger, S. L. (1996). Software quality: The elusive target. *IEEE Software, 13*(1), 12–21. doi:10.1109/52.476281

Koppol, P. V., Carver, R. H., & Tai, K. C. (2002). Incremental integration testing of concurrent programs. *IEEE Transactions on Software Engineering, 28*(6), 607–623. doi:10.1109/TSE.2002.1010062

Krishnamoorthi, R., & Sahaaya, M. A. S. A. (2009)/ Regression test suite prioritization using genetic algorithms. *International Journal of Hybrid Information Technology, 2*(3), 35-52. Sersc publication house Korea.

Mathur, A. P (2007). *Foundation of software testing*, 1st ed. India Pearson Education.McMinn, P. (2004). Search-based software test data generation: A survey. *Software Testing, Verification and Reliability, 14*(3), 212-223.

Ladan, M. A. (2001). A survey and a taxonomy of approaches for testing parallel and distributed programs. In *AICCSA '01: Proceedings of the ACS/IEEE International Conference on Computer Systems and Applications* (pp. 273-279).

Lamport, L. (1978). Time, clocks, and the ordering of events in a distributed system. *Communications of the ACM, 21*(7), 558–565. doi:10.1145/359545.359563

Lamport, L. (1990). A theorem on atomicity in distributed algorithms. *Distributed Computing, 4*(2), 59–68. doi:10.1007/BF01786631

Lamsweerde, A. V. (2000). *Requirements engineering in the year 00: A research perspective.* Paper Presented at the 22nd International Conference on Software Engineering (ICSE '00). New York, NY: ACM.

Land, F. (1999). *The management of change: Guidelines for the successful implementation of Information Systems.* Department of Information Systems, London School of Economics and Political Science.

Lanet, J. L., & Requet, A. (1998). Formal proof of smart card applets correctness. *Proceeding of the Third Smart Card Research and Advanced Application Conference (CARDIS'98)*, (pp. 85-97). Berlin, Germany: Springer.

Lazic, L. (2005). *The software testing challenges and methods.* Paper presented at the 9th WSEAS International Conference on Communications (ICCOM'05), Stevens Point, Wisconsin, USA.

Lee, K., Hon, H., & Reddy, R. (1990). Sphinx, an open source continuous speech recognition system. Retrieved from http://cmusphinx.sourceforge.net/sphinx4/

Lee, N. H., Kim, T. H., & Cha, S. D. (2002). Construction of global finite state machine for testing task interactions written in message sequence charts. *Proceedings of the 14th International Conference on Software Engineering and Knowledge Engineering (SEKE 2002)*, (pp. 369-376). ACM Press.

Lientz, B. P., & Swanson, E. (1981). Problems in application software maintenance. *Communications of the ACM, 24*(11), 763–769. doi:10.1145/358790.358796

Lientz, B., & Swanson, E. (1980). *Software maintenance management*. Reading, MA: Addison Wesley.

Li, H. F., Rilling, J., & Goswami, D. (2004). Granularity-driven dynamic predicate slicing algorithms for message passing systems. *Automated Software Engineering, 11*(1), 63–89. doi:10.1023/B:AUSE.0000008668.12782.6c

Linnenkugel, U., & Müllerburg, M. (1990). Test data selection criteria for (software) integration testing. *Proceedings of the 1st International Conference on Systems Integration*, (pp. 709-717). Piscataway, NJ: IEEE Press.

Löfstedt, U. (2007). Public e-services research- A critical analysis of current research in Sweden. *International Journal of Public Information Systems, 2007*, 2.

Loughran, S. (2000). *Apache Ant*. Retrieved from http://ant.apache.org/

Machado, P. D. L., Figueiredo, J. C. A., Lima, E. F. A., Barbosa, A. E. V., & Lima, H. S. (2007). Component-based integration testing from UML interaction diagrams. *IEEE International Conference on Systems, Man and Cybernetics (SMC 2007)*, (pp. 2679-2686). Washington, DC: IEEE Computer Society.

Mackinnon, T., Freeman, S., & Craig, P. (2000). *Endo-testing: Unit testing with mock objects*. eXtreme Programming and Flexible Processes in Software Engineering – XP2000.

Mahdian, A., Andrews, A. A., & Pilskalns, O. J. (2009). Regression testing with UML software designs: A survey. *Journal of Software Maintenance and Evolution, 21*(4), 253–286. doi:10.1002/smr.403

Makedonov, Y. (2005). *Managers guide to GUI test automation*. Software Test and Performance Conference 2005. Retrieved from http://www.softwaretestconsulting.com/Presentations_slides/Manager_sGuide_GUI_Test-Automation11wh.pdf

Mao, Y., Boqin, F., Zhenfang, H., & Li, F. (2006). Important usage paths selection for GUI software testing. *Information and Technology Journal, 5*(4), 648–654. doi:10.3923/itj.2006.648.654

Marick, B. (1998). When should a test be automated. In *Proceedings of the 11th International Software/Internet Quality Week. Software Research*, San Francisco, USA. Retrieved from http://www.testing.com/writings/automate.pdf

Martin, M. P. (1991). *Analysis and design of business information systems*. New York: Macmillan Publishing Company.

Mathworks. (2011, May 15). *Mathworks™ website: Simulink - Simulation and model-based design*. Retrieved from http://www.mathworks.com/products/simulink/

Mattern, F. (1989, October). Virtual time and global states of distributed systems. In *Proceedings of the International Workshop on Parallel and Distributed Algorithms* (pp. 215–226). Château de Bonas, France.

Mayer, J., & Schneckenburger, C. (2006). *An empirical analysis and comparison of random testing techniques*. Paper presented at the 2006 ACM/IEEE International Symposium on Empirical Software Engineering (ISESE '06). New York, NY: ACM.

McCarthy, V. (1999). *HP splits in two to focus on enterprise, e-services*. Retrieved from http://www.hpworld.org/hpworldnews/hpw903/news/01.html

Mcglade, L. (2008). *Structural testing of Web-based scripting programs*. Retrieved from http://www.cra.org/Activities/craw/dmp/awards/2001/mcglade/final_paper.htm

McGraw, G. (2006). *Software security: Building security in*. Boston, MA: Addison-Wesley.

Memon, A. (2001). *A comprehensive framework for testing graphical user interfaces*. Ph.D. thesis, Department of Computer Science, University of Pittsburgh, July 2001.

Memon, A., & Soffa, M. (2003). Regression testing of GUIs. In *Proceedings of ESEC/FSE'03*, September 2003.

Memon, A., Banerejee, I., & Nagarajan, A. (2003). GUI ripping: Reverse engineering of graphical user interfaces for testing. In *Proceedings of the 10th. Working Conference on Reverse Engineering* (WCRE'03), (pp. 1095-1350).

Memon, A. (2001). Hierarchical GUI test case generation using automated planning. *IEEE Transactions on Software Engineering, 27*(2), 144–155. doi:10.1109/32.908959

Memon, A. (2002). GUI testing: Pitfall and process. *Software Technologies, 35*(8), 87–88.

Memon, A. (2004). *Developing testing techniques for event-driven pervasive computing applications*. Department of Computer Science, University of Maryland.

Memon, A. (2008). Automatically repairing event sequence-based GUI test suites for regression testing. *ACM Transactions on Software Engineering and Methodology, 18*(2). doi:10.1145/1416563.1416564

Memon, A., & Xie, Q. (2005). Studying the fault detection effectiveness of GUI test cases for rapidly evolving software. *IEEE Transactions on Software Engineering, 31*(10), 884–896. doi:10.1109/TSE.2005.117

Metsa, J., Katara, M., & Mikkonen, T. (2007). Testing non-functional requirements with aspects: An industrial case study. Paper presented at the Seventh International Conference on Quality Software (QSIC '07). Washington, DC: IEEE Computer Society.

Meuter, M. L., Ostrom, A. L., Roundtree, R. I., & Bitner, M. J. (2000). Self-service technologies: Understanding customer satisfaction with technology-based service encounters. *Journal of Marketing, 64*, 50–64. doi:10.1509/jmkg.64.3.50.18024

MIT Software design group. (2008). *Computer science and artificial intelligence laboratory*. Retrieved from http://sdg.csail.mit.edu/index.html

Mitchell, A., & Power, J. (2004). An approach to quantifying the run-time behavior of Java GUI applications. In Proceedings of the Winter International Symposium on Information and Communication Technologies, Cancun, Mexico, (pp. 1–6).

Mittal, N., & Garg, V. K. (2001). Computation slicing: Techniques and theory. In *DISC '01: Proceedings of the 15th International Conference on Distributed Computing* (pp. 78–92). London, UK: Springer-Verlag.

Mohapatra, S. (2010). Improvised process for quality through quantitative project management; an experience from software development projects. *International Journal of Information and Communication Technology, 2*(4), 355–373. doi:10.1504/IJICT.2010.034977

Muccini, H., Bertolino, A., & Inverardi, P. (2004). Using software architecture for code testing. *IEEE Transactions on Software Engineering, 30*(3), 160–171. doi:10.1109/TSE.2004.1271170

Mustafa, G., Ali Shah, A., Asif, K. H., & Ali, A. (2007). A strategy for testing of Web based software. *Information Technology Journal, 6*(1), 74–81. doi:10.3923/itj.2007.74.81

Myers, G. (1979). *The art of software testing.* New York, NY: John Wiley and Sons.

Myers, G. L. (1979). *The art of software testing.* Wiley-Interscience.

Naunheimer, H., Bertsche, B., Ryborz, J., & Novak, W. (2011). *Automotive transmissions: Fundamentals, selection, design and application* (2nd ed.). Berlin, Germany: Springer.

Nistorica, G. (2005). Automated GUI testing. O'Reilly Network. Retrieved from http://www.perl.com/pub/a/2005/08/11/win32guitest.html

Nogueira, S., Sampaio, A., & Mota, A. (2008). Guided test generation from CSP models. *Proceedings of the 5th International Colloquium on Theoretical Aspects of Computing,* (pp. 258-273). Berlin, Germany: Springer.

Nuseibeh, B., & Easterbrook, S. (2000). *Requirements engineering: A roadmap,* (pp. 35-46). Paper presented at the Conference on The Future of Software Engineering (ICSE '00). New York, NY: ACM.

Oliveira, J. C., Gouveia, C. C., & Filho, R. Q. (2006). *A way of improving test automation cost-effectiveness. CAST 2006.* Indianapolis: EUA.

Omar, A. A., & Mohammed, F. A. (1991). A survey of software functional testing methods. *SIGSOFT Software Engineering Notes, 16*(2), 75–82. doi:10.1145/122538.122551

Onken, L., & Kueng, S. (2001). *Tortoise, a SVN client for Windows.* Retrieved from http://tortoisesvn.tigris.org/

Orso, A., & Silva, S. (1998). Open issues and research directions in object oriented testing. In *Proceedings of the 4th International Conference on "Achieving Quality in Software: Software Quality in the Communication Society" (AQUIS '98)*, Venice, Italy.

Parasuraman, A., & Grewal, D. (2000). The impact of technology on the quality-value-loyalty chain: A research agenda. *Journal of the Academy of Marketing Science, 28*(1), 168–174. doi:10.1177/0092070300281015

Park, S. S., & Maurer, F. (2008). *The benefits and challenges of executable acceptance testing.* Paper presented at the 2008 International Workshop on Scrutinizing Agile Practices or Shoot-out at the Agile Corral (APOS '08). New York, NY: ACM.

Parthasarathy, M., & Bhattacherjee, A. (1998). Understanding post-adoption behaviour in the context of online services. *Information Systems Research, 9*(4), 362–379. doi:10.1287/isre.9.4.362

Pelliccione, P., Muccini, H., Bucchiarone, A., & Facchini, F. (2005). TeStor: Deriving test sequences from model-based specifications. *Proceedings of the 8th International SIGSOFT Symposium on Component-Based Software Engineering,* (pp. 267-282). Berlin, Germany: Springer.

Compilation of References

Petrasch, R. (1999). *The definition of software quality: A practical approach*. Paper presented at the 10th International Symposium on Software Reliability Engineering.

Pettichord, B. (2004). *Homebrew test automation*. ThoughtWorks. Retrieved from www.io.com/~wazmo/papers/homebrew_test_automation_200409.pdf

Pilskalns, O., Andrews, A., Ghosh, S., & France, R. (2003). Rigorous testing by merging structural and behavioral UML representations. *Proceedings of the 6th International Conference on the Unified Modeling Language*, (pp. 234-248). Berlin, Germany: Springer.

Pnueli, A. (1977). The temporal logic of programs. In *FOCS: Proceedings of the 18th IEEE Symposium on Foundation of Computer Science* (pp. 46-57).

Pnueli, A. (1979). The temporal semantics of concurrent programs. In *Proceedings of the International Symposium on Semantics of Concurrent Computation* (pp. 1-20).

Pressman, R. S. (2005). *Software engineering: A practitioner's approach* (6th ed.). India: TMH.

Pretschner, A., Slotosch, O., Aiglstorfer, E., & Kriebel, S. (2004). Model based testing for real--The in house card case study. *International Journal on Software Tools for Technology Transfer*, *5*(2), 140–157. doi:10.1007/s10009-003-0128-3

Prowell, S. J., & Poore, J. H. (2003). Foundations of sequence-based software specification. *IEEE Transactions on Software Engineering*, *29*(5), 417–429. doi:10.1109/TSE.2003.1199071

Pursak, L. (1997). *Knowledge in organizations*. Oxford, UK: Butlerworth-Heinemann.

Rajanna, V. (2001). Automated software testing tools and their impact on software maintenance. In *Proceedings of the 3rd Annual International Software Testing*, India. Retrieved from Softwaredioxide.com

Ranjan, S. P. (2008). Test case prioritization. *Journal of Theoretical and Applied Information Technology*, *4*(2), 178-181. Asian Research Publishing Network. ISSN 1992-8645

Ranjan, S. P., et al. (2008). Generation of test data using meta heuristic approach. *Proceeding of IEEE TENCON 2008*.

Ranjan, S. P., & Raghurama, G. (2009). Function and path coverage based techniques for prioritization test cases for regression testing. *International Journal of Software Engineering and Computing*, *1*(2), 85–91.

Redmill, F. (2004). Exploring risk-based testing and its implications: Research articles. *Software Testing and Verifying Reliability*, *14*(1), 3–15. doi:10.1002/stvr.288

Rehman, M. J., Jabeen, F., Bertolino, A., & Polini, A. (2007). Testing software components for integration: A survey of issues and techniques: Research Articles. *Software Testing and Verifying Reliability*, *17*(2), 95–133. doi:10.1002/stvr.357

Reza, H., & Grant, E. S. (2007). A method to test concurrent systems using architectural specification. *The Journal of Supercomputing*, *39*(3), 347–357. doi:10.1007/s11227-006-0017-0

Riel, A. C. R., Liljander, V., & Jurriens, P. (2001). Exploring consumer evaluations of e-services: A portal site. *International Journal of Service Industry Management, 12*(4), 359–377. doi:10.1108/09564230110405280

Robinson-Mallett, C., Hierons, R., Poore, J., & Liggesmeyer, P. (2008). Using communication coverage criteria and partial model generation to assist software integration testing. *Software Quality Journal, 16*(2), 185–211. doi:10.1007/s11219-007-9036-1

Rogers, E. M. (1995). *Diffusion of innovations*. New York, NY: The Free Press.

Rothermel, G., & Harrold, M. J. (1994). Selecting tests and identifying test coverage requirements for modified software. *International Symposium on Software Testing and Analysis (ISSTA 94),* (pp. 169-184). New York, NY: ACM Press.

Rothermel, R. (1996). *Efficient effective regression testing using safe test selection techniques.* Ph.D Thesis, Clemson University, May, 1996.

Rothermel, G., Elbaum, S., Malishevsky, A. G., Kallakuri, P., & Qiu, X. (2004). On test suite composition and cost-effective regression testing. *ACM Transactions on Software Engineering and Methodology, 13*(3), 277–331. doi:10.1145/1027092.1027093

Rust, R. T., & Lemon, K. N. (2001). E-service and the consumer. *International Journal of Electronic Commerce, 5*(3), 85–101.

Ruyter, K. D., Wetzels, M., & Kleijnen, M. (2001). Customer adoption of e- services: An experimental study. *International Journal of Service Industry Management, 12*(2), 184–207. doi:10.1108/09564230110387542

Saglietti, F., & Pinte, F. (2010). Automated unit and integration testing for component-based software systems. *Proceedings of the International Workshop on Security and Dependability for Resource Constrained Embedded Systems* (S&D4RCES '10). New York, NY: ACM Press.

Sandhu, K. (2009). Measuring the performance of electronic services acceptance model (E-SAM). *International Journal of Business Information Systems, 5*(4).

Sandhu, K., & Corbitt, B. (2002). *WG8.6: Exploring an understanding of electronic service end-user adoption.* Sydney, Australia: The International Federation for Information Processing.

Sandhu, K., & Corbitt, B. (2008). A framework for electronic services system. *International Journal of Electronic Customer Relationship Management, 2*(1). doi:10.1504/IJECRM.2008.019568

Schätz, B., & Pfaller, C. (2010). Integrating component tests to system tests. *Electronic Notes in Theoretical Computer Science, 260,* 225–241. doi:10.1016/j.entcs.2009.12.040

Schwarz, R., & Mattern, F. (1994). Detecting causal relationships in distributed computations: In search of the holy grail. *Distributed Computing, 7*(3), 149–174. doi:10.1007/BF02277859

Seacord, R. C. (2005). *Secure coding in C and C++ (SEI series in software engineering).* Addison-Wesley Professional.

Sen, A. (2004). *Techniques for formal verification of concurrent and distributed program traces.* PhD thesis, University of Texas at Austin.

Sen, A., & Garg, V. K. (2002). Detecting temporal logic predicates on the happened-before model. In *IPDPS '02: Proceedings of the 16th International Parallel and Distributed Processing Symposium* (p. 116).

Sen, A., & Garg, V. K. (2003b). Partial order trace analyzer (pota) for distributed programs. In *In Runtime Verification 2003, volume 89 of ENTCS.*

Sen, A., & Garg, V. K. (2003a). *Detecting temporal logic predicates in distributed programs using computation slicing* (pp. 171–183). OPODIS.

Sengupta, G. J. (2010). Regression testing method based on XML schema for GUI components. *Journal of Software Engineering, 4*(2), 137–146. doi:10.3923/jse.2010.137.146

Seol, S., Kim, M., Kang, S., & Ryu, J. (2003). Fully automated interoperability test suite derivation for communication protocols. *Computer Networks: The International Journal of Computer and Telecommunications Networking, 43*(6), 735–759.

Shams, M., Krishnamurthy, D., & Far, B. (2006). A model-based approach for testing the performance of web applications. *The 3rd International Workshop on Software Quality Assurance* (SOQUA '06), (pp. 54-61). New York, NY: ACM.

Shen, L., & Su, S. Y. H. (1988). A functional testing method for microprocessors. *IEEE Transactions on Computers, 37*(10), 1288–1293. doi:10.1109/12.5992

Silva, F. R. C., Almeida, E. S., & Meira, S. R. L. (2009). An approach for component testing and its empirical validation. In *Proceedings of the 2009 ACM Symposium on Applied Computing* (SAC '09), (pp. 574-581). New York, NY: ACM.

Singh, Y., Kaur, A., & Bharti, S. (2010). Test case prioritization using ant colony optimization. *ACM SIGSOFT Software Engineering Notes, 35*(4), 1-7 Srikanth, H., & Williams, L. (2005). On the economics of requirements based test case prioritization. *Proceeding in EDSER*, (pp. 1-3). ACM Press.

Sneed, H. M. (2010). Testing object-oriented software systems. In *Proceedings of the 1st Workshop on Testing Object-Oriented Systems* (ETOOS '10). New York, NY: ACM.

Song, X., & Osterweil, L. J. (1994). Experience with an approach to comparing software design methodologies. *IEEE Transactions on Software Engineering, 20*(5), 364–384. doi:10.1109/32.286419

Souza, E., Gusmão, C., & Venâncio, J. (2010). Risk-based testing: A case study. In *Proceedings of the 2010 Seventh International Conference on Information Technology: New Generations* (ITNG '10), (pp. 1032-1037). Washington, DC: IEEE Computer Society.

Spender, J. C. (1996). Making knowledge the basis of a dynamic theory of the firm. *Strategic Management Journal, 17*, 45–62.

Spezialetti, M., & Kearns, P. (1986). *Efficient distributed snapshots* (pp. 382–388). ICDCS.

Spillner, A. (1995). Test criteria and coverage measures for software integration testing. *Software Quality Journal, 4*(4), 275–286. doi:10.1007/BF00402648

Sprenkle, S., Gibson, E., Sampath, S., & Pollock, L. (2005). Automated replay and failure detection for Web applications. *Proceedings of the 20th IEEE/ACM international Conference on Automated Software Engineering*, November 07-11, 2005, USA.

Sreedevi, S. (2006). *Cost effective techniques for user session based testing of Web applications*. PhD dissertation, University of Delaware. Retrieved from 128.4.133.74:8080/dspace/bitstream/123456789/168/1/-sampath.dissertation06.pdf

Srivastava, A., & Thiagarajan, J. (2002). *Effectively prioritizing test cases in development environment. Proceeding in ISSTA* (pp. 97–106). ACM Press.

Stepanov, A., & Lee, M. (1995). *The standard template library*. HP Laboratories Technical Report 95-11(R.1).

Stewart, F. (2008). *Practical use of Rational Robot in transactional monitoring*. IBM. Retrieved from http://www.ibm.com/developerworks/tivoli/library/trationalrobot/index.html

Szymanski, D. M., & Hise, R. T. (2000). E-satisfaction: An initial examination. *Journal of Retailing, 76*(3), 309–322. doi:10.1016/S0022-4359(00)00035-X

Takang, A. A., & Grubb, P. A. (1996). *Software maintenance concepts and practice*. London, UK: Thompson Computer Press.

Tarafdar, A., & Garg, V. K. (1998). *Predicate control for active debugging of distributed programs* (pp. 763–769). IPPS/SPDP.

Tomlinson, A. I., & Garg, V. K. (1993). Detecting relational global predicates in distributed systems. In *Workshop on Parallel and Distributed Debugging* (pp. 21-31).

Tretmans, J. (1996). Test generation with inputs, outputs, and quiescence. In *Proceedings of the Second International Workshop on Tools and Algorithms for Construction and Analysis of Systems, Passau, Germany, Lecture Notes in Computer Science,* 1055, (pp. 127–146).

Trevino, L. K., & Webster, J. (1992). Flow in computer-mediated communication: electronic mail and voice evaluation. *Communication Research, 19*(2), 539–573. doi:10.1177/009365092019005001

Tse, T. H., Chan, F. T., & Chen, H. Y. (1994). An axiom-based test case selection strategy for object-oriented programs. *IFIP Conference Proceedings, Software Quality and Productivity: Theory, Practice and Training,* London, UK, (pp. 107–114).

Tse, T. H., Chan, F. T., & Chen, H. Y. (1998). In black and white: An integrated approach to object-oriented program testing. *ACM Transactions on Software Engineering and Methodology, 7*(3), 250–295. doi:10.1145/287000.287004

Tubeishat, M., Alsmadi, I., & Al-Kabi, M. (2010). Using XML for user interface documentation and differential evaluation. *Journal of Theoretical and Applied Information Technology, 21*(2).

Turner, C. D., & Robson, D. J. (1993). The state-based testing of object-oriented programs. In *Proceedings of the IEEE Conference on Software Maintenance* (CSM- 93), Montreal, Canada, (pp. 302–310).

Ulrich, A., & König, H. (1997). Specification-based testing of concurrent systems. *Proceedings of the Joint International Conference Formal Description Techniques and Protocol Specification, Testing and Verification (FORTE/PSTV97)*, (pp. 7–22). Chapman & Hall.

Utting, M., Pretschner, A., & Legeard, B. (2011). A taxonomy of model-based testing. *Journal of Software Testing. Verification and Reliability*, *21*(2), 72–90.

van Riel, A. C. R., Liljander, V., & Jurriëns, P. (2001). Exploring consumer evaluations of e-services: a portal site. *International Journal of Service Industry Management*, *12*(40), 359–377. doi:10.1108/09564230110405280

Venkatesh, V. (2000). Determinants of perceived ease of use: Integrating control, intrinsic motivation, and emotion into the technology acceptance model. *Information Systems Research*, *11*(4), 342–365. doi:10.1287/isre.11.4.342.11872

Volk, E. (2004). *CxxTest: A JUnit/CppUnit/xUnit-like framework for C/C++*. Retrieved from http://cxxtest.sourceforge.net/guide.html

Walston, C. E., & Felix, C. P. (1977). A method of programming measurement and estimation. *IBM Systems Journal*, *16*(1), 54–73. doi:10.1147/sj.161.0054

Wang, Z., Wu, J., & Yin, X. (2004). Generating interoperability test sequence for distributed test architecture: A generic formal framework. *Proceedings of the International Conference on Information Networking (ICOIN 2004)*, (pp. 1135-1144). Berlin, Germany: Springer.

Weiser, M. (1984). Program slicing. *IEEE Transactions on Software Engineering*, *10*(4), 352–357. doi:10.1109/TSE.1984.5010248

White, L., & Almezen, H. (2000). Generating test cases from GUI responsibilities using complete interaction sequences. In *Proceedings of the International Symposium on Software Reliability Engineering (ISSRE'00)*, San Jose, USA, (pp. 110-121).

White, L., Al Mezen, H., & Alzeidi, N. (2001). User-based testing of GUI sequences and their interactions. In *Proceedings of the 12th International Symposium on Software Reliability Engineering* (ISSRE'01), Hong Kong, PRC, (p. 54).

Whittaker, J. A. (2002). *How to break software*. Boston, MA: Addison-Wesley.

Whittaker, J. A. (2009). *Exploratory software testing: Tips, tricks, tours, and techniques to guide test design* (1st ed.). Addison-Wesley.

Wieczorek, S., Kozyura, V., Roth, A., Leuschel, M., Bendisposto, J., Plagge, D., & Schieferdecker, S. (2009). Applying model checking to generate model-based integration tests from choreography models. *Proceedings of the 21st International Conference on Testing of Software and Communication Systems and 9th International FATES Workshop (TESTCOM '09/FATES '09)*, (pp. 179-194). Berlin, Germany: Springer.

Wiegers, K. A. (2002). *Peer reviews in software: A practical guide*. Addison-Wesley.

Wiegers, K. A. (2003). *Software requirements*. Microsoft Press.

Wiegers, K. A. (2006). *More about software requirements: Thorny issues and practical advice*. Microsoft Press.

Wiegers, K. A. (2007). *Practical project initiation - Best practices, a handbook with tools*. Microsoft Press.

Wilber, J., & Weishaar, G. (2002). *Executing visual test scripts with IBM Rational TestManager*. IBM. Retrieved from http://www.ibm.com/developerworks/rational/library/2962.html

Williams, C. (1999). Software testing and the UML. In *Proceedings of the International Symposium on Software Reliability Engineering* (ISSRE'99), Boca Raton, USA.

Wong, W. E., Horgan, J. R., London, S., & Aggrawal, H. (1997). *A study of effective regression in practice. Proceeding in ISSRE* (p. 264). IEEE Press.

Wright, K. M., & Granger, M. J. (2001). Using the Web as a strategic resource: an applied classroom exercise. *Proceedings of the 16th Annual Conference of the International Academy for Information Management*, New Orleans, Louisiana.

Wu, Y., Pan, D., & Chen, M.-H. (2001). Techniques for testing component-based software. *Proceeding of the 7th International Conference on Engineering of Complex Computer Systems (ICECCS 2001)*, (pp. 222-232). IEEE Computer Society.

Wu, F., & Yi, T. (2004). Slicing Z specifications. *SIGPLAN Notice, 39*(8), 39–48. doi:10.1145/1026474.1026481

Wysopal, C., Nelson, L., Dai Zovi, D., & Dustin, E. (2006). *The art of software security testing: Identifying software security flaws*. Boston, MA: Addison-Wesley.

Xie, Q. (2006). Developing cost-effective model-based techniques for GUI testing. In *Proceedings of The International Conference of Software Engineering 2006* (ICSE'06).

Xin, W., Feng-Yan, H., & Zheng, Q. (2010). Software reliability testing data generation approach based on a mixture model. *Information Technology Journal, 9*(5), 1038–1043. doi:10.3923/itj.2010.1038.1043

Xue, M., Harker, P. T., & Heim, G. R. (2004). *Incorporating the dual customer roles in e-service design. The working paper series*. The Wharton Financial Institutions Center.

Yang, X.-S., & Deb, S. (2009). Cuckoo search via Lévy flights. *Proceeding in World Congress on Nature & Biologically Inspired Computing* (NaBIC), (pp. 210–214). IEEE Publications.

Yang, X.-S., & Deb, S. (2010). Engineering optimisation by cuckoo search. *International Journal of Mathematical Modelling and Numerical Optimisation, 1*(4), 330–343. doi:10.1504/IJMMNO.2010.035430

Yin, R. K. (1994). *Case study research: Design and methods* (2nd ed.). Sage Publications.

Young, S. J., Russell, N. H., & Thornton, J. H. S. (1989). *Token passing: A simple conceptual model for connected speech recognition systems. Tech. Rep.* CUED.

Zeithaml, V. A., Parasuraman, A., & Malhotra, A. (2000). *A conceptual framework for understanding e-service quality: Implications for future research and managerial practice*. Marketing Science Institute, Working paper, Report no: 00-115.

Zeithaml, V. A., Berry, L., & Parasuraman, A. (1993). The nature and determinants of customer expectations of service. *Journal of the Academy of Marketing Science, 21*(1), 1–12. doi:10.1177/0092070393211001

Zeithaml, V. A., & Bitner, M. J. (2000). *Services marketing: Integrating customer focus across the firm*. Irwin McGraw-Hill.

Compilation of References

Zemke, R., & Connellan, T. (2001). *E-service: 24 ways to keep your customers when the competition is just a click away*. American Management Association.

Zhang, J., & Cheung, S. C. (2002). Automated test case generation for the stress testing of multimedia systems. *Software, Practice & Experience, 32*(15), 1411–1435. doi:10.1002/spe.487

Zhu, H., & He, X. (2000). A methodology of testing high-level Petri nets. *Journal of Information and Software Technology, 44*(8), 473–489. doi:10.1016/S0950-5849(02)00048-4

Related References

To continue our tradition of advancing information science and technology research, we have compiled a list of recommended IGI Global readings. These references will provide additional information and guidance to further enrich your knowledge and assist you with your own research and future publications.

Abait, E. S., Vidal, S. A., Marcos, C. A., Casas, S. I., & Sofia, A. A. (2010). An Integrated Process for Aspect Mining and Refactoring In Cipolla-Ficarra, F. V. (Ed.), *Quality and Communicability for Interactive Hypermedia Systems: Concepts and Practices for Design* (pp. 176–194).

Abdat, N., Spruit, M., & Bos, M. (2011). Software as a Service and the Pricing Strategy for Vendors In Strader, T. (Ed.), *Digital Product Management, Technology and Practice: Interdisciplinary Perspectives* (pp. 154–192).

Abdullah, M., Ahmad, R., Peck, L. S., Kasirun, Z. M., & Alshammari, F. (2012). Benefits of CMM and CMMI-Based Software Process Improvement In Fauzi, S. S., Nasir, M. N., Ramli, N., & Sahibuddin, S. (Eds.), *Software Process Improvement and Management: Approaches and Tools for Practical Development* (pp. 224–240).

Abels, S., Hasselbring, W., Streekmann, N., & Uslar, M. (2009). Model-Driven Integration in Complex Information Systems: Experiences from Two Scenarios In Rech, J., & Bunse, C. (Eds.), *Model-Driven Software Development: Integrating Quality Assurance* (pp. 431–446).

Abu-Taieh, E. M., El Sheikh, A. A., Abu-Tayeh, J. M., & El-Mahied, M. T. (2009). Information Technology Projects System Development Life Cycles: Comparative Study In Kidd, T. T. (Ed.), *Handbook of Research on Technology Project Management* (pp. 114–136). Planning, and Operations.

Abu-Taieh, E. M., & Rahman El Sheikh, A. A. (2007). Discrete Event Simulation Process Validation, Verification, and Testing In Dasso, A., & Funes, A. (Eds.), *Verification* (pp. 177–212). Validation and Testing in Software Engineering.

Related References

Adam, A. (2009). Trusting Computers Through Trusting Humans: Software Verification in a Safety-Critical Information Society In Gupta, M., & Sharman, R. (Eds.), *Social and Human Elements of Information Security: Emerging Trends and Countermeasures* (pp. 61–75).

Afzal, W., Torkar, R., Feldt, R., & Gorschek, T. (2010). Genetic Programming for Cross-Release Fault Count Predictions in Large and Complex Software Projects In Chis, M. (Ed.), *Evolutionary Computation and Optimization Algorithms in Software Engineering: Applications and Techniques* (pp. 94–126).

Ahmad, N., & Laplante, P. A. (2011). A Systematic Approach to Evaluating Open Source Software. [IJSITA]. *International Journal of Strategic Information Technology and Applications*, *2*(1), 48–67. doi:doi:10.4018/jsita.2011010104

Ahmed, N., & Jensen, C. D. (2012). Security of Dependable Systems In Petre, L., Sere, K., & Troubitsyna, E. (Eds.), *Dependability and Computer Engineering: Concepts for Software-Intensive Systems* (pp. 230–264).

Ajewole, A. I. (2008). Software Requirements for Cybercafés In Adomi, E. (Ed.), *Security and Software for Cybercafes* (pp. 125–146).

Alberti, M., Cattafi, M., Chesani, F., Gavanelli, M., Lamma, E., & Mello, P. (2011). A Computational Logic Application Framework for Service Discovery and Contracting. [IJWSR]. *International Journal of Web Services Research*, *8*(3), 1–25. doi:doi:10.4018/IJWSR.2011070101

Alkkiomäki, V., & Smolander, K. (2012). Service Elicitation Method Using Applied Qualitative Research Procedures In Liu, X., & Li, Y. (Eds.), *Advanced Design Approaches to Emerging Software Systems: Principles* (pp. 1–17). Methodologies and Tools.

Alzoabi, Z. (2012). Agile Software: Body of Knowledge In Rahman El Sheikh, A. A., & Alnoukari, M. (Eds.), *Business Intelligence and Agile Methodologies for Knowledge-Based Organizations: Cross-Disciplinary Applications* (pp. 14–34).

Angelis, L., Sentas, P., Mittas, N., & Chatzipetrou, P. (2011). Methods for Statistical and Visual Comparison of Imputation Methods for Missing Data in Software Cost Estimation In Dogru, A. H., & Biçer, V. (Eds.), *Modern Software Engineering Concepts and Practices: Advanced Approaches* (pp. 221–241).

Antunes, N., & Vieira, M. (2012). Detecting Vulnerabilities in Web Services: Can Developers Rely on Existing Tools? In Cardellini, V., Casalicchio, E., Castelo Branco, K. L., Estrella, J. C., & Monaco, F. J. (Eds.), *Performance and Dependability in Service Computing: Concepts, Techniques and Research Directions.* (pp. 402-426). doi:10.4018/978-1-60960-794-4.ch018

April, A., & Laporte, C. Y. (2006). An Overview of Software Quality Concepts and Management Issues In Duggan, E., & Reichgelt, J. (Eds.), *Measuring Information Systems Delivery Quality* (pp. 28–54).

Azevedo, S., Machado, R. J., Bragança, A., & Ribeiro, H. (2011). Systematic Use of Software Development Patterns through a Multilevel and Multistage Classification In Osis, J., & Asnina, E. (Eds.), *Model-Driven Domain Analysis and Software Development: Architectures and Functions* (pp. 304–333).

Bader, A., & Ramakrishnan, S. (2010). Software Components In Ramachandran, M., & de Carvalho, R. (Eds.), *Handbook of Research on Software Engineering and Productivity Technologies: Implications of Globalization* (pp. 351–363).

Barker, M., Matsumoto, K., & Inoue, K. (2010). Putting a TAG on Software: Purchaser-Centered Software Engineering In Ramachandran, M., & de Carvalho, R. (Eds.), *Handbook of Research on Software Engineering and Productivity Technologies: Implications of Globalization* (pp. 38–48).

Bartolini, C., Bertolino, A., Lonetti, F., & Marchetti, E. (2012). Approaches to Functional, Structural and Security SOA Testing. In Cardellini, V., Casalicchio, E., Castelo Branco, K. L., Estrella, J. C., & Monaco, F. J. (Eds.), *Performance and Dependability in Service Computing: Concepts, Techniques and Research Directions.* (pp. 381-401). doi:10.4018/978-1-60960-794-4.ch017

Berki, E., Siakas, K., & Georgiadou, E. (2007). Agile Quality or Depth of Reasoning? Applicability vs. Suitability with Respect to Stakeholders' Needs In Stamelos, I. G., & Sfetsos, P. (Eds.), *Agile Software Development Quality Assurance* (pp. 23–55).

Bettin, J. (2006). Managing Complexity with MDSD In Liu, L., & Roussev, B. (Eds.), *Management of the Object-Oriented Development Process* (pp. 200–230).

Bhattacharya, S., Kanjilal, A., & Sengupta, S. (2010). Tools and Techniques for Model Based Testing In Ramachandran, M., & de Carvalho, R. (Eds.), *Handbook of Research on Software Engineering and Productivity Technologies: Implications of Globalization* (pp. 226–249).

Bibi, S., Katsaros, D., & Bozanis, P. (2012). How to Choose the Right Cloud In Liu, X., & Li, Y. (Eds.), *Advanced Design Approaches to Emerging Software Systems: Principles* (pp. 219–240). Methodologies and Tools.

Blake, M. B. (2012). Semi-Automated Life-cycles for Eliciting Requirements for Service-Oriented Environments In Lee, J., Ma, S., & Liu, A. (Eds.), *Service Life Cycle Tools and Technologies: Methods* (pp. 22–34). Trends and Advances.

Blanco, C., Rosado, D., Gutiérrez, C., Rodríguez, A., Mellado, D., & Fernández-Medina, E. (2011). Security Over the Information Systems Development Cycle In Mouratidis, H. (Ed.), *Software Engineering for Secure Systems: Industrial and Research Perspectives* (pp. 113–154).

Bobkowska, A. E. (2009). Integrating Quality Criteria and Methods of Evaluation for Software Models In Rech, J., & Bunse, C. (Eds.), *Model-Driven Software Development: Integrating Quality Assurance* (pp. 78–94).

Related References

Bolanos, D., & Sierra, A. (2009). Integrated Software Testing Learning Environment for Training Senior-Level Computer Science Students In Ellis, H., Demurjian, S., & Naveda, J. (Eds.), *Software Engineering: Effective Teaching and Learning Approaches and Practices* (pp. 233–249).

Boldyreff, C., Nutter, D., Rank, S., Kyaw, P., & Lavery, J. (2005). Support for Collaborative Component-Based Software Engineering In Yang, H. (Ed.), *Advances in UML and XML-Based Software Evolution* (pp. 71–91).

Boulanger, J. (2010). Requirements Engineering in a Model-Based Methodology for Embedded Automotive Software In Ramachandran, M., & de Carvalho, R. (Eds.), *Handbook of Research on Software Engineering and Productivity Technologies: Implications of Globalization* (pp. 15–27).

Boulanger, J. (2011). Requirement Management and Link with Architecture and Components1 In Ramachandran, M. (Ed.), *Knowledge Engineering for Software Development Life Cycles: Support Technologies and Applications* (pp. 34–67).

Boulanger, J., Rasse, A., & Idani, A. (2010). Models Oriented Approach for Developing Railway Safety-Critical Systems with UML In Ramachandran, M., & de Carvalho, R. (Eds.), *Handbook of Research on Software Engineering and Productivity Technologies: Implications of Globalization* (pp. 305–330).

Brændeland, G., & Stølen, K. (2012). Using Model-Driven Risk Analysis in Component-Based Development In Petre, L., Sere, K., & Troubitsyna, E. (Eds.), *Dependability and Computer Engineering: Concepts for Software-Intensive Systems* (pp. 330–380).

Brandon, D. M. (2006). Managing Quality In Brandon, D. M. (Ed.), *Project Management for Modern Information Systems* (pp. 202–233).

Brandon, D. M. (2008). Project Management and Web Software Engineering In Brandon, D. M. (Ed.), *Software Engineering for Modern Web Applications: Methodologies and Technologies* (pp. 254–291).

Brehm, N., & Gómez, J. M. (2010). Secure Service Rating in Federated Software Systems Based on SOA In Gutiérrez, C. A., Fernández-Medina, E., & Piattini, M. (Eds.), *Web Services Security Development and Architecture: Theoretical and Practical Issues* (pp. 83–98).

Brosch, P., Langer, P., Seidl, M., Wieland, K., Wimmer, M., & Kappel, G. (2012). The Past, Present, and Future of Model Versioning In Rech, J., & Bunse, C. (Eds.), *Emerging Technologies for the Evolution and Maintenance of Software Models* (pp. 410–443).

Bryce, R. C., Lei, Y., Kuhn, D. R., & Kacker, R. (2010). Combinatorial Testing In Ramachandran, M., & de Carvalho, R. (Eds.), *Handbook of Research on Software Engineering and Productivity Technologies: Implications of Globalization* (pp. 196–208).

Burkhardt, P. (2009). Social Software Trends in Business In Deans, P. C. (Ed.), *Social Software and Web 2.0 Technology Trends* (pp. 1–16).

Byers, D., & Shahmehri, N. (2012). Modeling Security Goals and Software Vulnerabilities In Petre, L., Sere, K., & Troubitsyna, E. (Eds.), *Dependability and Computer Engineering: Concepts for Software-Intensive Systems* (pp. 171–198).

Carter, R. B., & Strader, T. J. (2012). Software Firm Cost Structure and Its Impact on IPOs in the E-Commerce Era In Lee, I. (Ed.), *Transformations in E-Business Technologies and Commerce: Emerging Impacts* (pp. 240–251).

Carver, A., & Halpin, T. (2010). Atomicity and Semantic Normalization. [IJISMD]. *International Journal of Information System Modeling and Design*, *1*(2), 23–39. doi:doi:10.4018/jismd.2010040102

Castro, C. C., Calero, C., & García, Y. M. (2008). A Quality-Aware Engineering Process for Web Applications In Calero, C., Angeles Moraga, M., & Piattini, M. (Eds.), *Handbook of Research on Web Information Systems Quality* (pp. 378–404).

Caudill, J. G. (2010). Helping to Bridge the Digital Divide with Free Software and Services In Reddick, C. (Ed.), *Politics, Democracy and E-Government: Participation and Service Delivery* (pp. 315–331).

Chen, Q., Wang, L., Guo, P., & Huang, H. (2011). Analyzing Concurrent Programs Title for Potential Programming Errors In Dogru, A. H., & Biçer, V. (Eds.), *Modern Software Engineering Concepts and Practices: Advanced Approaches* (pp. 380–415).

Chis, M. (2010). Introduction: A Survey of the Evolutionary Computation Techniques for Software Engineering In Chis, M. (Ed.), *Evolutionary Computation and Optimization Algorithms in Software Engineering: Applications and Techniques* (pp. 1–12).

Cho, H., Gray, J., Cai, Y., Wong, S., & Xie, T. (2011). Model-Driven Impact Analysis of Software Product Lines In Osis, J., & Asnina, E. (Eds.), *Model-Driven Domain Analysis and Software Development: Architectures and Functions* (pp. 275–303).

Choi, H., Lee, S., Fahmi, S. A., Ibrahim, A., Shin, H., & Park, Y. (2012). Towards an Integrated Personal Software Process and Team Software Process Supporting Tool In Fauzi, S. S., Nasir, M. N., Ramli, N., & Sahibuddin, S. (Eds.), *Software Process Improvement and Management: Approaches and Tools for Practical Development* (pp. 205–223).

Chroust, G., Kuhrmann, M., & Schoitsch, E. (2010). Modeling Software Development Processes In Cruz-Cunha, M. M. (Ed.), *Social* (pp. 31–62). Managerial, and Organizational Dimensions of Enterprise Information Systems.

Chroust, G., & Schoitsch, E. (2009). Choosing Basic Architectural Alternatives In Tiako, P. (Ed.), *Designing Software-Intensive Systems: Methods and Principles* (pp. 161–221).

Chu, W. C., Chang, C., Lu, C., Peng, Y., & Yang, D. (2005). PRAISE: A Software Development Environment to Support Software Evolution In Yang, H. (Ed.), *Advances in UML and XML-Based Software Evolution* (pp. 105–140).

Cicchetti, A., Di Ruscio, D., & Kolovos, D. (2012). A Test-Driven Approach for Metamodel Development In Rech, J., & Bunse, C. (Eds.), *Emerging Technologies for the Evolution and Maintenance of Software Models* (pp. 319–342).

Cinque, M., Coronato, A., & Testa, A. (2011). On Dependability Issues in Ambient Intelligence Systems. [IJACI]. *International Journal of Ambient Computing and Intelligence*, *3*(3), 18–27. doi:doi:10.4018/jaci.2011070103

Related References

Comino, S., & Manenti, F. M. (2007). On the Role of Public Policies Supporting Free/Open Source Software In St.Amant, K., & Still, B. (Eds.), *Handbook of Research on Open Source Software: Technological* (pp. 412–427). Economic, and Social Perspectives.

Conger, S. (2011). Software Development Life Cycles and Methodologies: Fixing the Old and Adopting the New. [IJITSA]. *International Journal of Information Technologies and Systems Approach, 4*(1), 1–22. doi:doi:10.4018/jitsa.2011010101

Constantinides, C., & Arnaoudova, V. (2009). Prolonging the Aging of Software Systems In Khosrow-Pour, M. (Ed.), *Encyclopedia of Information Science and Technology* (2nd ed., pp. 3152–3160).

Cooper, K. M., Dai, L., Steiner, R., & Mili, R. Z. (2009). A Survey of Software Architecture Approaches In Tiako, P. (Ed.), *Designing Software-Intensive Systems: Methods and Principles* (pp. 256–288).

Costa, G., Lazouski, A., Martinelli, F., & Mori, P. (2012). Application Security for Mobile Devices1 In Petre, L., Sere, K., & Troubitsyna, E. (Eds.), *Dependability and Computer Engineering: Concepts for Software-Intensive Systems* (pp. 266–284).

Crowston, K., & Scozzi, B. (2010). Bug Fixing Practices within Free/Libre Open Source Software Development Teams In Siau, K., & Erickson, J. (Eds.), *Principle Advancements in Database Management Technologies: New Applications and Frameworks* (pp. 51–81).

Dai, H., Murphy, C., & Kaiser, G. (2010). CONFU: Configuration Fuzzing Testing Framework for Software Vulnerability Detection. [IJSSE]. *International Journal of Secure Software Engineering, 1*(3), 41–55. doi:doi:10.4018/jsse.2010070103

Davis, A. (2008). Enterprise Resource Planning Under Open Source Software In Ferran, C., & Salim, R. (Eds.), *Enterprise Resource Planning for Global Economies: Managerial Issues and Challenges* (pp. 56–76).

de Oliveira, Í. R., Veiga Gimenes, R. A., & Rady de Almeida Jr, J. (2010). Component-Based Development of Aeronautical Software In Weigang, L., Barros, A. D., & Romani de Oliveira, I. (Eds.), *Computational Models, Software Engineering, and Advanced Technologies in Air Transportation: Next Generation Applications* (pp. 287–314).

de Souza, C. R., & Redmiles, D. F. (2009). On the Alignment of Organizational and Software Structure In Whitworth, B., & de Moor, A. (Eds.), *Handbook of Research on Socio-Technical Design and Social Networking Systems: (2-volumes)* (pp. 94–104).

del Sagrado Martinez, J., & del Aguila Cano, I. M. (2010). A Bayesian Network for Predicting the Need for a Requirements Review In Meziane, F., & Vadera, S. (Eds.), *Artificial Intelligence Applications for Improved Software Engineering Development: New Prospects* (pp. 106–128).

Deng, G., Schmidt, D. C., Gokhale, A., Gray, J., Lin, Y., & Lenz, G. (2009). Evolution in Model-Driven Software Product-Line Architectures In Tiako, P. (Ed.), *Designing Software-Intensive Systems: Methods and Principles* (pp. 102–132).

Deshmukh, A. (2006). Controls, Security, and Audit in Online Digital Accounting In Deshmukh, A. (Ed.), *Digital Accounting: The Effects of the Internet and ERP on Accounting* (pp. 318–383).

DiPardo, A., & DiPardo, M. (2010). Case Study - "Can You See Me?": Writing toward Clarity in a Software Development Life Cycle In Hewett, B. L., & Robidoux, C. (Eds.), *Virtual Collaborative Writing in the Workplace: Computer-Mediated Communication Technologies and Processes* (pp. 53–64).

Dogru, A., Senkul, P., & Kaya, O. (2011). Modern Approaches to Software Engineering in the Compositional Era In Ramachandran, M. (Ed.), *Knowledge Engineering for Software Development Life Cycles: Support Technologies and Applications* (pp. 1–20).

Donegan, P., Bandeira, L., Matos, C., da Cunha, P. L., & Maia, C. (2007). Automated Software Testing In Dasso, A., & Funes, A. (Eds.), *Verification* (pp. 82–110). Validation and Testing in Software Engineering.

Douce, C. (2011). Constructing and Evaluating Social Software: Lessons from Interaction Design In Papadopoulou, P., Kanellis, P., & Martakos, D. (Eds.), *Social Computing Theory and Practice: Interdisciplinary Approaches* (pp. 197–214).

Dragoni, N., Gadyatskya, O., & Massacci, F. (2012). Supporting Software Evolution for Open Smart Cards by Security-by-Contract In Petre, L., Sere, K., & Troubitsyna, E. (Eds.), *Dependability and Computer Engineering: Concepts for Software-Intensive Systems* (pp. 285–305).

Dubielewicz, I., Hnatkowska, B., Huzar, Z., & Tuzinkiewicz, L. (2011). Quality-Driven Database System Development In Osis, J., & Asnina, E. (Eds.), *Model-Driven Domain Analysis and Software Development: Architectures and Functions* (pp. 201–231).

Durand, J., Flores, J., Atkison, T., Kraft, N., & Smith, R. (2011). Using Executable Slicing to Improve Rogue Software Detection Algorithms. [IJSSE]. *International Journal of Secure Software Engineering*, *2*(2), 53–64. doi:doi:10.4018/jsse.2011040103

Dzega, D., & Pietruszkiewicz, W. (2012). The Technological Advancement of LMS Systems and E-Content Software In Babo, R., & Azevedo, A. (Eds.), *Higher Education Institutions and Learning Management Systems: Adoption and Standardization* (pp. 219–245).

Edwards, H. K., & Sridhar, V. (2006). Collaborative Software Requirements Engineering Exercises in a Distributed Virtual Team Environment In Hunter, M., & Tan, F. B. (Eds.), *Advanced Topics in Global Information Management* (*Vol. 5*, pp. 178–198).

Evaristo, R., Watson-Manheim, M. B., & Audy, J. (2007). E-Collaboration in Distributed Requirements Determination In Kock, N. (Ed.), *Emerging e-Collaboration Concepts and Applications* (pp. 119–135).

Fauzi, S. S., Ramli, N., & Noor, M. K. (2012). Implementing Internal Software Process Assessment: An Experience at a Mid-Size IT Company In Fauzi, S. S., Nasir, M. N., Ramli, N., & Sahibuddin, S. (Eds.), *Software Process Improvement and Management: Approaches and Tools for Practical Development* (pp. 78–99).

Related References

Favre, L. M. (2010). Towards MDA Software Evolution In Favre, L. (Ed.), *Model Driven Architecture for Reverse Engineering Technologies: Strategic Directions and System Evolution* (pp. 236–240).

Felderer, M., Atkinson, C., Barth, F., & Breu, R. (2012). Model-Driven Testing with Test Sheets In Rech, J., & Bunse, C. (Eds.), *Emerging Technologies for the Evolution and Maintenance of Software Models* (pp. 231–253).

Fernandez, L., Lara, P. J., & Cuadrado, J. J. (2007). Efficient Software Quality Assurance Approaches Oriented to UML Models in Real Life In Dasso, A., & Funes, A. (Eds.), *Verification* (pp. 385–426). Validation and Testing in Software Engineering.

Ferreira, R., Brisolara, L., Mattos, J. C., Spech, E., & Cota, E. (2010). Engineering Embedded Software: From Application Modeling to Software Synthesis In Gomes, L., & Fernandes, J. M. (Eds.), *Behavioral Modeling for Embedded Systems and Technologies: Applications for Design and Implementation* (pp. 245–270).

Fink, K., & Ploder, C. (2009). Integration Concept for Knowledge Processes, Methods, and Software for SMEs In Gupta, J. N., Sharma, S., & Rashid, M. A. (Eds.), *Handbook of Research on Enterprise Systems* (pp. 185–200).

Fioravanti, F. (2006). Project Maintenance In Fioravanti, F. (Ed.), *Skills for Managing Rapidly Changing IT Projects* (pp. 224–241).

Fioravanti, F. (2006). Agile and Defined Project Development In Fioravanti, F. (Ed.), *Skills for Managing Rapidly Changing IT Projects* (pp. 134–157).

Folmer, E., & Bosch, J. (2010). Experiences with Software Architecture Analysis of Usability. In Alkhatib, G. I., & Rine, D. C. (Eds.), *Web Engineering Advancements and Trends: Building New Dimensions of Information Technology.* (pp. 177-202). doi:10.4018/978-1-60566-719-5.ch010

Freeze, R., & Kulkarni, U. (2012). Understanding the Composition of Knowledge Management Capability. In Management Association, USA, I. (Ed.), *Organizational Learning and Knowledge: Concepts, Methodologies, Tools and Applications.* (pp. 208-226). doi:10.4018/978-1-60960-783-8.ch113

Frezza, S. (2009). How to Create a Credible Software Engineering Bachelor's Program: Navigating the Waters of Program Development In Ellis, H., Demurjian, S., & Naveda, J. (Eds.), *Software Engineering: Effective Teaching and Learning Approaches and Practices* (pp. 298–325).

Fu, Y., Dong, Z., & He, X. (2011). Architecture-Centered Integrated Verification In Dogru, A. H., & Biçer, V. (Eds.), *Modern Software Engineering Concepts and Practices: Advanced Approaches* (pp. 104–124).

Fuchs, C. (2010). Social Software and Web 2.0: Their Sociological Foundations and Implications In Murugesan, S. (Ed.), *Handbook of Research on Web 2.0, 3.0, and X.0: Technologies* (pp. 763–789). Business, and Social Applications.

Furquim, T. D., & do Amaral, S. A. (2011). Knowledge Management Practices in Brazilian Software Organizations: The Case of SERPRO In Al-Shammari, M. (Ed.), *Knowledge Management in Emerging Economies: Social* (pp. 213–226). Organizational and Cultural Implementation.

Gao, K., & Khoshgoftaar, T. M. (2009). Count Models for Software Quality Estimation In Wang, J. (Ed.), *Encyclopedia of Data Warehousing and Mining* (2nd ed., pp. 346–352).

Gary, K., & Koehnemann, H. (2008). Component-Based Deployment for Web Applications: Experiences with Duct Tape and Glue In Brandon, D. M. (Ed.), *Software Engineering for Modern Web Applications: Methodologies and Technologies* (pp. 123–137).

Genvigir, E. C., & Vijaykumar, N. L. (2010). Requirements Traceability In Ramachandran, M., & de Carvalho, R. (Eds.), *Handbook of Research on Software Engineering and Productivity Technologies: Implications of Globalization* (pp. 102–120).

Giese, H., Henkler, S., Hirsch, M., Rubin, V., & Tichy, M. (2009). Modeling Techniques for Software-Intensive Systems In Tiako, P. (Ed.), *Designing Software-Intensive Systems: Methods and Principles* (pp. 21–57).

Girardi, R., & Leite, A. (2011). Knowledge Engineering Support for Agent-Oriented Software Reuse In Ramachandran, M. (Ed.), *Knowledge Engineering for Software Development Life Cycles: Support Technologies and Applications* (pp. 177–195).

Goldschmidt, C., Dark, M., & Chaudhry, H. (2011). Responsibility for the Harm and Risk of Software Security Flaws In Dark, M. J. (Ed.), *Information Assurance and Security Ethics in Complex Systems: Interdisciplinary Perspectives* (pp. 104–131).

Gómez, J. M., & Lübke, D. (2008). Automatic Creation of GUI's for Web-Based ERP Systems In Brandon, D. M. (Ed.), *Software Engineering for Modern Web Applications: Methodologies and Technologies* (pp. 179–190).

Grace, L. (2009). The Philosophies of Software In Braman, J., Vincenti, G., & Trajkovski, G. (Eds.), *Handbook of Research on Computational Arts and Creative Informatics* (pp. 326–342).

Grotsev, D., Iliasov, A., & Romanovsky, A. (2012). Formal Stepwise Development of Scalable and Reliable Multiagent Systems In Petre, L., Sere, K., & Troubitsyna, E. (Eds.), *Dependability and Computer Engineering: Concepts for Software-Intensive Systems* (pp. 58–74).

Guillemot, C., Fondement, F., & Hassenforder, M. (2012). Model Evolution Leads by Users Interactions In Rech, J., & Bunse, C. (Eds.), *Emerging Technologies for the Evolution and Maintenance of Software Models* (pp. 146–162).

Guoqing Wei, G., & Sherrell, L. (2008). Applying Agility to Database Design In Brandon, D. M. (Ed.), *Software Engineering for Modern Web Applications: Methodologies and Technologies* (pp. 160–178).

Gupta, N., Saini, D., & Saini, H. (2010). Class Level Test Case Generation in Object Oriented Software Testing. In Alkhatib, G. I., & Rine, D. C. (Eds.), *Web Engineering Advancements and Trends: Building New Dimensions of Information Technology.* (pp. 203-211). doi:10.4018/978-1-60566-719-5.ch011

Halpert, B. J. (2007). Parental Rights to Monitor Internet Usage In Quigley, M. (Ed.), *Encyclopedia of Information Ethics and Security* (pp. 492–497).

Related References

Hamid, S. S., Nasir, M. H., Sahibuddin, S., & Nor, M. K. (2012). Managing Software Projects with Team Software Process (TSP) In Fauzi, S. S., Nasir, M. N., Ramli, N., & Sahibuddin, S. (Eds.), *Software Process Improvement and Management: Approaches and Tools for Practical Development* (pp. 149–182).

Hamouda, O., Kaâniche, M., & Kanoun, K. (2012). Dependability Assessment of Two Network Supported Automotive Applications In Petre, L., Sere, K., & Troubitsyna, E. (Eds.), *Dependability and Computer Engineering: Concepts for Software-Intensive Systems* (pp. 442–458).

Haraty, R. A., Mansour, N., & Daou, B. A. (2004). Regression Test Selection for Database Applications In Siau, K. (Ed.), *Advanced Topics in Database Research* (*Vol. 3*, pp. 141–165).

Hassan, S. Z. (2002). Software Development in Developing Countries: Framework for Analysis of Quality Initiatives In Dadashzadeh, M. (Ed.), *Information Technology Management in Developing Countries* (pp. 309–318).

Hazzan, O., & Dubinsky, Y. (2009). Teaching Agile Software Development Quality Assurance In Tiako, P. (Ed.), *Software Applications: Concepts* (pp. 2700–2713). Methodologies, Tools, and Applications.

Hazzan, O., & Tomayko, J. (2009). Tasks in Software Engineering Education: The Case of a Human Aspects of Software Engineering Course In Ellis, H., Demurjian, S., & Naveda, J. (Eds.), *Software Engineering: Effective Teaching and Learning Approaches and Practices* (pp. 61–74).

He, K., Wang, C., He, Y., Ma, Y., & Liang, P. (2010). Theory of Ontology and Meta-Modeling and the Standard: An Enabler for Semantic Interoperability In Ramachandran, M., & de Carvalho, R. (Eds.), *Handbook of Research on Software Engineering and Productivity Technologies: Implications of Globalization* (pp. 58–101).

Heimann, D. I. (2006). Implementing Software Metrics at a Telecommunications Company: A Case Study In Khosrow-Pour, M. (Ed.), *Cases on Telecommunications and Networking* (pp. 58–76).

Hernández-López, A., Colomo-Palacios, R., García-Crespo, Á., & Cabezas-Isla, F. (2011). Software Engineering Productivity: Concepts, Issues and Challenges. [IJITPM]. *International Journal of Information Technology Project Management, 2*(1), 37–47. doi:doi:10.4018/jitpm.2011010103

Hernández-López, A., Colomo-Palacios, R., García-Crespo, Á., & Soto-Acosta, P. (2010). Team Software Process in GSD Teams: A Study of New Work Practices and Models. [IJHCITP]. *International Journal of Human Capital and Information Technology Professionals, 1*(3), 32–53. doi:doi:10.4018/jhcitp.2010070103

Herrmann, A., & Morali, A. (2012). Interplay of Security Requirements Engineering and Reverse Engineering in the Maintenance of Undocumented Software In Rech, J., & Bunse, C. (Eds.), *Emerging Technologies for the Evolution and Maintenance of Software Models* (pp. 57–91).

Hill, J. H. (2011). Data Mining System Execution Traces to Validate Distributed System Quality-of-Service Properties In Kumar, A. (Ed.), *Knowledge Discovery Practices and Emerging Applications of Data Mining: Trends and New Domains* (pp. 174–197).

Höhn, S., Lowis, L., Jürjens, J., & Accorsi, R. (2010). Identification of Vulnerabilities in Web Services using Model-Based Security In Gutiérrez, C. A., Fernández-Medina, E., & Piattini, M. (Eds.), *Web Services Security Development and Architecture: Theoretical and Practical Issues* (pp. 1–32).

Houmb, S. H., Ray, I., & Ray, I. (2012). SecInvest: Balancing Security Needs with Financial and Business Constraints In Petre, L., Sere, K., & Troubitsyna, E. (Eds.), *Dependability and Computer Engineering: Concepts for Software-Intensive Systems* (pp. 306–328).

Hu, J. (2008). Computer Application Software Training via E-Learning In Kidd, T. T., & Song, H. (Eds.), *Handbook of Research on Instructional Systems and Technology* (pp. 571–581).

Hussain, K. (2009). A Practical Approach to Computerized System Validation In Lazakidou, A. A., & Siassiakos, K. (Eds.), *Handbook of Research on Distributed Medical Informatics and E-Health* (pp. 456–469).

Iandoli, L., & Zollo, G. (2005). Knowledge at Work in Software Development: A Cognitive Approach for Sharing Knowledge and Creating Decision Support for Life-Cycle Selection In Narayanan, V., & Armstrong, D. J. (Eds.), *Causal Mapping for Research in Information Technology* (pp. 312–342).

Jaroucheh, Z., Liu, X., & Smith, S. (2012). A Software Engineering Framework for Context-Aware Service-Based Processes in Pervasive Environments In Liu, X., & Li, Y. (Eds.), *Advanced Design Approaches to Emerging Software Systems: Principles* (pp. 102–127). Methodologies and Tools.

Jokonya, O., & Hardman, S. (2011). Boundary Critique and Stakeholder Collaboration in Open Source Software Migration: A Case Study. [IJSKD]. *International Journal of Sociotechnology and Knowledge Development*, *3*(4), 1–14. doi:doi:10.4018/jskd.2011100101

Jones, C. (2009). Positive and Negative Innovations in Software Engineering. [IJSSCI]. *International Journal of Software Science and Computational Intelligence*, *1*(2), 20–30. doi:doi:10.4018/jssci.2009040102

Jung, Y., & Kim, M. (2012). Community Computing: Multi-Agent Based Computing Paradigm for Cooperative Pervasive System In Liu, X., & Li, Y. (Eds.), *Advanced Design Approaches to Emerging Software Systems: Principles* (pp. 195–217). Methodologies and Tools.

Kacmar, C. J., McManus, D. J., Duggan, E. W., Hale, J. E., & Hale, D. P. (2009). Software Development Methodologies in Organizations: Field Investigation of Use, Acceptance, and Application. [IRMJ]. *Information Resources Management Journal*, *22*(3), 16–39. doi:doi:10.4018/irmj.2009070102

Kalnins, A., Smialek, M., Kalnina, E., Celms, E., Nowakowski, W., & Straszak, T. (2011). Domain-Driven Reuse of Software Design Models In Osis, J., & Asnina, E. (Eds.), *Model-Driven Domain Analysis and Software Development: Architectures and Functions* (pp. 177–200).

Related References

Kamthan, P. (2008). Using Patterns for Engineering High-Quality Web Applications In Brandon, D. M. (Ed.), *Software Engineering for Modern Web Applications: Methodologies and Technologies* (pp. 100–122).

Kamthan, P. (2008). Software Quality in Open Source Software Ecosystems In Putnik, G. D., & Cruz-Cunha, M. M. (Eds.), *Encyclopedia of Networked and Virtual Organizations* (pp. 1496–1501).

Kamthan, P. (2009). A Methodology for Integrating Information Technology in Software Engineering Education In Donnelly, R., & McSweeney, F. (Eds.), *Applied E-Learning and E-Teaching in Higher Education* (pp. 204–222).

Kamthan, P. (2009). Ethics in Software Engineering In Tiako, P. (Ed.), *Software Applications: Concepts* (pp. 2795–2802). Methodologies, Tools, and Applications.

Kamthan, P. (2010). A Social Web Perspective of Software Engineering Education In Murugesan, S. (Ed.), *Handbook of Research on Web 2.0, 3.0, and X.0: Technologies* (pp. 472–495). Business, and Social Applications.

Kanellopoulos, D. (2011). Localising E-Learning Websites in the Semantic Web Era In Lazarinis, F., Green, S., & Pearson, E. (Eds.), *Handbook of Research on E-Learning Standards and Interoperability: Frameworks and Issues* (pp. 284–299).

Keller, A., & Demeyer, S. (2012). Change Impact Analysis for UML Model Maintenance In Rech, J., & Bunse, C. (Eds.), *Emerging Technologies for the Evolution and Maintenance of Software Models* (pp. 32–56).

Kelly, D. (2011). An Analysis of Process Characteristics for Developing Scientific Software. [JOEUC]. *Journal of Organizational and End User Computing, 23*(4), 64–79. doi:doi:10.4018/joeuc.2011100105

Kelly, D., Hook, D., & Sanders, R. (2012). A Framework for Testing Code in Computational Applications. In Leng, J., & Sharrock, W. (Eds.), *Handbook of Research on Computational Science and Engineering: Theory and Practice (2 vol).* (pp. 150-176). doi:10.4018/978-1-61350-116-0.ch007

Kendall, K. E., Kong, S., & Kendall, J. E. (2010). The Impact of Agile Methodologies on the Quality of Information Systems: Factors Shaping Strategic Adoption of Agile Practices. [IJSDS]. *International Journal of Strategic Decision Sciences, 1*(1), 41–56. doi:doi:10.4018/jsds.2010103003

Khan, A. H., & Memon, A. M. (2010). Enhancing Testing Technologies for Globalization of Software Engineering and Productivity In Ramachandran, M., & de Carvalho, R. (Eds.), *Handbook of Research on Software Engineering and Productivity Technologies: Implications of Globalization* (pp. 49–60).

Khemakhem, S., Drira, K., & Jmaiel, M. (2011). Description, Classification and Discovery Approaches for Software Components: A Comparative Study In Dogru, A. H., & Biçer, V. (Eds.), *Modern Software Engineering Concepts and Practices: Advanced Approaches* (pp. 196–219).

Kizza, J., & Migga Kizza, F. (2008). Software Standards, Reliability, Safety, and Risk In Kizza, J., & Migga Kizza, F. (Eds.), *Securing the Information Infrastructure* (pp. 66–87).

Knapp, K. J. (2009). Security Considerations in the Development Life Cycle In Syed, M. R., & Syed, S. N. (Eds.), *Handbook of Research on Modern Systems Analysis and Design Technologies and Applications* (pp. 295–304).

Knight, L. V., Steinbach, T. A., & Kellen, V. (2003). System Development Methodologies for Web-Enabled E-Business: A Customization Framework In Murthy, V., & Shi, N. (Eds.), *Architectural Issues of Web-Enabled Electronic Business* (pp. 213–226).

Koch, S., & Neumann, C. (2009). Exploring the Effects of Process Characteristics on Products Quality in Open Source Software Development In Tiako, P. (Ed.), *Software Applications: Concepts* (pp. 3008–3036). Methodologies, Tools, and Applications.

Koch, S., & Neumann, C. (2010). Exploring the Effects of Process Characteristics on Product Quality in Open Source Software Development In Siau, K., & Erickson, J. (Eds.), *Principle Advancements in Database Management Technologies: New Applications and Frameworks* (pp. 132–159).

Kohan, S., Schneck de Paula Pessôa, M., & de Mesquita Spinola, M. (2008). QuickLocus: A Software Development Process Evaluation Method for Small-Sized Organizations In Oktaba, H., & Piattini, M. (Eds.), *Software Process Improvement for Small and Medium Enterprises: Techniques and Case Studies* (pp. 109–139).

Kosmatov, N. (2010). Constraint-Based Techniques for Software Testing In Meziane, F., & Vadera, S. (Eds.), *Artificial Intelligence Applications for Improved Software Engineering Development: New Prospects* (pp. 218–232).

Koumakis, L., Moustakis, V., & Potamias, G. (2009). Web Services Automation In Cruz-Cunha, M. M., Oliveira, E., Tavares, A., & Ferreira, L. (Eds.), *Handbook of Research on Social Dimensions of Semantic Technologies and Web Services* (pp. 239–258).

Král, J., & Žemlicka, M. (2008). Architecture, Specification, and Design of Service-Oriented Systems In Brandon, D. M. (Ed.), *Software Engineering for Modern Web Applications: Methodologies and Technologies* (pp. 68–83).

Kreps, D., & Adam, A. (2008). Failing the Disabled Community: The Continuing Problem of Web Accessibility In Tan, F. B. (Ed.), *Global Information Technologies: Concepts* (pp. 2287–2293). Methodologies, Tools, and Applications.

Kunti, K., Majumdar, B., & Dias, T. B. (2010). Testing Complex and Dynamic Business Processes In Wang, M., & Sun, Z. (Eds.), *Handbook of Research on Complex Dynamic Process Management: Techniques for Adaptability in Turbulent Environments* (pp. 470–485).

Kuri-Morales, A. F. (2010). The Application of Genetic Algorithms to the Evaluation of Software Reliability In Chis, M. (Ed.), *Evolutionary Computation and Optimization Algorithms in Software Engineering: Applications and Techniques* (pp. 29–49).

Kussmaul, C., & Jack, R. (2008). Outsourcing Issues in Web Development In Brandon, D. M. (Ed.), *Software Engineering for Modern Web Applications: Methodologies and Technologies* (pp. 217–238).

Related References

Kussmaul, C., & Jack, R. (2008). Prototyping in Web Development In Brandon, D. M. (Ed.), *Software Engineering for Modern Web Applications: Methodologies and Technologies* (pp. 191–206).

Lam, C. P. (2010). Computational Intelligence for Functional Testing In Meziane, F., & Vadera, S. (Eds.), *Artificial Intelligence Applications for Improved Software Engineering Development: New Prospects* (pp. 233–258).

Laporte, C., & Vargas, E. P. (2012). The Development of International Standards to Facilitate Process Improvements for Very Small Entities In Fauzi, S. S., Nasir, M. N., Ramli, N., & Sahibuddin, S. (Eds.), *Software Process Improvement and Management: Approaches and Tools for Practical Development* (pp. 34–61).

Laporte, C. Y., Renault, A., & Alexandre, S. (2008). The Application of International Software Engineering Standards in Very Small Enterprises In Oktaba, H., & Piattini, M. (Eds.), *Software Process Improvement for Small and Medium Enterprises: Techniques and Case Studies* (pp. 42–70).

Leung, H., & Chan, K. (2004). *Implementing Automated Testing* (pp. 508–521).

Lewis, A., Mostaghim, S., & Randall, M. (2008). Evolutionary Population Dynamics and Multi-Objective Optimisation Problems In Thu Bui, L., & Alam, S. (Eds.), *Multi-Objective Optimization in Computational Intelligence: Theory and Practice* (pp. 185–206).

Lin, S., Lin, C., Lu, C., Chen, Y., & Hsiung, P. (2011). Model-Driven Development of Multi-Core Embedded Software In Dogru, A. H., & Biçer, V. (Eds.), *Modern Software Engineering Concepts and Practices: Advanced Approaches* (pp. 357–379).

Liu, Y., & Khoshgoftaar, T. M. (2007). A Practical Software Quality Classification Model Using Genetic Programming In Zhang, D., & Tsai, J. J. (Eds.), *Advances in Machine Learning Applications in Software Engineering* (pp. 208–236).

Mahmood, Z. (2011). Knowledge Management in E-Commerce In Ramachandran, M. (Ed.), *Knowledge Engineering for Software Development Life Cycles: Support Technologies and Applications* (pp. 84–95).

Mahmoud, Q. H., & Maamar, Z. (2008). Engineering Wireless Mobile Applications In Brandon, D. M. (Ed.), *Software Engineering for Modern Web Applications: Methodologies and Technologies* (pp. 239–253).

Mala, D. J. (2011). Knowledge Engineering Support for Intelligent Software Test Optimization In Ramachandran, M. (Ed.), *Knowledge Engineering for Software Development Life Cycles: Support Technologies and Applications* (pp. 211–243).

Maly, K., Abdel-Wahab, H., Overstreet, C. M., Wild, J. C., Abdel-Hamid, A., Ghanem, S., & Farag, W. (2003). The Essential Elements of Interactive Multimedia Distance Learning Systems. [IJDET]. *International Journal of Distance Education Technologies, 1*(2), 17–36. doi:doi:10.4018/jdet.2003040102

Mana, A., Rudolph, C., Spanoudakis, G., Lotz, V., Massacci, F., Melideo, M., & Lopez-Cobo, J. S. (2008). Security Engineering for Ambient Intelligence: A Manifesto In Nemati, H. (Ed.), *Information Security and Ethics: Concepts* (pp. 3676–3690). Methodologies, Tools, and Applications.

Manzalini, A., Minerva, R., & Moiso, C. (2010). Exploiting P2P Solutions in Telecommunication Service Delivery Platforms. In Antonopoulos, N., Exarchakos, G., Li, M., & Liotta, A. (Eds.), *Handbook of Research on P2P and Grid Systems for Service-Oriented Computing: Models, Methodologies and Applications.* (pp. 937-955). doi:10.4018/978-1-61520-686-5.ch040

Mark, S. (2007). Test-Driven Development: An Agile Practice to Ensure Quality is Built from the Beginning In Stamelos, I. G., & Sfetsos, P. (Eds.), *Agile Software Development Quality Assurance* (pp. 206–220).

Martinho, R., Domingos, D., & Varajão, J. (2010). Goals and Requirements for Supporting Controlled Flexibility in Software Processes. [IRMJ]. *Information Resources Management Journal, 23*(3), 11–26. doi:doi:10.4018/IRMJ.2010070102

Mead, N. R., Allen, J. H., Ardis, M., Hilburn, T. B., Kornecki, A. J., Linger, R., & McDonald, J. (2010). Development of a Master of Software Assurance Reference Curriculum. [IJSSE]. *International Journal of Secure Software Engineering, 1*(4), 18–34. doi:doi:10.4018/jsse.2010100102

Memon, A., & Xie, Q. (2007). Agile Quality Assurance Techniques for GUI-Based Applications In Stamelos, I. G., & Sfetsos, P. (Eds.), *Agile Software Development Quality Assurance* (pp. 114–134).

Menzin, M. (2008). Resources on Web-Centric Computing In Brandon, D. M. (Ed.), *Software Engineering for Modern Web Applications: Methodologies and Technologies* (pp. 292–353).

Miller, J., Zhang, L., Ofuonye, E., & Smith, M. (2008). *The Theory and Implementation of Input Validator: A Semi-Automated Value-Level Bypass Testing Tool* (pp. 242–260). International Journal of Information Technology and Web e.

Miller, J., Zhang, L., Ofuonye, E., & Smith, M. (2010). Towards Automated Bypass Testing of Web Applications. In Alkhatib, G. I., & Rine, D. C. (Eds.), *Web Engineering Advancements and Trends: Building New Dimensions of Information Technology.* (pp. 212-229). doi:10.4018/978-1-60566-719-5.ch012

Mills, D. L. (2008). Testing for Web Applications In Brandon, D. M. (Ed.), *Software Engineering for Modern Web Applications: Methodologies and Technologies* (pp. 207–216).

Mirbel, I., Crescenzo, P., & Cerezo, N. (2011). Empowering Web Service Search with Business Know-How: Application to Scientific Workflows In Ramachandran, M. (Ed.), *Knowledge Engineering for Software Development Life Cycles: Support Technologies and Applications* (pp. 161–176).

Mnkandla, E. (2010). Agile Software Engineering In Ramachandran, M., & de Carvalho, R. (Eds.), *Handbook of Research on Software Engineering and Productivity Technologies: Implications of Globalization* (pp. 28–37).

Mnkandla, E., & Dwolatzky, B. (2007). Agile Software Methods: State-of-the-Art In Stamelos, I. G., & Sfetsos, P. (Eds.), *Agile Software Development Quality Assurance* (pp. 1–22).

Moser, L. E., & Melliar-Smith, P. (2008). Voice-Enabled User Interfaces for Mobile Devices In Lumsden, J. (Ed.), *Handbook of Research on User Interface Design and Evaluation for Mobile Technology* (pp. 446–460).

Related References

Murugesan, S., & Ginige, A. (2008). Web Engineering: Introduction and Perspectives In Brandon, D. M. (Ed.), *Software Engineering for Modern Web Applications: Methodologies and Technologies* (pp. 1–24).

Nair, T., Selvarani, R., & Ramachandran, M. (2010). Comprehensive Software Industry Analysis Model (CSIAM) In Ramachandran, M., & de Carvalho, R. (Eds.), *Handbook of Research on Software Engineering and Productivity Technologies: Implications of Globalization* (pp. 128–138).

Nasir, M. H., Alias, N. A., Fauzi, S. S., & Massatu, M. H. (2012). Implementation of the Personal Software Process in Academic Settings and Current Support Tools In Fauzi, S. S., Nasir, M. N., Ramli, N., & Sahibuddin, S. (Eds.), *Software Process Improvement and Management: Approaches and Tools for Practical Development* (pp. 117–148).

Neto, F. M., & Morais, M. J. (2011). Multiagent System for Supporting the Knowledge Management in the Software Process In Ramachandran, M. (Ed.), *Knowledge Engineering for Software Development Life Cycles: Support Technologies and Applications* (pp. 96–113).

Niazi, M., & Zahran, S. (2012). Software Process Lines: A Step towards Software Industrialization In Fauzi, S. S., Nasir, M. N., Ramli, N., & Sahibuddin, S. (Eds.), *Software Process Improvement and Management: Approaches and Tools for Practical Development* (pp. 1–17).

Nicolaysen, T., Sassoon, R., Line, M. B., & Jaatun, M. G. (2010). Agile Software Development: The Straight and Narrow Path to Secure Software? [IJSSE]. *International Journal of Secure Software Engineering, 1*(3), 71–85. doi:doi:10.4018/jsse.2010070105

Niessink, F. (2005). On the Maturity of Software Maintenance and Other IT Services In Khan, K. M., & Zhang, Y. (Eds.), *Managing Corporate Information Systems Evolution and Maintenance* (pp. 51–74).

Olszewska, M. P., & Waldén, M. (2012). Measuring the Progress of a System Development In Petre, L., Sere, K., & Troubitsyna, E. (Eds.), *Dependability and Computer Engineering: Concepts for Software-Intensive Systems* (pp. 417–441).

Omerovic, A., Karahasanovic, A., & Stølen, K. (2012). Uncertainty Handling in Weighted Dependency Trees: A Systematic Literature Review In Petre, L., Sere, K., & Troubitsyna, E. (Eds.), *Dependability and Computer Engineering: Concepts for Software-Intensive Systems* (pp. 381–416).

Ortmann, S., Maaser, M., & Langendoerfer, P. (2012). High Level Definition of Event-Based Applications for Pervasive Systems In Liu, X., & Li, Y. (Eds.), *Advanced Design Approaches to Emerging Software Systems: Principles* (pp. 128–172). Methodologies and Tools.

Osis, J., & Asnina, E. (2011). Is Modeling a Treatment for the Weakness of Software Engineering? In Osis, J., & Asnina, E. (Eds.), *Model-Driven Domain Analysis and Software Development: Architectures and Functions* (pp. 1–14).

Ovaska, E., Cinotti, T. S., & Toninelli, A. (2012). The Design Principles and Practices of Interoperable Smart Spaces In Liu, X., & Li, Y. (Eds.), *Advanced Design Approaches to Emerging Software Systems: Principles* (pp. 18–47). Methodologies and Tools.

Owens, D. M., & Khazanchi, D. (2009). Software Quality Assurance In Kidd, T. T. (Ed.), *Handbook of Research on Technology Project Management* (pp. 242–260). Planning, and Operations.

Özkan, B., & Demirörs, O. (2011). Formalization Studies in Functional Size Measurement In Dogru, A. H., & Biçer, V. (Eds.), *Modern Software Engineering Concepts and Practices: Advanced Approaches* (pp. 242–262).

Palomo-Duarte, M. (2012). Service Composition Verification and Validation In Lee, J., Ma, S., & Liu, A. (Eds.), *Service Life Cycle Tools and Technologies: Methods* (pp. 200–219). Trends and Advances.

Panfilenko, D., Seel, C., Phalp, K., & Jeary, S. (2012). Enriching the Model-Driven Architecture with Weakly Structured Information In Rech, J., & Bunse, C. (Eds.), *Emerging Technologies for the Evolution and Maintenance of Software Models* (pp. 121–145).

Papin-Ramcharan, J. (2007). Open Source Software: A Developing Country View In St. Amant, K., & Still, B. (Eds.), *Handbook of Research on Open Source Software: Technological* (pp. 93–101). Economic, and Social Perspectives.

Parsons, D. (2008). Evolving Web Application Architectures: From Model 2 to Web 2 In Brandon, D. M. (Ed.), *Software Engineering for Modern Web Applications: Methodologies and Technologies* (pp. 138–159).

Parthasarathy, S. (2010). Application of Software Metrics in EPR Projects In Parthasarathy, S. (Ed.), *Enterprise Information Systems and Implementing IT Infrastructures: Challenges and Issues* (pp. 51–60).

Patel, C., & Ramachandran, M. (2010). Best Practices Guidelines for Agile Requirements Engineering Practices In Ramachandran, M., & de Carvalho, R. (Eds.), *Handbook of Research on Software Engineering and Productivity Technologies: Implications of Globalization* (pp. 1–14).

Patel, C., & Ramachandran, M. (2010). Story Card Process Improvement Framework for Agile Requirements In Ramachandran, M., & de Carvalho, R. (Eds.), *Handbook of Research on Software Engineering and Productivity Technologies: Implications of Globalization* (pp. 61–54).

Pencheva, E., & Atanasov, I. (2010). Open Access to Control on Quality of Service in Convergent Networks. [IJITWE]. *International Journal of Information Technology and Web Engineering, 5*(2), 53–74. doi:doi:10.4018/jitwe.2010040104

Pendyala, V. S., & Holliday, J. (2012). Cloud As a Computer In Liu, X., & Li, Y. (Eds.), *Advanced Design Approaches to Emerging Software Systems: Principles* (pp. 241–249). Methodologies and Tools.

Pérez-Castillo, R., Rodríguez de Guzmán, I. G., & Piattini, M. (2011). Architecture-Driven Modernization In Dogru, A. H., & Biçer, V. (Eds.), *Modern Software Engineering Concepts and Practices: Advanced Approaches* (pp. 75–103).

Picone, J., Ganapathiraju, A., & Hamaker, J. (2007). Applications of Kernel Theory to Speech Recognition In Camps-Valls, G., Rojo-Alvarez, J., & Martinez-Ramon, M. (Eds.), *Kernel Methods in Bioengineering* (pp. 224–245). Signal and Image Processing.

Related References

Pillai, K. G., & Goldsmith, R. E. (2012). Knowledge Calibration and Knowledge Management. In Management Association, USA, I. (Ed.), *Organizational Learning and Knowledge: Concepts, Methodologies, Tools and Applications.* (pp. 127-135). doi:10.4018/978-1-60960-783-8.ch108

Polo, M., Piattini, M., & Ruiz, F. (2003). A Methodology for Software Maintenance In Piattini, M., Polo, M., & Ruiz, F. (Eds.), *Advances in Software Maintenance Management: Technologies and Solutions* (pp. 228–254).

Porto, J. B. (2012). Resistance Factors in Software Processes Improvement: A Study of the Brazilian Industry In Fauzi, S. S., Nasir, M. N., Ramli, N., & Sahibuddin, S. (Eds.), *Software Process Improvement and Management: Approaches and Tools for Practical Development* (pp. 100–116).

Pozzi, F. (2008). Teaching Dimension in Web-Based Learning Communities. [IJWLTT]. *International Journal of Web-Based Learning and Teaching Technologies, 3*(3), 34–43. doi:doi:10.4018/jwltt.2008070103

Prokhorova, Y., Troubitsyna, E., Laibinis, L., & Kharchenko, V. (2012). Development of Safety-Critical Control Systems in Event-B Using FMEA In Petre, L., Sere, K., & Troubitsyna, E. (Eds.), *Dependability and Computer Engineering: Concepts for Software-Intensive Systems* (pp. 75–91).

Raghavan, V. V. (2003). Toward an Integrative Model of Application-Software Security In Lloyd, S. J., & Peckham, J. (Eds.), *Practicing Software Engineering in the 21st Century* (pp. 157–163).

Rapp, B., & Bremer, J. (2010). Paving the Way towards Virtual Biorefineries In Teuteberg, F., & Marx Gomez, J. (Eds.), *Corporate Environmental Management Information Systems: Advancements and Trends* (pp. 85–105).

Raza, A., Capretz, L. F., & Ahmed, F. (2011). An Empirical Study of Open Source Software Usability: The Industrial Perspective. [IJOSSP]. *International Journal of Open Source Software and Processes, 3*(1), 1–16. doi:doi:10.4018/jossp.2011010101

Rech, J. (2007). Handling of Software Quality Defects in Agile Software Development In Stamelos, I. G., & Sfetsos, P. (Eds.), *Agile Software Development Quality Assurance* (pp. 90–113).

Rech, J., Decker, B., Ras, E., Jedlitschka, A., & Feldmann, R. L. (2007). The Quality of Knowledge: Knowledge Patterns and Knowledge Refactorings. [IJKM]. *International Journal of Knowledge Management, 3*(3), 74–103. doi:doi:10.4018/jkm.2007070105

Reformat, M., Musilek, P., & Igbide, E. (2007). Intelligent Analysis of Software Maintenance Data In Zhang, D., & Tsai, J. J. (Eds.), *Advances in Machine Learning Applications in Software Engineering* (pp. 14–51).

Reisman, S. (2006). Costs and Benefits of Software Engineering in Product Development Environments In Khosrow-Pour, M. (Ed.), *Cases on Strategic Information Systems* (pp. 199–215).

Rejas-Muslera, R., Davara, E., Abran, A., & Buglione, L. (2010). Intellectual Property Systems in Software In Portela, I. M., & Cruz-Cunha, M. M. (Eds.), *Information Communication Technology Law, Protection and Access Rights: Global Approaches and Issues* (pp. 121–135).

Rodrigues, D., Estrella, J. C., Monaco, F. J., Branco, K. R., Antunes, N., & Vieira, M. (2012). Engineering Secure Web Services. In Cardellini, V., Casalicchio, E., Castelo Branco, K. L., Estrella, J. C., & Monaco, F. J. (Eds.), *Performance and Dependability in Service Computing: Concepts, Techniques and Research Directions.* (pp. 360-380). doi:10.4018/978-1-60960-794-4.ch016

Rodriguez, L. C., Mora, M., Martin, M. V., O'Connor, R., & Alvarez, F. (2009). Process Models of SDLCs: Comparison and Evolution In Syed, M. R., & Syed, S. N. (Eds.), *Handbook of Research on Modern Systems Analysis and Design Technologies and Applications* (pp. 76–89).

Rosca, D. (2009). Continuous Curriculum Restructuring in a Graduate Software Engineering Program In Ellis, H., Demurjian, S., & Naveda, J. (Eds.), *Software Engineering: Effective Teaching and Learning Approaches and Practices* (pp. 278–297).

Rose, S., Lauder, M., Schlereth, M., & Schürr, A. (2011). A Multidimensional Approach for Concurrent Model-Driven Automation Engineering In Osis, J., & Asnina, E. (Eds.), *Model-Driven Domain Analysis and Software Development: Architectures and Functions* (pp. 90–113).

Ruiz, F., Garcia, F., Piattini, M., & Polo, M. (2003). Environment for Managing Software Maintenance Projects In Piattini, M., Polo, M., & Ruiz, F. (Eds.), *Advances in Software Maintenance Management: Technologies and Solutions* (pp. 255–291).

Ruiz, F., Piattini, M., Polo, M., & Calero, C. (2000). Audit of Software Maintenance Process In Piattini, M. (Ed.), *Auditing Information Systems* (pp. 67–108).

Safavi, S. A., & Shaikh, M. U. (2011). Effort Estimation Model for each Phase of Software Development Life Cycle In Al Ajeeli, A. T., & Al-Bastaki, Y. A. (Eds.), *Handbook of Research on E-Services in the Public Sector: E-Government Strategies and Advancements* (pp. 270–277).

Sahraoi, S. (2007). An Agile Perspective on Open Source Software Engineering In St.Amant, K., & Still, B. (Eds.), *Handbook of Research on Open Source Software: Technological* (pp. 141–153). Economic, and Social Perspectives.

Samuelis, L. (2009). Notes on the Emerging Science of Software Evolution In Syed, M. R., & Syed, S. N. (Eds.), *Handbook of Research on Modern Systems Analysis and Design Technologies and Applications* (pp. 161–168).

Saxon, A., Walker, S., & Prytherch, D. (2011). Measuring the Unmeasurable?: Eliciting Hard to Measure Information about the User Experience In Alkhatib, G. (Ed.), *Web Engineered Applications for Evolving Organizations: Emerging Knowledge* (pp. 256–277).

Related References

Schaffert, S. (2008). Semantic Social Software: Semantically Enabled Social Software or Socially Enabled Semantic Web? In Rech, J., Decker, B., & Ras, E. (Eds.), *Emerging Technologies for Semantic Work Environments: Techniques* (pp. 33–46). Methods, and Applications.

Schulz, T., Radlinski, L., Gorges, T., & Rosenstiel, W. (2011). Software Process Model using Dynamic Bayesian Networks In Ramachandran, M. (Ed.), *Knowledge Engineering for Software Development Life Cycles: Support Technologies and Applications* (pp. 289–310).

Seehusen, F., & Stølen, K. (2012). A Method for Model-Driven Information Flow Security In Petre, L., Sere, K., & Troubitsyna, E. (Eds.), *Dependability and Computer Engineering: Concepts for Software-Intensive Systems* (pp. 199–229).

Seethamraju, R. (2007). Enterprise Systems Software in the Business Curriculum: Aligning Curriculum with Industry Requirements In Lowry, G. R., & Turner, R. L. (Eds.), *Information Systems and Technology Education: From the University to the Workplace* (pp. 57–81).

Sekerinski, E. (2012). Exceptions for Dependability In Petre, L., Sere, K., & Troubitsyna, E. (Eds.), *Dependability and Computer Engineering: Concepts for Software-Intensive Systems* (pp. 11–35).

Seleim, A. A., Ashour, A. S., & Khalil, O. E. (2005). Knowledge Acquisitions and Transfer in Egyptian Software Firms. [IJKM]. *International Journal of Knowledge Management, 1*(4), 43–72. doi:doi:10.4018/jkm.2005100103

Seliya, N., & Khoshgoftaar, T. M. (2007). Software Quality Modeling with Limited Apriori Defect Data In Zhu, X., & Davidson, I. (Eds.), *Knowledge Discovery and Data Mining: Challenges and Realities* (pp. 1–15).

Selvarani, R., Nair, T., Ramachandran, M., & Prasad, K. (2010). Software Metrics Evaluation Based on Entropy In Ramachandran, M., & de Carvalho, R. (Eds.), *Handbook of Research on Software Engineering and Productivity Technologies: Implications of Globalization* (pp. 139–151).

Shan, T. C., & Hua, W. W. (2008). Model-Centric Architecting Process In Brandon, D. M. (Ed.), *Software Engineering for Modern Web Applications: Methodologies and Technologies* (pp. 53–67).

Shiell, D. J., Terry, L. H., Aleksic, P. S., & Katsaggelos, A. K. (2009). Audio-Visual and Visual-Only Speech and Speaker Recognition: Issues about Theory, System Design, and Implementation In Liew, A. W., & Wang, S. (Eds.), *Visual Speech Recognition: Lip Segmentation and Mapping* (pp. 1–38).

Simmons, D. B., Lively, W., & Nelson, C. (2007). Rapid Insertion of Leading Edge Industrial Strength Software into University Classrooms In St. Amant, K., & Still, B. (Eds.), *Handbook of Research on Open Source Software: Technological* (pp. 670–680). Economic, and Social Perspectives.

Singhera, Z., Horowitz, E., & Shah, A. (2009). A Graphical User Interface (GUI) Testing Methodology In Ang, C., & Zaphiris, P. (Eds.), *Human Computer Interaction: Concepts* (pp. 659–676). Methodologies, Tools, and Applications.

Siponen, M., Baskerville, R., & Kuivalainen, T. (2008). Extending Security in Agile Software Development Methods In Nemati, H. (Ed.), *Information Security and Ethics: Concepts* (pp. 845–858). Methodologies, Tools, and Applications.

Sneed, H. M. (2003). Software Maintenance Cost Estimation In Piattini, M., Polo, M., & Ruiz, F. (Eds.), *Advances in Software Maintenance Management: Technologies and Solutions* (pp. 201–227).

Solemon, B., Sahibuddin, S., & Ghani, A. A. (2012). Requirements Engineering Process Improvement and Related Models In Fauzi, S. S., Nasir, M. N., Ramli, N., & Sahibuddin, S. (Eds.), *Software Process Improvement and Management: Approaches and Tools for Practical Development* (pp. 18–33).

Solis, C., & Ali, N. (2011). Managing Requirements Elicitation Knowledge using a Spatial Hypertext Wiki In Ramachandran, M. (Ed.), *Knowledge Engineering for Software Development Life Cycles: Support Technologies and Applications* (pp. 68–83).

Soria, A., Diaz-Pace, J. A., Bass, L., Bachmann, F., & Campo, M. (2010). Supporting Quality-Driven Software Design through Intellectual Assistants In Meziane, F., & Vadera, S. (Eds.), *Artificial Intelligence Applications for Improved Software Engineering Development: New Prospects* (pp. 181–216).

Sousa, K., Schilling, A., & Furtado, E. (2007). Integrating Usability, Semiotic, and Software Engineering into a Method for Evaluating User Interfaces In Dasso, A., & Funes, A. (Eds.), *Verification* (pp. 55–81). Validation and Testing in Software Engineering.

Srivastava, P. R., & Baby,. (2010). Automatic Test Sequence Generation for State Transition Testing via Ant Colony Optimization. In Chis, M. (Ed.), *Evolutionary Computation and Optimization Algorithms in Software Engineering: Applications and Techniques.* (pp. 161-183). doi:10.4018/978-1-61520-809-8.ch009

Srivastava, P. R., Singh, A. P., & V., V. K. (2010). Assessment of Software Quality: A Fuzzy Multi-Criteria Approach. In Chis, M. (Ed.), *Evolutionary Computation and Optimization Algorithms in Software Engineering: Applications and Techniques.* (pp. 200-219). doi:10.4018/978-1-61520-809-8.ch011

Stamelos, I. (2009). Teaching Software Engineering with Free/Libre Open Source Projects. [IJOSSP]. *International Journal of Open Source Software and Processes, 1*(1), 72–90. doi:doi:10.4018/jossp.2009010105

Stevens, P. (2003). Patterns in Software Maintenance: Learning from Experience In Piattini, M., Polo, M., & Ruiz, F. (Eds.), *Advances in Software Maintenance Management: Technologies and Solutions* (pp. 93–113).

Stewart, O., & Chakraborty, J. (2010). Culturally Determined Preferences: Automatic Speech Recognition (ASR) Systems vs. Live Help In Blanchard, E. G., & Allard, D. (Eds.), *Handbook of Research on Culturally-Aware Information Technology: Perspectives and Models* (pp. 74–93).

Sticklen, D. J., & Issa, T. (2011). An Initial Examination of Free and Proprietary Software-Selection in Organizations. [IJWP]. *International Journal of Web Portals, 3*(4), 27–43. doi:doi:10.4018/jwp.2011100103

Related References

Stojanovic, Z., Dahanayake, A., & Sol, H. (2004). Agile Development Methods and Component-Orientation: A Review and Analysis In Siau, K. (Ed.), *Advanced Topics in Database Research* (*Vol. 3*, pp. 1–22).

Strecker, J., & Memon, A. M. (2009). Testing Graphical User Interfaces In Khosrow-Pour, M. (Ed.), *Encyclopedia of Information Science and Technology* (2nd ed., pp. 3739–3744).

Streitferdt, D., Kantz, F., Nenninger, P., Ruschival, T., Kaul, H., & Bauer, T. (2011). Model-Based Testing of Highly Configurable Embedded Systems in the Automation Domain. [IJERTCS]. *International Journal of Embedded and Real-Time Communication Systems, 2*(2), 22–41. doi:doi:10.4018/jertcs.2011040102

Struska, Z., Vanícek, J., & Závodný, M. (2011). Methods for Software Complexity and Development Effort Estimation and its Importance in the Area of ICT Governance In Rahman, H. (Ed.), *Cases on Adoption, Diffusion and Evaluation of Global E-Governance Systems: Impact at the Grass Roots* (pp. 117–147).

Studnicki, E. (2008). Software Evaluation In Tomei, L. A. (Ed.), *Encyclopedia of Information Technology Curriculum Integration* (pp. 789–792).

Suárez-Guerra, S., & Oropeza-Rodriguez, J. L. (2007). Introduction to Speech Recognition In Perez-Meana, H. (Ed.), *Advances in Audio and Speech Signal Processing: Technologies and Applications* (pp. 325–348).

Subramanian, N., & Whitson, G. (2008). Augmented WebHelix: A Practical Process for Web Engineering In Brandon, D. M. (Ed.), *Software Engineering for Modern Web Applications: Methodologies and Technologies* (pp. 25–52).

Subraya, B. M. (2006). Performance Test Automation In Subraya, B. (Ed.), *Integrated Approach to Web Performance Testing: A Practitioner's Guide* (pp. 201–233).

Sugiyama, S., & Burgess, L. (2012). Principle for Engineering Service Based System by Swirl Computing In Liu, X., & Li, Y. (Eds.), *Advanced Design Approaches to Emerging Software Systems: Principles* (pp. 48–60). Methodologies and Tools.

Sun, Y., Gray, J., Langer, P., Kappel, G., Wimmer, M., & White, J. (2012). A WYSIWYG Approach to Support Layout Configuration in Model Evolution In Rech, J., & Bunse, C. (Eds.), *Emerging Technologies for the Evolution and Maintenance of Software Models* (pp. 92–120).

Tappenden, A. F., Huynh, T., Miller, J., Geras, A., & Smith, M. (2006). Agile Development of Secure Web-Based Applications. [IJITWE]. *International Journal of Information Technology and Web Engineering, 1*(2), 1–24. doi:doi:10.4018/jitwe.2006040101

Tarasyuk, A., Troubitsyna, E., & Laibinis, L. (2012). Quantitative Reasoning About Dependability in Event-B: Probabilistic Model Checking Approach In Petre, L., Sere, K., & Troubitsyna, E. (Eds.), *Dependability and Computer Engineering: Concepts for Software-Intensive Systems* (pp. 459–472).

Tekinerdogan, B., & Aksit, M. (2011). A Comparative Analysis of Software Engineering with Mature Engineering Disciplines using a Problem-Solving Perspective In Dogru, A. H., & Biçer, V. (Eds.), *Modern Software Engineering Concepts and Practices: Advanced Approaches* (pp. 1–18).

Tomic, D., & Markic, B. (2010). Continuous Database Availability In Bajgoric, N. (Ed.), *Always-On Enterprise Information Systems for Business Continuance: Technologies for Reliable and Scalable Operations* (pp. 129–148).

Tsai, W., Paul, R., Yu, L., & Wei, X. (2005). Rapid Pattern-Oriented Scenario-Based Testing for Embedded Systems In Yang, H. (Ed.), *Software Evolution with UML and XML* (pp. 222–262).

Twala, B., Cartwright, M., & Shepperd, M. (2007). Applying Rule Induction in Software Prediction In Zhang, D., & Tsai, J. J. (Eds.), *Advances in Machine Learning Applications in Software Engineering* (pp. 265–286).

Unhelkar, B. (2009). Creation of a Process Framework for Transitioning to a Mobile Enterprise In Unhelkar, B. (Ed.), *Handbook of Research in Mobile Business* (2nd ed., pp. 63–72). Technical, Methodological and Social Perspectives.

Urquiza, A. (2007). A Survey of Competency Management Software Information Systems in the Framework of Human Resources management In Sicilia, M. (Ed.), *Competencies in Organizational E-Learning: Concepts and Tools* (pp. 41–82).

Uzoka, F. E. (2009). Examining the Effects of TAM Constructs on Organizational Software Acquisition Decision. [IRMJ]. *Information Resources Management Journal, 22*(3), 40–58. doi:doi:10.4018/irmj.2009070103

Vacher, M., Portet, F., Fleury, A., & Noury, N. (2011). Development of Audio Sensing Technology for Ambient Assisted Living: Applications and Challenges. [IJEHMC]. *International Journal of E-Health and Medical Communications, 2*(1), 35–54. doi:doi:10.4018/jehmc.2011010103

van Staaden, P. (2008). A Case Study on the Selection and Evaluation of Software for an Internet Organisation In Adomi, E. (Ed.), *Security and Software for Cybercafes* (pp. 205–219).

Vaquero, L. M., Rodero-Merino, L., Cáceres, J., Chapman, C., Lindner, M., & Galán, F. (2012). Principles, Methodology and Tools for Engineering Cloud Computing Systems In Liu, X., & Li, Y. (Eds.), *Advanced Design Approaches to Emerging Software Systems: Principles* (pp. 250–273). Methodologies and Tools.

Vardaki, M., & Papageorgiou, H. (2008). Statistical Data and Metadata Quality Assessment In Garson, G. D., & Khosrow-Pour, M. (Eds.), *Handbook of Research on Public Information Technology* (pp. 604–614).

Vargas, E. P. (2012). Quality, Improvement and Measurements in High Risk Software In Fauzi, S. S., Nasir, M. N., Ramli, N., & Sahibuddin, S. (Eds.), *Software Process Improvement and Management: Approaches and Tools for Practical Development* (pp. 62–77).

Related References

Ven, K., Van Nuffel, D., & Verelst, J. (2007). The Migration of Public Administrations Towards Open Source Desktop Software: Recommendations from Research and Validation through a Case Study In Sowe, S. K., Stamelos, I. G., & Samoladas, I. (Eds.), *Emerging Free and Open Source Software Practices* (pp. 191–214).

Verma, S. (2008). Software Quality and Open Source Process In Tan, F. B. (Ed.), *Global Information Technologies: Concepts* (pp. 1096–1109). Methodologies, Tools, and Applications.

Verma, S. (2009). Software Quality and the Open Source Process In Tiako, P. (Ed.), *Software Applications: Concepts* (pp. 2665–2679). Methodologies, Tools, and Applications.

Vidyasankar, K., & Vossen, G. (2011). Multi-Level Modeling of Web Service Compositions with Transactional Properties. [JDM]. *Journal of Database Management, 22*(2), 1–31. doi:doi:10.4018/jdm.2011040101

Vitharana, P., & Mone, M. A. (2008). Measuring Critical Factors of Software Quality Management: Development and Validation of an Instrument. [IRMJ]. *Information Resources Management Journal, 21*(2), 18–37. doi:doi:10.4018/irmj.2008040102

Vitharana, P., & Mone, M. A. (2010). Software Quality Management: Measurement and Research Directions In Khosrow-Pour, M. (Ed.), *Global, Social, and Organizational Implications of Emerging Information Resources Management: Concepts and Applications* (pp. 225–247).

Wagner, S., Deissenboeck, F., Teuchert, S., & Girard, J. (2009). Assuring Maintainability in Model-Driven Development of Embedded Systems In Rech, J., & Bunse, C. (Eds.), *Model-Driven Software Development: Integrating Quality Assurance* (pp. 352–373).

Wan, V. (2007). Building Sequence Kernels for Speaker Verification and Word Recognition In Camps-Valls, G., Rojo-Alvarez, J., & Martinez-Ramon, M. (Eds.), *Kernel Methods in Bioengineering* (pp. 246–262). Signal and Image Processing.

Wang, A. I., & Sørensen, C. (2009). Differentiated Process Support for Large Software Projects In Tiako, P. (Ed.), *Designing Software-Intensive Systems: Methods and Principles* (pp. 1–20).

Wang, Y. (2009). On the Cognitive Complexity of Software and its Quantification and Formal Measurement. [IJSSCI]. *International Journal of Software Science and Computational Intelligence, 1*(2), 31–53. doi:doi:10.4018/jssci.2009040103

Wang, Y., & Patel, S. (2009). Exploring the Cognitive Foundations of Software Engineering. [IJSSCI]. *International Journal of Software Science and Computational Intelligence, 1*(2), 1–19. doi:doi:10.4018/jssci.2009040101

Wiewiora, A., Trigunarsyah, B., & Murphy, G. (2012). Knowledge Transfer in Project-Based Organisations: The Need for a Unique Approach. In Management Association, USA, I. (Ed.), *Organizational Learning and Knowledge: Concepts, Methodologies, Tools and Applications.* (pp. 262–274). doi:10.4018/978-1-60960-783-8.ch116

Winschiers-Theophilus, H. (2009). Cultural Appropriation of Software Design and Evaluation In Whitworth, B., & de Moor, A. (Eds.), *Handbook of Research on Socio-Technical Design and Social Networking Systems: (2-volumes)* (pp. 699–710).

Wong, B. (2006). The Different Views of Software Quality In Duggan, E., & Reichgelt, J. (Eds.), *Measuring Information Systems Delivery Quality* (pp. 55–89).

Wong, Y. K. (2006). Recommendations for Conducting Software Reviews In Wong, Y. (Ed.), *Modern Software Review: Techniques and Technologies* (pp. 268–280).

Wong, Y. K. (2006). Software Review, Inputs, Process, and Performance In Wong, Y. (Ed.), *Modern Software Review: Techniques and Technologies* (pp. 81–114).

Wong, Y. K. (2006). Software Review Tools and Technologies In Wong, Y. (Ed.), *Modern Software Review: Techniques and Technologies* (pp. 37–52).

Worth, D., Greenough, C., & Chin, S. (2012). Pragmatic Software Engineering for Computational Science. In Leng, J., & Sharrock, W. (Eds.), *Handbook of Research on Computational Science and Engineering: Theory and Practice (2 vol).* (pp. 119-149). doi:10.4018/978-1-61350-116-0.ch006

Xu, B., Xie, X., Shi, L., & Nie, C. (2007). Application of Genetic Algorithms in Software Testing In Zhang, D., & Tsai, J. J. (Eds.), *Advances in Machine Learning Applications in Software Engineering* (pp. 287–317).

Yang, D. X. (2012). QoS-Oriented Service Computing: Bringing SOA Into Cloud Environment In Liu, X., & Li, Y. (Eds.), *Advanced Design Approaches to Emerging Software Systems: Principles* (pp. 274–296). Methodologies and Tools.

Yeh, C., Chang, C., & Lin, P. (2011). Ontology-Based Personal Annotation Management on Semantic Peer Network to Facilitating Collaborations in e-Learning. [IJHCR]. *International Journal of Handheld Computing Research*, 2(2), 20–33. doi:doi:10.4018/jhcr.2011040102

Yildiz, M., Oktem, M. K., & Bensghir, T. K. (2011). The Adoption Process of Free & Open Source Software (FOSS) in Turkish Public Organizations In Rahman, H. (Ed.), *Cases on Adoption, Diffusion and Evaluation of Global E-Governance Systems: Impact at the Grass Roots* (pp. 148–170).

Yilmaz, A. E., & Yilmaz, I. B. (2011). Natural Language Processing Techniques in Requirements Engineering In Ramachandran, M. (Ed.), *Knowledge Engineering for Software Development Life Cycles: Support Technologies and Applications* (pp. 21–33).

Yu, D., & Deng, L. (2008). Speech-Centric Multimodal User Interface Design in Mobile Technology In Lumsden, J. (Ed.), *Handbook of Research on User Interface Design and Evaluation for Mobile Technology* (pp. 461–477).

Yu, E., Liu, L., & Mylopoulos, J. (2009). A Social Ontology for Integrating Security and Software Engineering In Tiako, P. (Ed.), *Software Applications: Concepts* (pp. 743–772). Methodologies, Tools, and Applications.

Related References

Zhang, Y., Deng, Q., Xing, C., Sun, Y., & Whitney, M. (2012). A Service Component Model and Implementation for Institutional Repositories In Liu, X., & Li, Y. (Eds.), *Advanced Design Approaches to Emerging Software Systems: Principles* (pp. 61–81). Methodologies and Tools.

Zhang, Z. J. (2010). Social Software for Customer Knowledge Management In Dumova, T., & Fiordo, R. (Eds.), *Handbook of Research on Social Interaction Technologies and Collaboration Software: Concepts and Trends* (pp. 496–508).

Zhou, J., Ovaska, E., Evesti, A., & Immonen, A. (2011). OntoArch Reliability-Aware Software Architecture Design and Experience In Dogru, A. H., & Biçer, V. (Eds.), *Modern Software Engineering Concepts and Practices: Advanced Approaches* (pp. 48–74).

Zhu, H., & Huo, Q. (2005). Developing Software Testing Ontology in UML for a Software Growth Environment of Web-Based Applications In Yang, H. (Ed.), *Software Evolution with UML and XML* (pp. 263–295).

Zhu, Y., & Pahl, C. (2008). Data Integration Through Service-Based Mediation for Web-Enabled Information Systems In Brandon, D. M. (Ed.), *Software Engineering for Modern Web Applications: Methodologies and Technologies* (pp. 84–99).

Zulkernine, M., & Ahamed, S. I. (2006). Software Security Engineering: Toward Unifying Software Engineering and Security Engineering. In Warkentin (Foreward), M., & Vaughn, R. (Eds.), *Enterprise Information Systems Assurance and System Security: Managerial and Technical Issues.* (pp. 215-233). doi:10.4018/978-1-59140-911-3.ch014

About the Contributors

Izzat Mahmoud Alsmadi is an Assistant Professor in the Department of Computer Information Systems at Yarmouk University in Jordan. He obtained his Ph.D degree in Software Engineering from NDSU (USA). His second Master's is in Software Engineering from NDSU (USA) and his first Master's is in CIS from University of Phoenix (USA). He had B.sc degree in Telecommunication Engineering from Mutah University in Jordan. Before joining Yarmouk University he worked for several years in several companies and institutions in Jordan, USA, and UAE. His research interests include: software engineering, software testing, e-learning, software metrics, and formal methods.

* * *

Thomas Bauer, after studying software engineering at the University of Potsdam (Germany, 1999-2005), has been working as a researcher at the department of Embedded Systems Quality Assurance at the Fraunhofer IESE. His research interests are cost-efficient application of quality assurance, test automation, and model-based testing. Mr. Bauer has been involved in several industrial and research projects focusing on the quality assurance of software-intensive technical systems. He was the IESE-project leader of the ITEA2-project D-Mint which was about developing and transferring model-based testing technologies to industrial practice. Furthermore, he is co-founder and co-organizer of the workshop series on model-based testing in practice (MoTiP).

Daniel Bolanos received his undergraduate degree in Computer Science from the Universidad Autonoma de Madrid (Spain) in 2002 and his PhD in Computer Science and Electrical Engineering in 2008 from the same university. Since then he has worked as a Research Associate at the University of Colorado in Boulder (USA) and as a Research Scientist in the company Boulder Language Technologies. His research is focused on automatic speech recognition with a focus on children's speech. As another area of interest he has worked on automatic testing tools and techniques. Dr. Bolanos is the author of several conference and journal articles in the field of speech recognition as well as a book and two book chapters in the field of automated software testing.

Robert Eschbach is the Embedded Systems Quality Assurance department head at Fraunhofer IESE, where he is mainly engaged in projects with safety-critical and software intensive systems. His research in software and systems engineering centers on modeling theory, model-based testing, dependability engineering and formal methods. He is the author of more than 60 refereed publications. Dr. Eschbach has been a principal investigator in numerous research and industrial development projects, including the standardization of an important formal description technique for the telecommunication sector. He has given more than 30 industrial talks at different important industrial workshops and conferences. Dr. Eschbach earned his Ph.D. in Informatics at the University of Kaiserslautern, Germany.

Alexander Roy Geoghegan graduated summa cum laude from Jackson State University in May 2011 with Bachelor of Science degrees in Computer Science and Physics. Since graduation, he has been working as a Software Engineer at L-3 Communications, TX, a Fortune 500 company. He had participated in the NSF-sponsored Research Experiences for Undergraduates (REU) program in Wireless Ad hoc Networks and Sensor Networks at Jackson State University during Summer 2009. He had worked as an Undergraduate Research Assistant during the academic year 2010-11 at Jackson State University, focusing on Web development, software security, and virtualization. He had also served as a Research Assistant for the Department of Civil Engineering in 2009, developing materials for a freshman orientation course with the goal of fostering teamwork and critical thinking skills through the use of Lego Mindstorm robots.

Seifedine Kadry is an Associate Professor of Applied Mathematics in the faculty of general education at American University of the Middle East Kuwait. He received his Masters' degree in Modeling and Intensify Calculus (2001) from the Lebanese University – EPFL -INRIA. He did his doctoral research (2003-2007) in Applied Mathematics from Blaise Pascal University-Clermont Ferrand II, France. He worked as Head of Software Support and Analysis Unit of First National Bank where he designed and implemented their data warehouse and business intelligence; he has published one book and many papers on applied math, computer science, and stochastic systems in peer-reviewed journals.

Eslam Al Maghayreh is currently an Assistant Professor in the Department of Computer Science at Yarmouk University in Jordan. Al Maghayreh received his PhD degree in Computer Science from Concordia University (Canada) in 2008, his Master's degree in Computer Science from Yarmouk University in 2003, and his Bachelor's degree in Computer Science from Yarmouk University in 2001. Al Maghayreh research interests include: multi-agent systems, distributed systems, and runtime verification.

Zaigham Mahmood is a Principal Researcher and Reader in Applied Computing in the School of Computing and Mathematics, University of Derby, UK. He has an MSc in Mathematics, an MSc in Computer Science, and a PhD in Modeling of Phase Equilibria. He is also a Chartered Engineer and a Chartered Information Technology Professional. Dr. Mahmood has in excess of 50 papers published in proceedings of international conferences and journals as well as chapters in books. He is also a member of advisory and editorial boards of several journals and international conferences. His research interests are in the areas of software engineering, project management, enterprise computing, and e-government.

Srikanth Reddy Malipatel is currently pursuing M.Sc Tech. Information System at BITS-PILANI.

Farrukh Masood holds a Master degree in Embedded Systems engineering from University of Stuttgart, Germany and bachelors in computer science from International Islamic University Islamabad, Pakistan. He has got extensive industrial experience in well-known multinational companies like Ericsson Telecommunication Frankfurt, Altran Technologies Frankfurt, Micronas GmbH Munich, Marconi Communications Stuttgart and Agilent Technologies Stuttgart. His expertise lie in the area of software verification and quality assurance.

Natarajan Meghanathan is a tenured Associate Professor of Computer Science at Jackson State University, Jackson, MS. He graduated with a Ph.D. in Computer Science from The University of Texas at Dallas in May 2005. Dr. Meghanathan has published more than 110 peer-reviewed articles (more than half of them being journal publications). He has also received federal education and research grants from the U. S. National Science Foundation and the Army Research Lab. Dr. Meghanathan has been serving in the editorial board of several international journals and in the technical program committees and organization committees of several international conferences. His research interests are wireless ad hoc networks and sensor networks, graph theory, network and software security, bioinformatics, and computational biology. For more information, visit http://www.jsums.edu/cms/nmeghanathan.

I.Ch Manikanta Nath is currently pursuing M.Sc Tech. Information System at BITS-PILANI.

Ch. V.B. Ramaraju is currently pursuing M.Sc Tech. Information System at BITS-PILANI.

D. V. Pavan Kumar Reddy is currently pursuing M.Sc Tech. Information System at BITS-PILANI.

Saqib Saeed is a final year Ph.D. student at University of Siegen, Germany. He holds a Master's degree in Software Technology from Stuttgart University of Applied Sciences, Germany. He is also a certified software quality engineer. He was working as Lecturer at the department of Computer Sciences and Engineering at Bahria University Islamabad, Pakistan before coming to Siegen. His area of interest lie in computer supported cooperative work, ICT4D, and empirical software engineering.

Kamaljeet Sandhu is a Senior Lecturer of Accounting and Information Systems at the School of Business, Economics and Public Policy of the University of New England. He earned his Ph.D. in Information Systems from Deakin University, Melbourne. His teaching and research expertise are in electronic services and services management at universities, corporate governance, accounting Information Systems, management accounting, asset management, and e-learning.

Praveen Ranjan Srivastava is working in Software Engineering and Software Testing Research group in Computer Science and Information Systems Department at Birla Institute of Technology and Science (BITS), Pilani India. He is currently doing research in the area of software testing. His research areas are software testing, quality assurance, testing effort, software release, test data generation, agent oriented software testing, stopping testing, and soft computing techniques. He has a number of publications in the area of software testing; also he is reviewers of various leading international conference and journals.

Index